Across Genres, Generations and Borders

Italian Women Writing Lives

Edited by Susanna Scarparo and Rita Wilson

Newark: University of Delaware Press

Monash Romance Studies

General Editor: Brian Nelson

Monash Romance Studies is a series of refereed scholarly publications devoted to the study of any aspect of French, Italian and Spanish literature, language, culture and civilization. It will publish books and collections of essays on specific themes, and is open to scholars associated with academic institutions other than Monash University.

Proposals for the series should be addressed to the general editor, from whom details of volumes previously published in the series are available:

Professor Brian Nelson
School of Languages, Cultures and Linguistics
Building 11
Monash University
Melbourne Vic. 3800
Australia

Fax: (+61 3) 9905 5437
Email: brian.nelson@arts.monash.edu.au

Financial assistance from the Instituto Italiano di Cultura (Melbourne)

First American edition published 2004

Associated University Presses
2010 Eastpark Blvd
Cranbury, NJ 08512

ISBN 0-87413-918-X

Cataloging-in-Publication Data is available from the Library of Congress

Cover illustration: Dosso Dossi, "Risveglio di Venere" (detail)
Rolo Banca Collection

Acknowledgements

The Editors would like to thank all the readers who kindly gave their advice on the contributions published in this volume. We are particularly grateful to Klaus Neumann for his invaluable help in the preparation of the final manuscript, to Richard Wilson for his industry and skill in formatting the text, and to Susi Walker, Paula Green, Bernadette Luciano and Denise Formica for their assistance and perceptive translations. Thanks are also due to the series editor, Brian Nelson, for his encouragement and support.

Paola Bono's essay, "Women's Biographies and Autobiographies: A Political Project in the Making", first appeared in *Resources for Feminist Research*, 25(3-4), 1997, Special Issue: "Passionate Ethics: Kathleen Martindale, 1947-1995", pp. 38-45, and is re-printed here by kind permission of the publishers, OISE/UT (University of Toronto, Canada).

Unless otherwise indicated, translations from the Italian are by the authors of the individual essays.

The Editors gratefully acknowledge the financial contribution of the Istituto Italiano di Cultura (Melbourne) towards the publication costs of the volume and we thank the Director, Dott.ssa Simonetta Magnani, for her enthusiasm in fostering collaboration between the Institute and the academy.

MELBOURNE
ITALIAN GOVERNMENT CULTURAL OFFICE

Contents

Across Borders

Across the Nation

Re-Thinking the Politics and Practice of Life Writing

Susanna Scarparo and Rita Wilson

ACROSS: *prep.* from one side to the other side of; intersecting; passing over at any angle; opposite; in contact with; *adv.* crosswise; transversely from one side to the other. (*Webster's New Twentieth Century Dictionary*)

As the title, *Across Genres, Generations and Borders: Italian Women Writing Lives,* suggests, the essays in this volume question, investigate and problematise the terms 'life,' 'writing,' and 'woman.' We have deliberately chosen a title that is open to multiple interpretations to highlight the book's two interrelated aims: namely, to examine the processes involved in writing the lives of women, both as autobiographies and as biographies, and to link the process of narration (*narrazione*) to the act of writing lives and the search for the subject-woman. The accounts of identities which emerge from this collection of essays are set off by an understanding of life writing as a political practice. All of the essays in this collection give voice to practices and traditions which are usually lost in monolithical representations of dominant (especially male) culture, and show ways in which such representations can be challenged. Some essays are more autobiographical, emphasising the importance of self-articulation for creating possibilities for self-direction. Others are theoretical discussions about the constructions of self-articulation in women's life writing.

The two chapters by Paola Bono and Ida Dominijanni, frame the theoretical arguments of the collection. Bono's essay refers specifically to women's auto/biography as a political project in the making, while Dominijanni's contribution is an example of the practice of this politics. All of the essays develop and defend the insight that there can be no fixed identity, that there is no ultimate knowledge, and that representation is no longer a matter of veracity or accuracy but merely of competing discourses. Notions of authenticity and truth are, by all accounts, outdated. Yet, within certain discourses there emerges the desire for affirmation of self or origin. In particular, in women's life writing the need to reconsider, reclaim and reconcile hybrid forms of self-definition is not just a moral, but also an epistemological requirement – a necessary condition for understanding one's 'place in the world.'

As Paola Bono and Graziella Parati have argued, there are risks in but also good reasons for avoiding clear definitions of biography and autobiography. Parati writes that "autobiography as a genre allows for a constant redefinition of its boundaries and limitations." As such, it is "a hybrid and malleable genre that partakes of other genres and becomes a literary space where a woman can experiment with the construction of a female 'I' and, sometimes, a feminist identity" (Parati 2). We take Parati's definition of autobiography to include the more encompassing label of life writing. Escaping clearly defined genre boundaries, this form stands neither merely for autobiography or personal narratives, nor solely for biography. In its varied incarnations, it is also neither entirely fictional, nor purely historical writing, and often includes elements of metafictional and self-reflexive styles.

The term life writing, first proposed by feminist critics who wanted to expand the genre of autobiography to include personal narratives such as diaries, memoirs and letters, is currently used to account for narratives that cross the line between fact and fiction, and to describe writing that is located on the cusp of autobiography and fiction. Such writing presents different strategies for negotiating hybrid (and therefore more fluid) identity/identities. These writers shape a place in-between, a space with elusive borders that fluctuate between the real and the imaginary, and which is produced as much by the interstices as the conjunction of the selves inscribed in the conventions of different genres.

Feminist discussions about women's life writing have focused mainly on autobiographical practices, including the writing of personal narratives such as journals, memoirs and letters. The interest in biography has come mostly from women historians and feminist biographers reflecting on the processes involved in the act of writing other women's lives. Since the late 1980s, the theorising of women's autobiography has increasingly included women's biography under the generic definition of women's life writing. Broadly speaking, feminist scholars in this field have mostly been concerned with debunking the notion of a unified, rational and autonomous self as the universal norm and with challenging the boundaries between women's private and public roles. Feminist analyses have also focused on the attempts of auto/biographers to claim authority and legitimacy while seeking self-representational agency.

In her contribution to this collection, Paola Bono describes women's biographies and autobiographies as "sharing a fluctuating border, or perhaps intersecting on a changeable common ground" (20). Ambiguity is a necessary component of a collection like this, in which genres, generations and borders are deliberately crossed. However, the act of crossing has specific political purposes. Following Bono's proposition, it may be useful to view such crossing as a political practice. Both terms, 'political' and 'practice,' need to be understood in the context of terms proposed and developed by the Italian feminist theory of sexual difference. As Bono explains, women's biographies and autobiographies "are a form of relationship between/among women resulting from and giving strength to the activation of female subjectivity," which in the writing and reading of a woman's life "can produce its own representations and evaluations of itself and the world." The same energy and the same desire "to produce a socio-symbolic change circulate in both types of narration, involving the self and the life of the writing, written, reading subjects" (13).

Wishing to exploit this notion of "political practice," Ida Dominijanni offers an analysis of the auto/biography of the Italian nation as recounted by three recent films viewed through the lens of a feminist journalist. Dominijanni's reading of the Italian transition from the First to the Second Republic offers an interpretation of the auto/biography of the Italian nation which came out of the crisis of traditional political institutions in the light of the role that Italian feminism has played in identifying, analysing and deconstructing the fragmentation of paternal authority, which is a fundamental cause of the political crisis. Dominijanni argues that the transition did not result from the political crisis of the 1980s but can be traced to the death of Aldo Moro.

Fundamental to Dominijanni's argument is a re-reading of the conventional story that 1970s feminism "was a great social revolution but [that] it failed to make a bridge in the world of politics which is still entirely a male bastion, impenetrable then and now to women, as is evidenced by the insignificant percentages of women in parliament and in top party or government jobs" (202). This version of events, however, as Dominijanni convincingly explains, undermines the effects that the Italian feminist revolution has had on the system of traditional politics understood as the exercise of power. As Dominijanni writes, "Italian feminism has been and continues to be, not only a social, but an intrinsically political movement, not because it asserted women's right to enter politics but because it demolished the traditional idea, scope and ways of politics. Moreover, its *criticism* of traditional politics cuts across the *crisis* of politics, thereby showing an alternative that did not mean adding women to an existing scenario but, rather, creating a new scenario" (202).

In this reading, the auto/biography of the Italian nation also needs to be understood in relation to the concomitant crisis of (national) identity and the need to re-invent it as homogeneous and unifying. Many social scientists consider identity to be a discursive phenomenon. Research built on this insight consequently assumes that a phenomenon such as collective identity is a social construct. If discourse is understood in a Foucauldian sense, it is reproduced not just verbally, but also through political, institutional, and everyday practices. Ida Dominijanni's essay attempts to present a socio-political analysis of practices in which meanings around Italian national identity are produced, and to explain how they work. She shows that the challenge is to explain their power. This is at once intriguing and frustrating, as such practices tend to be concealed by what has been called "naturalisation" (Hall 204). Systems of meaning through which identities are cultivated – understandings of how things are and how they are connected – are so taken for granted that they ultimately take on a natural guise and are, as Barthes put it, "innocently consumed" (131).

Scholars from a broad range of disciplines have found the concept of narrative helpful when trying to gain analytical purchase on this trait: on what Veronique Mottier has referred to as the central mechanism of the discursive construction of identity (3). Narrative analysis provides a tool for explaining the relationship between ideas, experience and action; for understanding how identities are constructed and reconstructed in specific contexts and over time; and for explicating 'how things are connected.' It becomes possible to understand why certain identities occur and recur when we see that social identities are constituted through narrativity, social action is guided by narrativity, and social processes and interactions are narratively mediated (Somers 621).

A central issue which is presented or foreshadowed in almost all of the essays included in this volume centres around the question: how do we construct what we call our lives and how do we create ourselves in the process? Perhaps what remains most stable about the self as an enduring concept over time is a sense of commitment to a set of beliefs and values that we are unable (or unwilling) to submit to radical scrutiny (Taylor). It is this commitment which provides the engine, as it were, for the rhetorical aspect of autobiography – seen in the evaluative component in autobiographical discourse. For what makes the telling justifiable is also a commitment to a set of presuppositions about oneself, one's relations to others, and one's view of the world and one's place in it. So, given that autobiography is also a form of 'taking a stand,' it is perforce rhetorical.

Combining the rhetoric of self-justification with the requirements of a genre-linked narrative, we come close to 'world-making,' a process whereby agentive powers become the gravitational centre of the world. The force that relates the centre to the rest of the world is a commitment that endures over time. It ensures a certain stability in self-conception, but also permits the auto/biographer to maintain a sense of alliance with, and opposition to, others. In this sense, autobiography (like the novel) involves not only the construction of self, but also a construction of one's culture.

What is apparent from recent studies in child psychology (Nelson) is that self-construction begins very early and is a strikingly systematic process that is deeply enmeshed with the mastery of language itself, not just its syntax and lexicon, but its rhetoric and its rules for constructing narrative. Like all other aspects of world-making, self-making (or 'life-making') depends heavily upon the symbolic system in which it is conducted, its opportunities and constraints. These opportunities and constraints come under scrutiny in the contributions by Paula Green, Maria Pallotta-Chiarolli and Suzanne Branciforte. They combine and juxtapose their academic and creative work, thus creating self-making narratives in which the process of discovery and construction of the self become a cognitive and political practice.

Other contributors to this volume consider how self-making narratives by women portray changes in the cultural representations of *italianità* (as defined by Dickie in "Imagined Italies" and "The Notion of Italy"), particularly at crucial times in the making of Italy as a nation. Dana Renga and Maja Mikula focus on fascism and the anti-fascist resistance, respectively. Dominijanni problematises the transition from the First to the Second Republic, taking into account the events of 1968, the kidnapping of Aldo Moro and the ascendancy to power of Silvio Berlusconi. Most of the contributors also make a connection between *italianità*, and the relationship between private stories and public identity. Finally, the writers of the essays in the section entitled "Across Borders" reflect on the notion of *italianità* when used as a category for theorising social identity and belonging. It is in this context that we locate the second part of the title of this volume, recognising that our use of the term "Italian" is deliberately ambiguous.

Within the theoretical frameworks previously discussed, chapters in this collection highlight the connections between subjectivity and history, feminist concerns about mothering and the mother-daughter relationships, autobiography, discourse and its framing of the relationship between text and life, and the ethics of constructing biographies. In order to emphasise the intersecting nature of these issues, the book is divided into three parts. Part I, "Across Genres," includes contributions which examine the process of writing lives as expressed but also contested in epistolary narratives, autobiography and historical fiction. Gabriella Romani seeks to explore the overlapping of literary and non-literary phenomena, which made the letter "a viable and visible strategy for communication" in nineteenth-century Italian culture (24). Romani suggests that "the appearance of epistolary narratives during the second half of the *ottocento* is connected to the rise of new practices of communication, which affected significantly the way in which women experienced and represented their entrance into the public discourse of unified Italy" (24-25). More specifically, letter narratives typify the complex and contradictory participation of women to the post-unification reconstruction of Italy (25).

Patrizia Guida plays with the idea of "a novel, almost an autobiography" to foreground the relationship between fictional and autobiographical selves in Grazia Deledda's *Cosima*. The interplay between the two creates Deledda's feminist message, which for Guida lies in the "binary, escape/emancipation" narrative that brings to light the "moral isolation of a female artist in a society whose cultural codes did not contemplate issues beyond motherhood, bringing up children, and looking after a family" (Guida 49). Guida also argues that the autobiographical self gives her reader a role model.

Focusing on Elsa Morante's *La Storia: Romanzo*, Dana Renga examines the sexual politics of fascism by illustrating how Morante critiques the "rhetoric of virility" and challenges "traditional definitions of the 'sexual' and 'political' in her re-presentation of the *ventennio*" (58). In so doing, Renga argues that Morante discloses new practices of "reading sexuality and politics that feminises" dominant patriarchal structures. While Renga proposes a reading of Morante's novel as a transgressive rewriting of fascist discourses, Dominijanni deconstructs current revisionist interpretations of those discourses. She argues that, since the early 1990s, historical revisionists – both right- and moderate left-wing – have been tenacious in their insistence on rewriting the history of the Republic's founding struggle. This struggle between fascism and antifascism has been turned into a story of 'national reconciliation' with the purpose, on the one hand, of lifting the blame from fascism and placing it on communism and, on the other hand, of turning what was apparently a divisive and partisan national identity into a 'single' one that all 'Italians' can embrace (198-200).

Maja Mikula discusses Carla Capponi's construction of her gendered and national identity "interpreting it as a politically charged act of resistance" (71-72), highlighting the intersections between history and autobiography, genre, gender and *italianità*. Carla Capponi's autobiography, *Con cuore di donna* (With the Heart of a Woman) is a prime example of narrative life writing, aimed both at constructing the self-identity of the author through her moral dilemmas and choices at a crucial moment in the history of contemporary Italy, and at representing that historical moment through the eyes of one of its prominent protagonists. Published in late 2000 and officially launched a week before the author's death, the text may be read as her bequest to posterity, in which memory of personal experience is offered to validate the truthfulness of historical interpretation.

The book's title, as well as its discursive framework, reveal the author's subjectivity as highly gendered. With the 'heart of a woman,' Capponi does not engage in acts of violence lightly. Her choices are seen as forced upon her by particular historical circumstances. Furthermore, Capponi sees the resistance movement as primarily motivated by a desire to 'protect Italy's honour,' constructing her version of *italianità* first and foremost on moral grounds. It is an *italianità* based on a belief in tolerance, freedom and an imagined better future for the country. It is a patriotism based on the author's reading of universal values, which goes hand in hand with communist internationalism and the rhetoric of inclusion.

If we start from the hypothesis that writings such as Capponi's are essential sources to diagnose the gap between the image of women portrayed by tradition and the self-awareness developed by individual women, it is possible to imagine a history which may take into account women's roles. Furthermore, in considering such writings in relation to the existing literary tradition, we may reconstruct the cultural horizon of those years. Indeed, cultural history, with its attention to the rituals of everyday life, proves to be a useful method for reclaiming the life of those who were erased from political history. This is particularly evident in Mirna Cicioni's interpretation of Clara Sereni's life writing as a microtext in which Sereni's narrated self engages in a variety of political and personal projects in the context of developments in Italian society from the 1970s to the new century. The narrated self moves through and across several interconnected positions: a woman, a writer, a Jew, a public intellectual, a participant in political activities of the Italian Left, a wife and a mother of a son suffering from mental illness (Cicioni 86). According to Cicioni, Sereni situates her autobiographical self at the centre of the tangle of contradictions between the private and the public spheres and uses irony to foreground contradictions. As becomes evident in *Passami il sale*, the narrated self can find continuity for various identities through the concrete gesture of her daily life: "sorting out her clothes and her son's, planning meals, shopping for them, and above all preparing food" (Cicioni 94). Ultimately, however, Cicioni suggests that it is irony – which, in Linda Hutcheon's words, can only "complexify" and never "disambiguate" – which allows for new knowledge but also new uncertainties.

Part II, "Across Generations," is concerned with the notion of female genealogy and the relationship with the maternal, both biological and symbolic. Bernadette Luciano discusses the works of writers from three distinct generations: Sibilla Aleramo's *Andando e stando*, Lalla Romano's *Un sogno del nord* and Gina Lagorio's *Inventario*. Luciano calls these texts inventories and points out that while they refer to geographical and domestic landscapes, cultural figures, friends and relations, and literary ideologies, each author invents her life "via a dialogue with her literary mother(s), at times reflecting herself in her image, at times resisting her, at times assisting her, always reinventing her." Furthermore, Luciano argues that the dialogue within and between the works she analyses, reveals a "principle of literary *maternage*" (101).

Establishing a type of literary *maternage* with Fabrizia Ramondino, Paula Green inserts a poetic text from her own volume of poetry *Chrome* (which, as she states, "owes a great debt to Ramondino's novel") into her discussion of Ramondino's *Althènopis*. In both her poetic and in her scholarly analysis, Green writes of the desire to conceive versions of the mother, rooted in a desire to write versions of home. She proposes that writing home can be interpreted as a form of writing the mother; and similarly writing the mother can be interpreted as a form of writing home. Green argues that Ramondino's *Althènopis* builds "a compelling example of a woman beginning to come to terms with her maternal origins" and that "the figure of the mother, both absent and present, propels a narrative that in seeking home is seeking the mother herself" (115).

Part III, "Across Borders," comprises articles which deal with "writing outside the borders" (to use Maria Cristina Mauceri's title) geographically and metaphorically. Mauceri discusses the works of two writers who left their native Silesia (now part of Poland and formerly of Germany) and Germany, respectively, moved to Italy and chose to write and publish in Italian. Mauceri also makes a connection between mothers, mother countries and autobiographical writing. Quoting Brodzki, she argues that the mother is the "pre-text for the daughter's autobiographical project" (138).

Maria Pallotta-Chiarolli uses tapestry as a metaphor to describe the interweaving of her "multiple lifeworlds" as an Italo-Australian woman, academic, writer, and social activist. Positioned "outside/inside/no-side" on account of her Italian parents and of the Italian and Australian identities she claims as her own, Pallotta-Chiarolli explores the tensions and points of confluence between constructs of 'social diversity' and 'multiculturalism.' Her article is itself a textual tapestry made of theory, research and personal narrative.

The issue of being an insider/outsider is also at the centre of our investigation of the early works of the Italo-Australian writer Anna Maria Dell'Oso. As we point out, her writing crosses the boundaries of both culture and genre. Standing between two cultures, she writes stories that are on the cusp of autobiography and fiction, and that allow her simultaneously to stage and to question her own desire to construct a narrative of the self (165).

In "My Other, My Self," Suzanne Branciforte, stages her journey of self-discovery from being 'simply' an American Italianist to becoming an Italian American American Italianist. Once again, the slippage between identities prompts a search for a narrative of the self. As Branciforte explains: "more Italian when in America, more American when in Italy, I shifted languages and personalities like I changed planes, and sometimes, quite honestly, I missed my connection" (180). Missing connections is perhaps typical also of life writing, with its obvious relationship between *narrazione* and self-construction in relation to individuals and nations. We feel that this book shows how creative such missed connections can be, and presents a dynamic series of rhetorical, discursive, theoretical and practical strategies that resist a coherent prescription of ways in which women may write lives. We hope that readers will find such fluidity liberating (and even necessary) and will concur with Ida Dominijanni's view that moving across traditional forms of representation helps constitute cultural meanings and political reality, and contains the potential for engaged critical intervention.

From Private to Public

Women's Biographies and Autobiographies: A Political Project in the Making

Paola Bono

One could look at life as a narrative process, the making of a story which is narrated in its experiential development and created in its narration; so that a life truly *exists*, becoming both visible and – most importantly – valuable, only when it is signified for others, and is in turn recognised, reinterpreted, used by others. Signified in the act itself, already offered to their reading/s, and, even more, textualised in the communicative exchange. Narrated and represented: in its experiential roots, but also transcending experience in order to enter symbolic construction.

Just as it happened, for example, in the feminist practice of *autocoscienza* in Italy, and elsewhere in consciousness-raising groups.[1] It was there that for many women the seeming senselessness of their single lives could find a meaning, also becoming a political project:

> the small *autocoscienza* group was for many women the social place where they could for the first time talk openly about their experience; where this kind of talk was acknowledged as valuable. Before, it was an invisible and dispersed human matter which the social body consumed almost unknowingly; a matter which, having no value, was devalued and scorned. (Libreria delle Donne di Milano 33)

A previously invisible matter could find a form and a value through the process of narration, through the discovery of an infinite echo which modified both the narrating self and the self of the addressee of the narration; the exchange and coincidence of these roles was in that situation a constituent part of the processes of signification and sense production. The signifier 'woman,' where all those selves met in the discovery, was also questioned, investigated and modified – an ongoing modification, still involving experience and narration, which will be taken up later.

The example means taking up and declaring a *position* in writing, as well as asking for a specific mode of reading; it is in the highly contextualised perspective evoked by that illustration that these brief considerations on women's biographies and autobiographies are written and should be read. They are the mere beginning of a discourse; I will rapidly outline the complex question of the identification of the narrative forms of biography and autobiography, both in general and when they concern women's lives, touching upon the terms of the problem without accepting or proposing an answer;[2] then I will address the peculiar relationship that women's authored biographies and autobiographies can establish with the (woman) reader in the process of fruition. The frame of reference is feminist criticism, but even more feminism/s as a political movement, as a close-knit texture of theories and practices. Especially, though not exclusively, the Italian feminism of sexual difference; so that by 'practices' I mean of course 'political practices,' in the sense in which this phrase is used in Italian feminism, where it points to a fundamental and well understood notion. As Ida Dominijanni has written:

> It refers to the forms the relationship between/among women has taken through the years [...]; *autocoscienza*, 'practice of the unconscious,' *affidamento* (entrustment) and so on. It signifies the political 'mode' of the feminism of sexual difference, according to which politics is not primarily founded on the identification and vindication of women's rights, with its attendant objectives and requests, but rather on the activation of female subjectivity in order to produce a socio-symbolic change. In this kind of politics, the relationship among/between women is not a matter of organisation, a way to bring women together. It is the site, the 'setting,' where female subjectivity can come into being, taking shape from its dis-symmetries with regard to the dominant symbolic order; where it can produce its own representations and evaluations of itself and the world, thereby also modifying its relationship with reality, and reality itself.[3] (Dominijanni, "Politica" 68)

This conception of what constitutes a 'political practice' in feminist politics has played a relevant role in my coming to see women's biographies and autobiographies as a political project.

Biography and autobiography: intertwining of life and writing, meeting of the self with the word. Language gives form to events and to the perception/ representation of events in order to construct a narration, and in the narration a subject. Or rather, two (at least): in the narration there is an effect of doubling, which points at a distance but also at a similarity bordering on identity, and which asks for an investigation of the relationship between the narrating and the narrated subjects. Thus a fissure can be detected in the deceiving simplicity of their seeming coincidence in autobiography, on the one hand, and on the other, of their seeming diversity in biography.

In looking at these narrative forms, there are three elements to bear in mind and to investigate: the self of the subject/s in question; the life which is the pre-text of the narration; the writing where they meet, both giving and taking shape from it. These elements are present in biography and autobiography according to varying and mobile modes, linked to the 'recognisability' of the (narrating and narrated) subjects, as well as to the changes in the narrative possibilities opened up or denied to them by their experiential and writing contexts. Especially for autobiography, where the coexistence of the three elements *appears* obvious and immediately visible, criticism and theory have centred and developed around the meaning and the relationship of these concepts – *autós*, the self; *bíos*, life; *graphía*, writing.

Denying the assumption of an easy identification, there have been changes of focus as all three were in turn questioned and problematised, with the adoption of a series of critical approaches and the creation, discarding and re-creation of different theoretical models. Initially and for quite a while, autobiography was allowed only a marginal space in critical discourse. It was considered at most a historiographical document, useful in as much as it could provide one with 'secondary' information which would help recapture the atmosphere of a period, the rules of a temporally and spatially delimited daily life, the individualised workings of a culture. Or it was seen (with the exception, of course, of 'great personalities') as a sub-type of biography, guilty moreover of a damning partiality. Actually, for a long time biography itself was granted a critical attention focused mainly upon the *bíos* of the narrated subject, neglecting the subjectivity of the narrating self and the forms of narration (again, with the exception of biographers who were recognised a literary or historical relevance).

More recently, both genres have become the object of increasingly sophisticated inquiries and theoretical proposals.[4] In trying to identify their conventions and to develop adequate analytical categories, the critical hierarchy has even been turned upside down. They have been accepted in the realm of literature, and studied as literary genres; the narrating function, and with it the subjectivity of the narrator, have been emphasised. Underlining the inscription of the narrating subject in any narration, it has been suggested that not only biography but the whole of literature is a form of autobiography. Coming to be seen as an all pervading mode of expression active in any representational system, autobiography has risked losing its status of genre almost as soon as it had been granted one – certainly before it could be defined.

It is true that the more autobiography is investigated, the more it escapes any search for a 'stable' definition; and the same happens for biography. For both, the instability of the descriptive and analytical categories is greater in the case of women's autobiographies or biographies, stories of women's lives by women narrated. In retracing the stages of a critical interest for these narrative forms, their 'feminine' side must be further problematised, questioning the partiality and inadequacy of methodological frameworks which either implicitly exclude it or naturally assimilate it (a discursive move which is another form of exclusion).

As Sidonie Smith argues in the opening chapter of *A Poetics of Women's Autobiography*, something which seemed without shadows and mysteries has been revealed as unexpectedly complex: complex as the subject who tries to represent him/herself, entering a difficult relationship and having to negotiate a mediation with language and with the rhetorical forms through which one's subjectivity is written and read into the world. Just think of an example which is for many a part of daily life, that is to say the writing of a letter. Think of the – more or less conscious – process of selection concerning the information to be included/excluded; then of their careful combination in the construction of a narrative, in the *mise-en-scène* of a self which is presented to the addressee bearing in mind all possible 'moves' in the reception. It is an activity which actually underlies all communicative exchanges. The relationship – be it friendly, amorous, or conflictual – is put at stake by and in the necessity/possibility of keeping under control the represented identity, also taking into account one's readiness to acknowledge and accept the same necessity/possibility for the other.[5]

This aspect of self-construction and self-representation exists and can be detected also in biographical writing, certainly in women-authored women's biographies. For a woman, writing another woman's life – as well as reading it (an increasingly common exercise) – means engaging in a difficult and rewarding *pas de deux*. In the issue "Biografie: effetti di ritorno," the editorial board of the Italian feminist journal *DWF* maintain that "investigating another woman's life means for a female subject a peculiar involvement which plays a role in the space of interpretation" (*DWF* 5), then to argue that this special involvement asks for – and indeed provokes – a multiplication in the relationship with the (female) addressee of the narration, who today experiences and expresses a desire which is "almost a political request." Thus the *pas de deux* becomes a multiple meeting, a collective dance creating continuous refractions in the diffusion of *effetti di ritorno* – 'feedback effects.'

In this sense, already in their production, and/or in their reception, women's biographies and autobiographies can be considered a political project in the making. At the very least, they can be said to belong in the conception of a 'political practice' quoted above; they are a form of relationship between/ among women resulting from and giving strength to the 'activation of female subjectivity,' which in the writing and reading of a woman's life 'can produce its own representations and evaluations of itself and the world.' The same energy and the same desire 'to produce a socio-symbolic change' circulate in both types of narration, involving the self and the life of the writing, written, reading subjects.[6]

It is not by chance that these narrative forms are privileged in and by feminist theory and practice. Rather, it is a necessity, as Carolyn Heilbrun reminds us: "Women must turn to one another for stories; they must share the stories of their lives and their hopes and their unacceptable fantasies." (Heilbrun 44) The search into history – the need for her/story and stories – is part of the feminist tension towards the construction of a female symbolic, which takes shape (also) through the investigation of *life*, one's own and other women's lives. Like a shuttle moving between the signification of the self and the signification of the other (woman), this tension weaves a plot of references in which an individual and collective foundation can be retraced.

It is a search which can take many forms; privileging an intellectual biography of thought, focusing upon an element of such significance as to mark the whole of an existence, twining together events and encounters, sketching many single lives to outline a collective her/story. It is the multifaceted response to a desire which sparks more desire. This passion for narrated lives, for the risky exercise of the textualisation of experience, could fill shelves upon shelves – and indeed it has, feeding upon the growing production of women's biographies fostered by feminism. Heilbrun's experience has been a shared one:

> In 1984, I wrote in an article in the *New York Times Book Review* that, since 1970, I had added seventy-three new biographies of women to my library. That number has certainly doubled by now, and yet there are countless biographies of women that I have not acquired. (Heilbrun 12)

And they have kept and keep growing – in all languages.

Moreover, especially since the mid-eighties, this passion has engendered a form of writing where theoretical reflection is rooted in and mixes with personal narration. The process has been put into motion also by the need to re-problematise the signifier 'woman,' giving a greater relevance to inter- and intra-subjective differences, and taking into account identity variables such as race, class, nationality, sexuality etc. – an endeavou which has been in the last ten years the focus of much feminist reflection and of a sometimes heated debate. The fruitful encounter of feminist thought, psychoanalytic theory, and postmodern philosophy on the one hand, and on the other the renewed awareness of the differences among women, in a postcolonial world and in multicultural, multi-ethnic contexts, have also played a significant role. The crisis of the universal/unitary subject has met the reflections on/of a new subject – the female/feminist subject. The proposition of *experience* as a cognitive category has brought about a revision of given definitions of the feminine, as well as a questioning of the concept of experience itself. The critique of these definitions and the investigation of a new – also female/feminist – subjectivity have increasingly focused on the mechanisms of language and representation.

The emphasis on the nexus between language, subjectivity and consciousness in the constitution of the (social) subject, and therefore the shifting of the borders between the personal and the political as a result of the subjective links joining the two in the subject's experience, have implied the full acknowledgement of the peculiar discursive and epistemological character of feminist theory. Being both *inside* the given social determination-s and *outside* them, it calls for a comprehensive re-examination and re-conceptualisation of the terms and categories of inquiry.[7]

The need has emerged of analysing anew the relationship between 'women' – plural and different, each woman historically placed and identified according to multiple components – and 'woman,' trans-historical product of an hegemonic discourse. The focus of inquiry is the gap between 'woman' and 'women;' the question is how the normativity of the signifier 'woman' marks the life of single women, what dynamics of adaptation and resistance are set in motion by *each* woman, also in relation to other relevant features of her life and story. And furthermore, the question is if and how feminist discourse may run the risk on the one hand of reproposing some normative traits of that signifier, and on the other hand of creating new norms in the name of a new feminist ethos.[8] In both cases this would entail simplifications which would re-enforce the paradox of exclusion/inclusion.

Women of the so-called Third World, and, in Western countries, Black, Asian, Amerindian women, *chicanas* (all 'women of colour,' in their own definition), as well as many lesbians, have developed a feminist critique of feminism. They have exposed the limits of white-Western-heterosexual theory which indeed could end up in proposing a new norm without taking into due account the differences among women. Speaking up *within and against* feminism, they have interrupted a feminist discourse proceeding on the single axis of the difference between man and woman; they have asserted the necessity to re-negotiate the signifier 'woman' having in mind differences and power-relationships not accountable for by that axis.[9]

In the recognition of a multiple subjectivity, and responding to this conflictual emergence of differences between/among women, many feminist thinkers have started to investigate their own complex and contradictory subject positions in texts which question and trespass the borders between theory, fiction and autobiography. An in-between territory has taken shape, in a sort of continuum of fictional and theoretical writing.

There is no paucity of examples,[10] coming from different countries and different cultural/political feminist backgrounds. A few will suffice here to show the variety of ways in which these explorations and contaminations of genres take place: inserting autobiographical passages in a theoretical argumentation, addressing theoretical questions under the guise of an autobiographical narration, combining different registers and styles to evoke a multiple subject, often traversing and intersecting several disciplines whose borders are also called into question.

Joan Nestle's fiction/theory in *A Restricted Country* and Audre Lorde's 'biomythography' in *Zami: A New Spelling of My Name* privilege the narrative mode, but always with a cutting political analysis. Writing with her usual lucidity and passion about Nestle's and Lorde's texts, Kathleen Martindale has discussed this tendency towards a contamination and reshaping of genres in women's writing, be it fictional or theoretical; she has looked at the ways in which the process of subjectivisation in/through writing takes on a collective political meaning in the feminist community, riddled though it is with unsolved conflicts and questions (see Martindale 1991).

The pages of her diary become for Barbara Godard a form of investigation, as she offers them to the reader in a theoretical and theorised reflection on her existential/ intellectual itineraries as well as on her writing strategies. "Essay/ons Traduction" is the site of a *redde rationem* on issues involving both language and life; it is a relentless self-analysis of Godard's work as a literary critic and a translator, and also of her everyday experience as a white, anglophone, Canadian, feminist woman. And it is a linguistic construction – Godard *par* Godard – openly acknowledged as the 'private' and 'spontaneous' action of writing a diary turns into a paper to be read at a conference and published in a book.

Nancy K. Miller's "Decades" is the self-portrait of a scholar whose personal and professional life has been deeply related to the development of academic feminism in the USA. Episodes of her life and significant moments of the collective adventure of establishing women's studies in the university alternate and combine; subjective changes sparkle, reflect, interact with the growth of a feminist literary theory, and they become symptoms of a larger process, as the passing years witness the successes and *empasses* of the 'institutionalisation' of feminism. She is 'getting personal', practising a form of criticism which she also theorises, one in which "there is a self-narrative woven into critical argument" and which includes "self-representation as political representativity." (Miller, *Getting Personal* 2) Her purpose is to discuss a represented self, the autobiographical "I" of a woman critic whose feminist involvement entails a questionable but only too easy slippage into representativity. Autobiography is a way of refocusing the 'I' as a singular subject, in order to problematise the meaning of her shared identities as a woman and a feminist in a specific time and place.

In *Autoritratto di gruppo* and *Storie di donne e femministe*, Italian historian Luisa Passerini looks at the experiences of the student movement of 1968 and of the feminist movement to investigate an individual/collective history, filtered through her subjective involvement; especially in her "group self-portrait," "Passerini writes a woman's life and at the same time personalises within an autobiographical text her theories of history in order to reconstruct the 'history' that she has witnessed" (Parati 24)[11]. The same could be said of Emma Baeri's *I lumi e il cerchio*, where in order to investigate political and theoretical issues such as the role of the researcher (and of sexual difference) in the construction of history, the search for a feminist epistemology and methodology, the happiness and frustrations of the discovery of the self, Baeri – also an Italian historian – mixes passages of her diary and archival documents, leaflets produced by her feminist collective and reflections about her teaching, poems and pages of scholarly research about an eighteenth century Sicilian thinker. In moving between the distant past of *i lumi* (the Enlightenment), the more recent past of her *autocoscienza* group and of the impact of feminism on her life, and the present of her writing about both, Baeri creates her/story – that is to say, a narration and a history where experiential elements and theoretical questions are not separated from one another, both speaking to (and often for) many other women.

As Julia Swindells has underlined, the 'not quite discourse' of autobiography has seeped into and modified many discursive fields which had previously belittled it, and it has come to be seen as a worthy object of analysis. At times it has even become a bone of contention among historical and literary disciplines, since the growing interest in proletarian autobiography has led social history to claim it as its own privileged object; so that feminist historian Carolyn Steedman was the target of much criticism by her colleagues when she refused to define as 'history' her (auto)biographical/theoretical book.[12]

It is a change clearly discernible also if we return to the development of the critical discourse on autobiography, especially in the literary field; and these remarks can apply as well to biography, obviously bearing in mind the different relationship with the sources and the issue of a double self/representation. As already said, the awareness of the complexity of this kind of text has come with the shifting of emphasis – from *bíos* to *autós* to *graphía*. A critical attention totally focused on 'life,' where any textual difficulty was solved in terms of factual truthfulness, has given way to a greater centrality of questions of identity and identification of the narrating self in relation to the narrated self (be they coincident or not in "reality"); then the interest has turned to the linguistic and rhetorical strategies influencing, limiting, dictating the construction of these selves and of their narration.[13] Truthfulness has been revealed as a pretence to be constantly subverted, and the autobiographical text as a narrative artifice; neither it nor its 'subject' exist outside language. Therefore, the focus is on the *graphía*, the ways and forms of the inscription/invention of oneself and one's life; not giving shape to something which somehow already existed, but *making it be* through and in language. This perspective implies a new relevance to be attributed to the reader – an element which is in turn modifying the critical discourse in various ways.

In this repeated shift of emphasis, in spite (or because of?) the importance of psychoanalytic theories – Freud, of course, but also and especially Lacan – and of post-structuralist thought in general, sexual difference has long remained untold; as all feminist critics have remarked who have worked on autobiography, trying to break its in-difference, trying to en-gender its analysis. We can apply to the theory of women's autobiographical writing what John Stuart Mill – or perhaps Harriet Taylor, true inspirator of many of his 'protofeminist' intuitions – maintained in general in *The Subjection of Women* about the wretchedly imperfect and superficial knowledge that men can acquire of women, until women themselves have told all they have to tell.

But now we also know that telling what we have to tell is not enough, for much depends on the quality and modes of listening, on the acknowledgement of sexual difference as it works with and upon words and the meaning they are given. Stuart Mill's assertion sounds a little naive – or, if it is Harriet Taylor's, a little provocative. Even the *same* sentence can have a different meaning if told by a man or a woman, and if interpreted by a man or a woman. For a long time, listening and interpretation have been biased. In retracing the stages of the development of autobiography criticism, in re-reading the most significant texts in this development, one can see how sexual difference has been paid little attention, with the attendant formulation of universal models which were inevitably moulded on the male subject. An example is the privileged place granted to the public dimension, and the consequent use of this yardstick to measure the importance of a life and therefore of its being written.

Feminist criticism, a gendered mode of listening, has partly shared the general features of this field of study; but with its 'partiality' it has thrown a different light on the whole set of problems. Therefore it has produced its own questions about the definition and delimitations of its "object," with other reasons and other consequences. The importance of a common belonging to the female sex in the meeting of 'object' and 'subject,' lends weight also to the centrality of this same belonging in the fruition. A web of 'feedback effects' is woven, in the reading and writing of a life which does not forget one's own self, but rather reinterprets it together with the other woman's. The difference between literary genres is questioned in the light of sexual difference.

It is a matter of writing, of writing a life; but is *a woman's* life, and this matters; once again, we can turn to Carolyn G. Heilbrun, alter-ego of crime-writer Amanda Cross, whom she invented to have a new mental space of her own, to gain the pleasure and freedom of living another life. Her search for 'honesty' in biography is different from that 'truthfulness' which many critics have long assumed as a measuring rod. Heilbrun upsets the hierarchy of facts and experiences, she does not observe the conventions; she looks for the founding 'move' or 'act' of a life, making sayable what could not be said before. This is how, starting from a feeling of unease – of danger, rather – she motivates her apparently anti-theoretical choice, openly accepted as a risk:

> there is a real danger that in re-writing the patriarchal text, scholars will get lost in the intellectual ramifications of their disciplines and fail to reach out to the women whose lives must be rewritten with the aid of the new intellectual constructs. [...] we are in danger of refining the theory and scholarship at the expense of the lives of the women who need to experience the fruits of research. For this reason, I have chosen to write of women's lives, rather than of the texts I have been trained to analyse and enjoy. (Heilbrun 20)

It is as though she were answering the "political request" of an ideal woman reader, her own request perhaps, but one which she feels is shared by many other women. Her stories, told interlacing and disentangling different threads of biographical narrations and inter-textual reflections on other writings about those same lives, have among their characters George Sand and Charlotte Brontë, Adrienne Rich and Anne Sexton, Dorothy Sayers and Ivy Compton-Burnett, Vera Brittain and herself/Amanda Cross; and many, many others. They are also full of theoretical implications and are clearly rooted in the wealth of feminist thought on these issues.

Heilbrun touches upon many of the problems discussed here. For example, when talking about Dorothy Sayers and discussing James Brabazon's biography of the English writer, there arises the problem of the relationship between who writes and who is written, and of the role of sex in this relationship. The latter is certainly relevant with reference to the 'product,' i.e. the form and structure taken by the narration of a specific life, but also concerning the 'process' and therefore the narrating subject. As the editorial board of *DWF* suggest, in the case of a woman biographer, signifying oneself in relation to the other woman, leaving the territory of comparison with the one and only (male) sex to enter that of a (female) sexed point of view, points to the self-determined desire to become a speaking and speakable subject; for language is as risky as life, both running the risk of interpretation. (*DWF*, "Biografie" 6)

When writing about George Sand, but not only there, Heilbrun underlines the importance of a net of gendered points of reference for a true change in women's lives and in the ways of narrating them; in other words, she underlines the political function of women's biographies, the possibility of inhabiting them as "the site where female subjectivity can come into being" – to quote once again Dominijanni's definition of a 'political practice.' Sylvia Plath, Anne Sexton and Adrienne Rich lead her – and us with her – to think upon the meanings (plural) of maternity in a woman's life, as well as on its social and cultural meanings. She also looks at the role played by marriage, or by the refusal to marry; at the consequences of choosing another woman as a life partner, or of choosing – sometimes having to choose – a man. She wishes to understand what happens when one tries to narrate her own story, and when one reads or writes another woman's life.

These are issues of remarkable theoretical importance, but also of remarkable experiential importance for many women; and of remarkable political importance. They have been investigated by feminist criticism in all disciplines as well as in its many fruitful contaminations and transgressions of disciplinary fields. These questions, still without answers, point to the difficult problem of the inscription of the self in the text of the world. They can perhaps be summarised by Louise Cotnoir's words, when in her introduction to the "Auto-graph(e)" issue of *Tessera* she asks: "Comment cela, le féminin, (s') écrit. Ce corps qui se trace, déborde et se déploi, comment inscrit-il sa marque dans les mots?" (Cotnoir 15)

"Le féminin," women's subjectivity, experience, life: how is it written, how does it write itself, how is it read? An auto/biography, a woman's life by a woman written, how does it mark words with its meaning to make them meaningful? Today, in relation to a demanding woman reader, who claims also for herself a political use of life and narration; for the *autocoscienza* groups and the practice of consciousness-raising are things of the past, but the interrogation and problematisation of experience are not. The ever stronger intervention of the reader asks for a further revision of already destabilised categories: a task for feminist theoretical work, also for that 'borderline' work of feminist theory mentioned above. Not (only) to question those categories anew, but to propose a shared, though mobile and changeable, approach to that political use, thus opening a new phase in the recent and already complex history of critical inquiry into auto/biographical writing.

Notes

1. Around the end of the 1960s groups of women formed all over Italy, adopting – but also transforming – the American consciousness-raising model, a practice which continued until the middle/end of the 1970s. In *Non credere di avere dei diritti* ("Don't think you have any rights," a quotation from Simone Weil), a highly subjective, idiosyncratic and therefore fascinating reconstruction of the history of Italian feminism, the women of the Libreria delle donne di Milano write: "It was a simple and a genial practice. [...] Women have always met to talk together about their own affairs, safe from the male listening ear. 'Autocoscienza' grafted itself upon this social practice, which was as common as it was belittled, and gave it political dignity" (Libreria delle donne di Milano 33). *Autocoscienza*, the name given to this practice in Italy, indicates its distinctive character as a cognitive and political practice. An age-old debased costume, women meeting "to talk about their own affairs" – it is usually called gossip! – was turned into the self-directed and self-determined process of achieving a new consciousness or awareness. Moving from the analysis of oppression on to a search for autonomous interpretative categories of reality, *autocoscienza* was a process of discovery and reconstruction of the self – both the self of the individual woman, and a collective sense of self: the search for the subject-woman.

2. *Not* proposing a clear definition of 'biography' and 'autobiography' is a choice taken in the full awareness of its risks. As will become apparent, ambiguity is a necessary component of my discourse; especially in the case of women's biographies and autobiographies, I see these forms as sharing a fluctuating border, or perhaps intersecting on a changeable common ground. So I had rather accept a measure of confusion than renounce this ambiguity; definitions will be only implicit, and will tend to combine the two forms. They will also be plural and constantly shifting; underlining the unstable and multiform status of these narratives is one of the purposes of this chapter. I agree with Graziella Parati when she writes that "autobiography as a genre allows for a constant redefinition of its boundaries and limitations. Autobiography is a hybrid and malleable genre that partakes of other genres and becomes a literary space where a woman can experiment with the construction of a female 'I' and, sometimes, a feminist identity;" (Parati 2) and I think that the same can be said of biography in the case of women-authored women's biographies.

3. For a more in-depth discussion of this and other central issues in the Italian feminism of sexual difference, see Cigarini and Muraro, Dominijanni 1992, Libreria delle donne di Milano 1987, 1989; Bono and Kemp 1991 may be useful, also for a general introduction to Italian feminism/s.

4. See for example – also for further bibliographical information: Mehlman 1974, Lejeune 1975, Bruss 1976, Spengemann 1980, Olney ed. 1980 (a rich and very useful collection, comprising essays representative of different approaches), Pilling 1981, Fleishmann 1983, Jay 1984, Derrida 1985, Eakin 1985, Agazzi and Canavese eds. 1992 (again, a good and varied collection, with a focus on narration and fictionality). Among previous studies, see at least Shumaker 1954 and Pascal 1960. Specifically focused on women's autobiography, but including – from a critical perspective – relevant material on the general theoretical framework, are Spaces 1976, Julienne ed. 1980, Station ed. 1987, S. Smith 1987, Brodzsky and Schenk eds. 1988, Benstock ed. 1988, Personal Narrative Group ed. 1989, Arru and Chialant eds. 1990, De Clementi 1991, Mattesini 1993, S. Smith 1993, Gilmore 1994, Miller 1994.

5. See Mizzau 1988, especially chapter 2, "Il detto e il non detto."

6. It is also for this reason that I have avoided to define these forms; definitions entail a separation and a distinction. Especially as a political project, it was important for me to look at them together, using the two terms (biography and autobiography) almost as synonyms, each somehow referring to and partly including the other; so that the specific choice would point to a different emphasis rather than to a mutually excluding diversity.

7. On these issues, see the works by de Lauretis included in the list of references.

8. As Judith Butler puts it: "identity categories tend to be instruments of regulatory regimes, whether as the normalising categories of oppressive structures or as the rallying points of a liberatory contestation of that very oppression." (Butler 13-14)

9. Among the fascinating and often theoretically sophisticated production on these questions, see for example Anzaldùa and Moraga eds 1981, Hull, Bell Scott and B. Smith eds 1982, B. Smith ed. 1983, Lorde 1984, Anzaldùa 1987, Spivak 1987 and 1989, Ward Jouve 1991.

10. Many of the texts just mentioned in note 9 are also instances of this composite style of writing.

11. Parati analyses Passerini's book together with the autobiographical writings of four other Italian women (Camilla Faà Gonzaga, Enif Robert, Fausta Cialente, Rita Levi Montalcini) in order to raise questions on the negotiation/representation of identity, or rather identities; with a destabilising aim, the focus is also on the dichotomies between male and female, paternal and maternal, and, especially, between the private and the public spheres.

12. Swindells 1989; Steedman 1987 combines a theoretical reflection on autobiography and history with the story of her own and her mother's lives, contextualising them in a larger web of proletarian women's lives in Great Britain.

13. As Sidonie Smith acutely summarises: "A kind of moralist, the autobiography critic evaluated the quality of life as it was lived and the veracity of the autobiographer as he or she narrated the story of that life. By contrast, the second generation of critics has attuned itself to the "agonising questions" inherent in self representation. [... T]ruthfulness becomes a much more complex and problematic phenomenon [and] autobiography is understood to be a process through which the autobiographer struggles to shape an 'identity' out of amorphous subjectivity. [...] Whatever the critical agenda, two underlying assumptions motivate these approaches to autobiography – confidence in the referentiality of language and a corollary confidence in the authenticity of the self. But a third generation of critics, the structuralists and poststructuralists, has challenged the notion of referentiality and undermined comfortable assumptions about an informing 'I'. These critics suggest that the *autos*, shattered by the influence of the unconscious and structured by linguistic configurations beyond any single mind, may be nothing more, and certainly nothing less, than a convention of space and time where symbolic systems, existing as infinite yet always as structures possibility, speak themselves in the utterance of a *parole*." (Smith, *A Poetics* 5)

Across Genres

Women Writing Letters: Epistolary Practices in Nineteenth-Century Newspapers, Manuals and Fiction

Gabriella Romani

Women's access to reading and writing represents, as Lucia Re has recently noted, one of the "central strategies in the post-Risorgimento consolidation of the Italian state and in the struggle for social hegemony in the nineteenth century" (162). One of the most basic forms of writing available to women in the nineteenth century was letter writing, which required little schooling or formal training. An emblem of the private, in the *ottocento* the letter became also an actual agent of the public exchange of knowledge and an instrument in the formation of public opinion. Starting from the end of the eighteenth century, the letter frequently appeared in newspapers and fiction addressed to a female readership. As a result of technological advances and institutional reforms, by the second half of the nineteenth century epistolary exchanges became a reality in the life of women, especially from the middle classes, and a vehicle for the creation of a network of cultural and social activities, which favoured the entrance of women into the public discourse.

Late nineteenth-century fiction and journalism featured the letter as a common narrative strategy. In literature, in addition to Verga's popular *Storia di una capinera* (1871), which sold more than 20 000 copies (Tortorelli 160), one may find several publications written with this literary device by women writers. Both Matilde Serao and Marchesa Colombi (*nom de plum* of Maria Antonietta Torriani), for example, wrote a novel and several short stories in the epistolary form. The decline of this genre in other European countries by the middle of the nineteenth century raises the question of why these writers adopted this literary strategy for their narrative production. Was it merely an attempt to capitalise on a genre that had already met with popular consent in Italy, especially among women?[1] Or was it determined by specific historical circumstances and, thus, resulted from the intersection of various 'discursive practices' connected to the social uses of the letter?[2] If so, then, what were these practices and how and why did they affect the writings of the time? This study seeks to explore the overlapping of literary and non-literary phenomena, which made the letter a viable and visible strategy for communication in nineteenth-century Italian culture. I suggest that the appearance of epistolary narratives during the second half of the *ottocento* is connected to the rise of new practices of communication, which significantly affected the way in which women experienced and represented their entrance into the public discourse of unified

Italy. At a time when the national rhetoric, focused on the female mission in society, emphasised woman's domestic role as mother and wife, the development of national entities, such as the postal service and the print industry, provided women with unprecedented opportunities to access and connect with the world surrounding their domestic sphere of life. Such contacts with the public sphere, however, were seen as deviations from a traditionally defined mode of domestic femininity and were at once encouraged and restrained. They were welcomed as a sign of advancement in women's contribution to the process of modernisation of Italy, but were also feared for their potential transgression. In this sense, nineteenth-century letter narratives exemplify the complex and, at times, contradictory relationship between women's expected participation in the post-unification reconstruction of Italy and the realities of a prevailing conservative approach to modernisation, which prevented any meaningful transformation of the status quo. If women were encouraged to read and write letters as a sign of their improved education and involvement in the life of the household and, more generally, of society, that same participation was closely monitored and at times censored for fear that such activities may be conducive to inappropriate behaviour.[3]

As the analysis of letter-fictions ultimately raises questions not only about the production of culture but also, and, foremost, about its distribution and consumption (reading being an essential component of the epistolary experience), this study seeks further to explore the interconnections between production and reception of the literary product, between the formulation and the interpretation of the cultural representations, understood as part of the national efforts to promote specific identities based on gender and class definitions. The focus therefore of this study will be on women writers' letter-productions, which have traditionally received little critical attention. Because late nineteenth-century women's epistolary writings arose in the midst of major political and cultural transformations, the study of the letter will also take into consideration some of the institutional innovations introduced in Italy after its political unification. Both metaphorically and practically the letter allowed writers to travel throughout the newly unified Italian territory and communicate with a public they strove to simultaneously educate and entertain.

Nineteenth-century epistolary writings by women can be inscribed within the vast array of cultural products with which the bourgeoisie sought to create a rhetorical vocabulary and a gallery of images for the representation of its social and cultural identity (Alberto Banti xii-xvi; Armstrong 4-10). In the popular fiction and journalism of the *ottocento,* the image of a woman reading or writing a letter belonged in fact more to the realm of the imaginary than to that of reality.[4] More evocative than descriptive, it expressed a vision of female readership that yet did not exist in the aftermath of the political unification, but which was considered a necessary component in the process of modernisation. Given the reality of high female illiteracy, even among the middle classes, the image, whether real or fictional, of a woman in the act of reading or writing a letter epitomised nineteenth-century bourgeois efforts to educate Italians and guide them in the maze of social and cultural transformation. The epistolary mode of writing, in fact, with it's advantage of facilitating communication between sender and receiver of the missive, synthesised the writers' efforts to connect with and ultimately influence their readers. It is not a coincidence that the same authors who wrote letter fictions, produced also conduct books and moralistic treatises. As the rising middle classes sought to create a consensus on social propriety and political hegemony, the production of a didactic literature fostered the cultivation of a collective identity based on a shared set of values. In this sense, the letter facilitated the process of such identification and the creation of a seemingly dialogical discourse between the producers and consumers of the cultural product.

To practice letter writing in the nineteenth century meant to relate to a larger community of individuals and engage with them in a dialogue which was supposed to follow the rules of a "civilised conversation" (Botteri 13). The introduction of epistolary norms in nineteenth-century conduct books instantiates the importance of exchanging epistles in accordance with a specific set of rules. It was not, however, a practice that involved the intellectual community alone, the nineteenth-century Republic of Italian Letters, but it comprised a larger social group: the literate citizenry, male or female, who, by the mere act of entertaining a correspondence with Italians located in different parts of the national territory, evoked and conceptually validated the idea that a community of Italians truly existed. For women, in addition, whom nineteenth-century social mores placed squarely within the confines of the household, writing letters represented a unique opportunity to escape domestic constraints, and develop a network of social and cultural activities which encouraged a sense of belonging to a social body more extensive than the exclusively familial one. While men, in their leisure time, frequented evening-clubs, coffee houses, and other public venues, women read novels, manuals, and wrote letters, engaging, thus, in social and cultural activities that allowed them to reach beyond the confines of the home without ever leaving it. The epistolary fiction and the correspondences published in newspapers during the second half of the nineteenth century exemplify the workings of such escape, as the letter, bridging worlds of distant interlocutors, facilitated cultural exchanges among a growing female readership.

A study on female epistolary writing at a time when only a small percentage of women was literate must begin with some preliminary considerations on women and reading. In spite of the nineteenth-century pervasive negative stereotype of the educated woman, with the school reforms enacted in 1859 and 1877 (the Casati and Coppino laws), women's rates of illiteracy (82 per cent in 1861) began to decrease. While precise data on female readership is difficult to obtain, the fragmentary, and yet valuable, records on female school attendance, publishing sales, and female newspaper subscriptions allow scholars to infer that, while not numerically conspicuous, the public of female readers was a growing and significant one.[5] Despite the high rates of female illiteracy or, perhaps, because of them, the female reader enjoyed a certain visibility in the cultural discourse of nineteenth-century Italy. In a recent volume by Anna Finocchi, one can see, for example, that starting in 1864 with the famous *La lettrice* by Federico Faruffini, several painters, many from the Tuscan artistic movement known as the *Macchiaioli,* strove to capture a moment of women's life as portrayed in the act of reading (Finocchi). Silvestro Lega (*La lettura,* 1864-65) Mosè Bianchi (*La lettrice,* 1867), Adriano Cecioni (*La zia Erminia,* 1867-1870), Francesco Netti (*Lettrice,* 1873), among many others, all attempt to portray in a realistic vein the contemporary life of Italy as they saw it. The frequency with which these painters chose the theme of a woman reading for their paintings suggests not only that that image had to correspond to some extent to an actual practice, but also that in their conception of a painting striving to be innovative and visionary, the female figure served as a symbol of an Italian modernity *in fieri.*[6] Although a controversial topic at the time, women's education was viewed as "il grado di vita moderna al quale un popolo è arrivato (the degree of modernity to which a people has arrived)," (147) as Aristide Gabelli, a renowned pedagogue, noted in 1870, and along the same lines, a woman with a letter in her hands, a symbol of her newly acquired education, projected an image of modern femininity in sharp contrast to the reality of past and present female illiteracy.[7]

The perception of letter writing as a sign of personal advancement and social modernisation derived also from the fact that nineteenth-century epistolary practices were stemming from technological developments and institutional reforms such as the railway, which, together with the nationalised postal service, was then considered a major symbol of progress (Maggi 7-8). Female epistolary writing may very well be considered a symbol of that same progress; the combination of these two images, the train and the letter, is less far-fetched that it may at first appear.

Two of the main promoters of political unification for Italy, Count Camillo Benso di Cavour and Cesare Balbo, recognised in the train a strong vehicle for the circulation of the "spirito di nazionalità italiana" throughout the Italian territory (Maggi 16-23). The train became instrumental for the circulation of people as well as ideas and news across Italy. In the period immediately following unification it proved to be a crucial factor in the government's creation of a nationalised postal service. With the invention of the railway, the mail was no longer being carried by horses, and its delivery became more efficient and extensive. While the railway already existed at the regional level, with a complex and differentiated fare system, it was only after 1862 that mail and prints started circulating throughout the national territory with relative ease.[8] Within only ten years the volume of mail and prints circulating nationally had more than doubled.[9] More people wrote and read letters: from being limited to a privileged circle of aristocrats and bureaucrats, epistolary exchanges became a daily reality in the lives of a much larger group of people and entered the imaginary of nineteenth-century female writers.

That writing letters was not just a commercial endeavour is proven by the many publications and chapters of books dedicated to the subject throughout the nineteenth century.[10] As Giovanni Mestica put it in 1882 in his *Istituzioni di letteratura*, where the topic of letter writing occupies 129 pages, the letters, "servendo alle persone di ogni età e condizione, dall'umile artigiano all'uomo di stato, è il componimento più comune negli usi della vita ed il più necessario"[11] (127). Women were seen as particularly talented in the art of writing letters; Paolo Mantegazza, for example, in his best-selling *Fisiologia della donna*, notes that "le donne emergono e brillano nello spirito e nel talento epistolare [...] L'uomo scrive in fretta perché ha altre occupazioni più serie [...] la donna invece ha quasi sempre meno da fare di noi"[12] (194). In the nineteenth century, women, especially those from the middle classes, had more free time to devote to leisure activities, as Mantegazza pointed out, but their assumed natural talent in the art of writing letters was also steeped in a tradition that harked back to ancient times.

Traditionally, epistolary writing was considered the best expressive form for the female voice (Goldsmith vii-xii). In ancient Greece, it was believed that a woman had initiated the tradition of writing letters, and throughout time, the letter form became a literary trope in which the speaking I, the sender of the missive, was often a woman.[13] The authenticity and naturalness of the female speaking subject is a feature that can be found *ab origine* in epistolary writing. Women were supposed to write in a simple and natural style, and the letter form seemed the genre most conducive to the expression of such qualities. Moreover, this form of writing reflected at best the oral nature of utterance and required little, if any, formal training. Marchesa Colombi' s conduct book, *Gente per bene* (1877), for instance, emphasises this aspect of letter writing as the author encourages young women to avoid formalities and write "con il linguaggio dell'intimità (with the language of intimacy)," with a register and language that most reflected their conversational style (82-83). Marchesa Colombi's narrative of conduct is at once a discourse on normalised behaviour constructed on the remains of old aristocratic norms (signalled by the author's choice of an 'aristocratic' pseudonym) and a formulation of new paradigms of social conduct that reflected the changing times, the process of modernisation, which in the chapter on epistles is symbolically expressed by the image of a woman following new standards of letter writing. Marchesa Colombi writes: "L'introduzione, la chiusa, sono storie del tempo trapassato remoto [...] La lettera comincia con quello che s'ha da dire, e finisce quando non s'ha più nulla da dire"[14] (82-83). The style and register of the written communication, in other words, had to comply with the rules of conversation, as if the writer of the letter were conversing with an absent interlocutor.

The notion of absence is a crucial component of nineteenth-century women's epistolary narratives. As for the missive, in which the sender strives to make the absent interlocutor present (the epistolary exchange begins in fact on this assumption of a missing interlocutor), writers of narratives in the letter form evoke the presence of a public which becomes the 'you' of the epistolary message. In a certain sense, the epistolary format invents the reader,[15] as it makes the figure of the interlocutor part of the exchange even if she is not present. At a time when the female readership was still numerically limited and scattered throughout the newly unified Italian territory, the letter form afforded writers a strategy with which they could project a readership which was at that point still in formation. Such projection was based on the fact that epistolary narratives are conceived as an exchange with an internal fictional reader, whom the real reader tends to identify with or distance oneself from. In short, the reader of epistolary narratives is always faced with the presence of someone else, and this process of multiple readings is likely to create the perception that the narrative is ultimately addressed to a body of readers larger than it truly is. Two main venues of epistolary practices promoted the creation of such imagined female readership: newspapers and fiction.

The letter and newspapers

The development of the postal service during the *ottocento* proceeded alongside another phenomenon of great cultural and institutional significance, the widespread increase in the number and circulation of newspapers. Jürgen Habermas notes that:

> one could speak of 'mail' only when the regular opportunity for letter dispatch became accessible to the general public, so there existed a press in the strict sense only once the regular supply of news became public, that is, again accessible to the general public. (16)

Habermas traces the origin and development of mail along with that of news print as phenomena related to the rise of the bourgeois public sphere. In the second half of the nineteenth century, when the Italian bourgeoisie was solidifying its cultural and political hegemony,[16] Italy saw the publication of hundreds of newspapers and periodicals – a small number if compared with other European countries, but a considerable one for Italy where in 1871, 69% of the population was still illiterate (Farinelli et all 165-72). While many of these publications had only a local readership and a short life span, the ones that were particularly popular had a national following, and had to be mailed to reach the increasing numbers of readers. Naturally, the nascent postal service could not always guarantee the delivery of 'fresh news;' still, readers from all over Italy relied on the postal service for the reception of cultural, political and literary information originating in cities other than their own.

During the second half of the nineteenth century, female readership, however limited in total number, became increasingly visible. It is evident from the number of newspapers and columns specifically addressed to women that a significant and important share of the Italian readership was composed of women.[17] Women not only read newspapers, but these newspapers provided readers with forums in which current issues could be discussed in the form of published correspondence exchanged between editors, journalists, and readers. Far from being a mere outpour of personal concerns, these spaces became an opportunity for women who lived in different parts of the newly formed nation to discuss issues of relevance to them and express their opinion in matters relating to national debates.

The practice of including letters in a journalistic format began in Italy towards the end of the eighteenth century – coming from England and France, where this tradition was already consolidated (Cook 16-17). Two of the first Italian papers devoted to a female readership made the letter a central feature of their format. *La Toelette*, a late eighteenth-century Florentine monthly, opened six of its twelve issues with a letter (two of which were addressed to the Venetian writer Elisabetta Caminer); *Il Corriere delle dame*, founded in Milan in 1804 and later renamed *La Ricamatrice*, included educational articles in the epistolary form and was the first paper to incorporate a permanent column of *piccola posta*, which was supposed to foster communication with the readers and help the editors gain a sense of the readership's opinions, expectations and tastes (Franchini 186-87). However, my study of a later periodical, *Passatempo*, shows to what extent in the second half of the *ottocento*, the letter had become an integral part of the journalistic discourse and a real tool to which both editors and journalists resorted in order to create a direct channel of communication with their readers.

Founded in Turin in 1869 by Amerigo Vespucci (sic), *Passatempo*, a monthly which in 1872 became a biweekly called *Giornale delle donne*, represented (along with *La donna* by Gualberta Alaide Beccari) one of the most outspoken newspapers for the social and cultural advancement of Italian women. Among its objectives, as stated in the paper's first issue, was that of "opporsi alle mollezze d'oltr'Alpi con morali, dilettevoli ed istruttive pubblicazioni."[18] The emphasis lay on "dilettevole," because "gli scritti puramente e semplicemente didattici sono troppo prolungati, annoiano e non possono raggiungere quindi la propria meta."[19] The idea, therefore, was that of creating a paper with a modern approach to journalistic writing, and a specific ideological agenda, one in which didactic purposes complemented commercial objectives of entertainment. It was a matter of responding to a national call for the cultural and spiritual awakening of women, but also of competing against other papers in order to gain the readers' attention and subscriptions. The letter-articles and fiction included in these newspapers conformed precisely to this double proposition: educate the readership and reach commercial success by responding to the readers' expectations. Because "the epistolary experience, as distinguished from the autobiographical one, is a reciprocal one [and] the letter writer simultaneously seeks to affect the reader and be affected by him" (Altman 88), the letter-narrative facilitated this process of mutual influence between writers and readers of newspapers. In this sense, it provided the space where readers' expectations and writers'/editors' didactic purposes converged, and where the public opinion of the time was forged.

Readers reacted immediately to Vespucci's initial definition of his journalistic approach. In the second issue, the editor published several letters he had received from his readers. Among them, a woman who lived in the Veneto region, praised the format and content of the paper because "se v'ha un bisogno urgente ed oltremodo urgente per questa nostra patria è quello di dare un indirizzo utile e nuovo affatto all'educazione della donna."[20] The letter appeared in the appendix, in a permanent column called *Conversazioni*. The name clearly suggests that the publication of the letters was conceived within a project that was supposed to evoke and encourage the creation of a dialogue among readers. But this project represented not only an abstract definition of group identity, meaningful insofar as it demonstrated the workings of cultural productions within a rhetoric advocating national identities, but also a concrete tool for the social and cultural advancement of women as it created spaces and opportunities in which to overcome what was then, and still is today, perceived as one of the main sources of female backwardness: domestic isolation. The reality of most Italian households was in fact such that outside of these cultural spaces, women had very few opportunities to escape the *hortus conclusus* of their domestic life in order to take part in the current intellectual activities and national debates.

Not only did readers write letters, but writers did too. Neera, Marchesa Colombi, Matilde Serao, Tommasina Guidi, Erminia Fuà Fusinato, Emila Nevers, to name some of the most famous female intellectuals of the time, wrote articles and fiction in the letter form for *Passatempo* and *Giornale delle donne*. Erminia Fuà Fusinato, educator and writer, published first in 1870 and then again in 1876 a series of seven letter-articles on the topic of female education. While formally addressed to the director of the paper, Amerigo Vespucci, these articles were meant to engage the larger public of female readers in a 'conversation' ("come se si conversasse tra noi" – "as if we were conversing") (Fuà Fusinato) on the controversial and much discussed topic of women's emancipation, which for Fusinato could be attained only through education and a gradual liberation from obsolete customs and atavistic ignorance. On the same topic, Caterina Pigorini Beri wrote in 1873 three letter-articles discussing the current state of the newly created "scuole normali femminili (high schools for women)." The articles, which complained about the administrative and didactic disarray in which these schools were forced to operate, were then reported by other newspapers and provoked a lively discussion among and beyond the readership of *Giornale delle donne*. Though addressed to the school superintendent of the Marche region, Piero Giuliani, these articles along with those by Fuà Fusinato were clearly meant to spark a debate that would, and did, involve a larger group of interlocutors than that suggested by the formal addressee. In all these articles, the epistolary form, far from being merely ornamental, significantly influenced the way in which the narrative implicitly evoked the presence of multiple interlocutors urging them to provide a response. Since epistolary writing is based on what has been defined as an "epistolary pact" (Altman 89) – the call for response from the reader – articles published in the letter form, unlike normal first-person writings, provided the writers with narratives that required interpretation by, and commentary from, their readers, who in response would write letters to the editor.

While the practice of writing letter-articles was not a unique feature of women's newspapers, women seemed to use it more frequently. The following examples illustrate the ample use that famous female journalists made of this narrative strategy. In March 1905, Marchesa Colombi published a letter-article, "La padrona (The mistress)," in *La Stampa* in response to Matilde Serao's article, published in the same paper a week before, "La serva (The maid);" in *L'illustrazione italiana,* Marchesa Colombi's letter-article "La donna povera (The poor woman)" responded in 1876 to Neera's "La donna libera (The free woman);" and in *La lega della democrazia,* Anna Maria Mozzoni wrote in 1880 "Lettera aperta a Matilde Serao." All articles touched upon some of the most controversial issues of the time, social and gender relations, female education and emancipation, and the letter form led a general discussion. Marchesa Colombi's letter-article "La padrona" was written in the epistolary format not only to respond personally to Serao's provocative criticism of the domestic workforce, but also to encourage readers themselves to ponder the thorny issue of class mobility and social protest. In a similar vein, Marchesa Colombi's letter-article "La donna povera," in which she rebuked Neera's argument against women working outside of the household, implicitly invited readers to see the question of female professional work from multiple perspectives.

That these writers tended to adopt the letter form for their opinionated columns or articles should not be surprising given their intense correspondences not only with fellow writers and friends but also with their readers. These letters, far from existing as a distinct part of their production, had a tremendous influence not only on their journalistic writings but also on their fiction. "Bisogna avere come ho la fortuna di aver io, un'immensa corrispondenza con le signore, per farsi un'idea del gusto della grazia, dell'eleganza che ci mettono,"[21] Marchesa Colombi wrote, stressing the intrinsic value of the correspondence provided by her readers, and also the need for a writer to understand and sympathise with the readers' world of cultural values and expectations. And indeed, both Marchesa Colombi's and Serao's fiction may be considered a response to this notion of 'correspondence,' understood as a commonality of taste, concerns and intents between writers and readers.

The letter and fiction

Matilde Serao's and Marchesa Colombi's epistolary fiction is embedded in romance. Not all of their sentimental fiction is developed with this literary strategy, but the letter with its narrative of union and separation, and its language of intimate communication seems to be particularly suited for the love plot (Altman 14). Historically, many writers of love narratives, from Ovid, Héloïse and Abelard, to Laclos, have employed the epistolary form; Italian nineteenth-century female authors of romance also relied on this tradition. In addition to this, however, one should not underestimate the role played by the reader in the construction of their sentimental texts. In light of the epistolary property of portraying the experience of reading (the writing of a letter implicitly or explicitly always outlines the figure of a reader), my analysis of Serao's and Marchesa Colombi's fiction demonstrates that the reader is here almost as important an agent as the writer (Altman 88). In addition to this, it further illustrates the intricate relation and interdependence between the writers' journalistic writings and their fiction as they both strove to engage the same audience of readers.

Matilde Serao wrote several short stories in the epistolary form, which appeared in collections such as *Fior di passione* (1899), *Lettere d'amore* (1901), *Novelle sentimentali* (1902), *Gli amanti* (1908) and *La vita è così lunga* (1918), all centered, as can be inferred from their titles, on passion and love intrigues. Serao also published a novel written entirely in the letter-form, *Ella non rispose* (1914), which, in thematic content and narrative strategy, does not differ from her *novelle*. Marchesa Colombi's letter novel, *Prima morire* (1881), and the short stories, "Un sogno azzurro" and "Cartolina postale," both in the collection *Dopo il caffè* (1878), similarly develop a plot of love desires that inescapably remain unrealised. Thematically repetitive and ideologically conservative, both Serao's and Colombi's romantic fictions have traditionally been neglected by critics for their presumed lack of literary merit. The problem with this critical approach is that by placing the attention on the 'what,' the content, rather than on the 'event' of the literary experience itself, the performance that brings the text to fruition, one invariably misses a central aspect of this type of literature: that textual meaning lies primarily in the relationship between reader and writer, and on the mechanism that supports such relation, rather than in an objective and universally binding set of literary canons.

In the last twenty years, reader-response criticism and theories of popular fiction have stressed the fact – often taken for granted and critically disregarded – that "all stories are implicitly or explicitly addressed to an audience, whose presence is as variable and as problematic as that of a story-teller" (Suleiman 3). In light of these studies, Serao's and Marchesa Colombi's romance fiction may be viewed as a collaborative effort, one in which textual meaning derives in a temporally defined intersection between the writer's creative impulses and the reader's interpretative act. Further, such effort reflects what may be considered a 'pact' – similar to the epistolary pact described by Janet Altman – made between authors and the public, whose active participation is *a sine qua non* of the historical actualisation of textual meaning. According to Robert Hans Jauss, the literary work represents "a moment of a process, in which two horizons are always at play in a synthesis of understanding" (23). In this sense, then, if, from the point of view of the author, the romantic fiction reflects the formulation of a project *a priori*: on the one hand, to secure consensus and commercial success by way of meeting the reading expectations and tastes of the audience; on the other, the readers make themselves available to that same project only on the condition that their literary experience enters "into the horizon of expectations of [their] lived praxis, performs [their] understanding of the world, and thereby also has an effect on [their] social behavior" (Jauss 23). In short, to be able to take part in and enjoy the literary experience, the reader has to be able to relate to, and often identify with, the topic, characters and language of the fiction. In the specific case of Matilde Serao and Marchesa Colombi, the popularity of their sentimental fiction can be explained by their ability to understand and interact with the realities and expectations of their readers who belonged to a world, specific in its social and gender identity (middle class and female), which they themselves inhabited. Serao's famous self-definition as "cronista della memoria (chronicler of memory),"[22] traditionally interpreted by critics as referring to her realistic novels, in this regard accurately describes the writer's 'hands-on' approach to her writing in general. This definition, it seems, applies also to Serao's later career, when she became the interpreter and chronicler of nineteenth-century bourgeois values as well as erotic desires. In this light, Serao's later sentimental short stories represent a continuation of, rather than a deviation from, her initial literary approach. The same conclusions can be drawn about Marchesa Colombi's literary production.

As in all popular fiction, the romantic text influences and is, at the same time, informed by the current beliefs and norms of behaviour of a specific social or gender group. Jauss speaks of the literary text as a "norm-creating experience," and in Serao's and Marchesa Colombi's epistolary fiction, and perhaps in their whole literary production, to read means not only to entertain but also to educate and fulfil a project of social amelioration. It is therefore a fiction that works in conjunction with other normative publications (conduct books, newspaper articles) written by the same authors and intended to be an instrument of cultural intervention in the social body. This is not to suggest that the two writers can be perfectly assimilated into a single mode of creative writing, as they differ on many levels, but they did conform to a similar principle of artistic inspiration which entailed a sort of social and civic 'engagement' in the literary production. Even late in their career, when writing sentimental fiction, the act of reading is never presented as an end in itself. Marchesa Colombi makes this point clear in *Serate d'inverno* where her short stories, though ironically described as 'little' and 'delightful,' ultimately aim at making reading, no matter what its content, an experience of self-improvement. The epistolary form, in particular, exemplifies the way in which the writers reach out to the readers and call upon their intervention in turning the text into a meaningful experience.

Thematically, texts written in the epistolary form do not differ from other stories produced during the same period, as they all refer to and describe the life of middle class women, and revolve around the happy and unhappy love stories of the protagonists. The plots are quite repetitive and narrate, with minor variations, the downfall of women who search for the satisfaction of their sentimental desires outside of their conjugal relationship. Structurally, however, the letter form invites the reader to interpret the message contained in the missive, thus making the writer's call for the reader's intervention more compelling. Such interpretation does not, however, occur directly but is always mediated by the figure of the internal reader (the character who is the recipient of the fictional letter) with whom the external reader (or 'real' reader of the book) is naturally prone to identify. The identification between fictional and factual reader takes place because the latter reads the text through the 'eyes' of the former and 'voyeuristically' experiences the event, the tormented love in the case of romance narrative.

In the nineteenth century, women's capacity to express themselves in letters presented a somewhat paradoxical situation. Seen as an example of women's improved education, the popularity of letter writing was interpreted as proof of women's increasing ability to read and write, but at the same time, as a dangerous realm within which women could act independently and without proper supervision. Many of Serao's stories that feature the letter represent women who secretly write and read letters that are exchanged with their lovers. The ambiguity embodied in the literary representation of epistolary exchange is maintained in those works in which the letter functions as the vehicle for both the expression and censorship of female emotions. The letter is written to express desire but also to instruct, to explain a situation, and in most cases to rectify what the sender of the missive perceives as an incorrect interpretation of the facts.

This double representation has inspired different critical interpretations of Serao's sentimental fiction. Most critics have underlined the writer's essentially conservative outlook on women's sexual behavior, while others, such as Deanna Shemek, have seen in Serao's love stories a "positive force struggling within a repressive and enclosing society" (245). My study of the epistolary form of these stories makes the conservative interpretation more compelling, because the structure of the texts forces us to read her narrative as constructing an essentially didactic discourse. The external reader cannot elude identification with the fictional recipient of the letter, as her reading is always mediated by the figure of the internal reader, created by the writer. The letter is used, therefore, as an instrument of relation, and, ultimately, of constraint. Exposed to the grave consequences of illicit love affairs or illusionary sentimental fantasies, the female readers of romance novels are taught how to avoid errors in life and how to improve their existence, but the final moral lesson that each story advances inescapably brings the reader back to an unquestionable moralistic norm of female virtuosity.

Nineteenth-century sentimental fiction written in the epistolary form conformed to this conservative outlook towards gender roles, and provided the female readership with an exemplary narration of negative female behaviour. The fact that these stories were written in the epistolary form confirms the authors' desire to convey a strong message to their readers, enabling identification among the middle class women who looked up to female public figures for guidance through the maze of social conventions attached to a class still in formation: the Italian bourgeoisie.

Whether in a journalistic format or in fiction, Matilde Serao's and Marchesa Colombi's use of the letter form can be interpreted in light of a utilitarian conception of art, one in which writing is intended to be an instrument used to engage the readers in a 'conversation.' Further, by using this literary strategy, the authors took advantage of the letter's inherent property to deliver a narrative infused with a message that was supposed to spark a reaction in the readers, whether in the form of an opinion or of restrained behaviour. Both Serao and Marchesa Colombi were familiar with their readers' concerns, tastes and expectations, and included these factors in the very fabric of their writings. Not surprisingly, these women were very popular and represented some of the best-selling authors of the time. Their romance fiction and journalistic work might not be original in content or artistically innovative, as the lack of critical interest has implicitly suggested, but they have a lot to say about the way in which during the late *ottocento* culture was produced and consumed by women. They demonstrate how for female authors of popular narratives writing was not just a matter of providing escape or entertainment, but of creating opportunities for women to access and participate in the national discourse on matters of relevance to women, such as female education or social mores; it was a matter of making reading pertinent to the daily experience of nineteenth-century women's life.

Notes

1. I am not referring only to the great success of readership that Foscolo's *Ultime lettere di Jacopo Ortis* enjoyed in the second half of the nineteenth century, especially among women, to which both Serao and Marchesa Colombi attest in their fiction (*Romanzo della fanciulla* and *Serate d'inverno*, respectively) but also to the popularity in Italy of Pietro Chiari's eighteenth-century novels in the letter form and his translations of English epistolary fiction. See Madrignani

2. For cultural historicisation of the epistolary form, see Gilroy and Verhoeven, and Beebee.

3. In this regard, Aristide Gabelli lamented: "è quasi comune il canone prudenziale, che alle donne sia cosa arrischiata insegnare a scrivere, perché altrimenti se ne servono per fare all'amore, come se non vi fossero amori senza scrittura." "Italia e l'istruzione femminile." Quoted in Perugi 194.

4. I am clearly drawing from Anderson's notion of imagined communities, and his theory that nationalism is first and foremost imagined as a cultural construct and then created as a political entity. The figure of the literate woman belongs to the same group of cultural artifacts of which Andersen speaks in his analysis of nationalism.

5. See Palazzolo 87-96. Palazzolo suggests that nineteenth-century efforts to control and limit women's education resulted in a vast production of publications, which exposed women to an inclusive rather than exclusive typology of reading material. See also Tortorelli 153-69.

6. Dario Durbè writes on the Macchiaioli that their work is "a warm and authentic expression of the dynamics and ideals of an entire society" (16). See also Dini; and Albert Boime, who wrote: "The Macchiaioli attempted to overturn convention and create a landscape appropriate to modern Italy." (71)

7. See, for example, Odoardo Borrani's painting *L' analfabeta* (1869), in which a middle class woman is writing a letter for one of her supposedly illiterate female employees.

8. For the history of the Italian postal service see: Melillo; Majorana; Caizzi; and Fedele.

9. According to the records included in the yearly report provided by the director of the Italian postal office, 72, 563, 346 letters were mailed in Italy in 1863, while ten years later, in 1873, the number increased to 104,502,431. See *Prima Relazione sul Servizio Postale in Italia, Anno 1863* and *Undicesima Relazione sul Servizio Postale in Italia:1873.*

10. The nineteenth century saw a proliferation of manuals and conduct books dedicated to the topic of letter writing. See for example: Picci; Bianchetti; Bertolotti; Montanari; Gamba; and Gozzi.

11. "being useful to people of all ages and social status, from the simple craftsman to the man of state, it is the most common and most necessary type of writing there is in life."

12. "women emerge and master the spirit and talent of letter writing. Man writes in a rush because he has other more serious occupations [...] a woman instead almost always has less to do than us."

13. See Doglio; Zancan, "La donna" and her *Il doppio itinerario della scrittura. La donna nella tradizione letteraria italiana;* and Zarri.

14. "The introduction and the closing are things long passed. The letter starts with what one has to say and ends when one has nothing else to say."

15. For a theoretical discussion on the figure of the reader, see: Eco; Iser; and Thompkins.

16. See Alberto Banti; and Lanaro.

17. Such publications included *Cordelia, L'Aurora, La Cornelia, La Donna e la famiglia, Corriere delle Maestre, Museo di Famiglia, Il giornale delle donne, La Donna, La Missione della donna, Margherita,* and all the main newspapers like *L'Almanacco italiano, Il Corriere di Milano, Il Mattino, La Vita italiana* in which appeared special columns dedicated to women and to family issues and special editions like the "strenne di Natale." See Zambon, *Letteratura e stampa nel secondo Ottocento* and *Le donne a scuola: l'educazione femminile nell'Italia dell'Ottocento;* Buttafuoco; Dappio; and Kroha.

18. "to face the feebleness from across the Alps with moral, delightful and educational publications."

19. "purely and simply didactic writings are too long and boring and therefore cannot reach the intended objective." *Passatempo: letture per il Gentil sesso* I (Jan 1869) 1.

20. "if there is a single and most urgent need for our country, it is that of giving a useful and altogether new direction to women's education." *Passatempo: letture per il Gentil sesso* I I (Feb 1869) Appendix, 1.

21. "It is necessary to have, as I have, an immense correspondence with the ladies, to be able to have an idea of the taste, grace, and elegance that they use in it." Quoted by Giuliana Morandini in her introduction to Colombi, *Un Matrimonio in provincia* 12.

22. Serao defined her writing as a process of excavation through the sediment of memories: "Io scavo nella mia memoria dove i ricordi sono disposti a strati successivi, come le tracce della vita geologica nella crosta terrestre, e vi do così come le trovo, senza ricostruire degli animali fantastici[...] Dal primo giorno che ho scritto, io non ho mai voluto e saputo esser altro che una fedele e umile cronista della mia memoria." Quoted by Giannatonio, 154.

Cosima, quasi Grazia: A Novel, Almost an Autobiography[1]

Patrizia Guida

The life and literary activity of Grazia Deledda stand out as a special 'case' in the whole of Italian literature, since the writer, known for her reserve and unpretentious image, has been conceptualised in terms of a sort of literary parthenogenesis, based on her lack of formal education, and her provincial beginnings far from dominant cultural circles. From 1888 onwards, Deledda's stories appeared in local publications; she died the author of more than fifty works of fiction,[2] which had been translated into many languages. In 1926 she was awarded the Nobel Prize for Literature, only the second woman, the first being Selma Lagerlöf, to receive such prestigious recognition[3] "for her idealistically inspired writings which with plastic clarity picture the life on her native island and with depth and sympathy deal with human problems in general," as the official citation reads. As Baiardo notes, the Deledda case would seem to contradict "le tesi sull'emarginazione della donna nel campo della creatività"[4] (58), however, it is the author herself who provides an insight into her success as a writer:

> Ho l'anima quasi maschile e non temo nulla, né vivi né morti, né le superstizioni né la critica, personale o artistica, né pregiudizi, nulla, ma sono nervosa e spesso i nervi si impongono dispoticamente sulla mia anima e mi fanno tremare per cose da nulla, e mi fanno piangere e smaniare come una bimba.[5]

This "almost masculine" temperament to some extent explains the writer's ability to find her bearings in the world of publishing, to establish relationships with publishers and men of letters and, in short, to control the public dimension of her work as a writer.

Literary criticism has not been in agreement with regard to the literary value of the Sardinian writer's works,[6] situating them, somewhat precariously, between *verismo* and *decadentismo*. In actual fact, Deledda's work is closer to *verismo* in its focus on social issues and customs, and its use of a language which is spontaneous and down-to-earth; however, the touches of originality in her way of interpreting everyday happenings fall outside the tenet of impersonality typical of *verismo*. In her novels, life's vicissitudes appear as an unceasing struggle between sin and the desire for redemption, between primitive, unrestrained passion and the inner striving for justice and purity. In this struggle human beings show themselves to be, as in the title of one of her novels, "like reeds in the wind," in other words, fragile beings battling destiny, which they oppose in the name of their fundamental values, without taking on the stance of heroes. Deledda's realism takes on a fatalistic slant: free will is denied and God is immanent. It is this vision of life and her primitive and natural settings (enlivened by frequent references to Sardinian culture and folklore), which form the backdrops to her stories, and are the key to the appeal and artistic merit which characterise many of her novels, such as *Anime oneste* (1895), *Canne al vento* (1913), *Marianna Sirca* (1915), and *La madre* (1920). On the other hand, though, the conflict between her desire for objectivity and her tendency to draw a lyrical halo around dramatic events, means that the naturalism of her portrayal moves more towards symbolism; a symbolism which, Sapegno (*Pagine*) maintains, is completely instinctive and unconscious.

Critical commentary surrounding Deledda's work focuses almost exclusively on its relationship to life on the island of her birth, but her work offers other themes to reflect upon, related to social development and the emancipation of women. In this context, of primary importance are the autobiographical and emotional aspects, which Deledda constantly brings to life on the page.

Leaving aside any consideration of the literary merit of Deledda's work, it clearly represents an extraordinary achievement, as Floris points out:

> francamente non si può non ammirare questa giovinetta autodidatta, sola, senza un retroterra culturale alle spalle, che era riuscita a farsi stampare, lei donna, non muovendosi d'un passo da Nuoro, fra l'incomprensione di un ambiente diffidente e ostile, migliaia e migliaia di pagine di prosa e di versi [...] e a scrivere centinaia e centinaia di lettere ad uomini più navigati di lei [...] per questo ci pare che si possa affermare che la Deledda, anche da giovanissima, come fatto culturale sia meritevole di grande rispetto e di notevole.[7] (32)

In this light, the autobiography of the writer, an expression of the *condition humaine* (Bruner), takes on a particular significance in that it constitutes the spatio-temporal dimension which triggers the typically phenomenological cognitive process.

In this chapter I attempt to focus on some issues of particular relevance to an analysis of the autobiographical novel *Cosima* (1936). I will also explore the application of theoretical frameworks regarding self-inscription to Deledda's text. The first point to consider is whether Deledda's novel belongs to the autobiographical genre, which in turn requires some discussion of the limits of autobiography.

Unfinished autobiography or fiction?

Following the studies of Misch (1955) and Pascal (1960), research into the genre of autobiography intensified in the seventies, taking as a starting point the well-known theory of the "autobiographical pact" as postulated by Lejeune in *Le pacte* (1975). This theory holds that the autobiographer enters into a pact with the reader, based on the identity of author, narrator and protagonist, and on the undertaking on the part of the author to tell the truth. Another significant influence on the study of autobiography has been Olney, according to whom autobiography is no more than a metaphor for the person writing, since, at the moment of writing, the autobiographer constructs "a monument of self as it is becoming, a metaphor of the self at a summary moment of composition" (35). These studies paid little attention to autobiographical texts written by women. It was not until the 1980s that the first theoretical studies appeared dealing with the role of the female subject in the writing of the self.[8]

Many studies have attempted to analyse autobiographical writing in its various forms. Battistini examines "possibili diffrazioni, moltiplicandone le varianti combinatorie situate all'intersezione con generi vicini"[9] (24), variables which lead Briganti to describe autobiography as an ultragenre (*ultragenere*) which "insinuates" itself into other genres (see Pickering-Iazzi 178). Clearly, it is in this sense that the phrase 'all autobiography is fiction' must be interpreted, since autobiography is not only "an attempt to retell one's past life on a linear scale, but rather in effect a novel written in the present with one's past life as its subject" (Pike 328). The coexistence of reality and fiction, which underlies all writing, is confirmed by Eakin, according to whom, in every autobiography "the materials of the past are shaped by memory and imagination to serve the needs of present consciousness" (56). At the moment of writing, the autobiographical writer is historically distant from the narrated events. This distance leads the reader to doubt their authenticity, and to believe that they may have been altered as a result of imperfect memory, or of the fact that not all of the events in the past receive the same amount of attention from the writer. In addition, some events may not be considered *a posteriori* relevant to the general economy of the text, or to the pact which is being forged with the reader.

The autobiographical writer's selection of narrative material is determined by its distance in time from the present (memory), by personal feelings such as reserve, shame or pride, and by external factors which lead to self-censorship. In addition to this, the act of writing is preceded not only by the choice of material, but also by the structuring of that material into narrative form. These two aspects, the selection and the organisation of material, are what characterise the written text. The dimensions of present and future, and the objectives the writer is trying to reach through a particular portrayal of self, are major influences on the autobiographer's perspective.

In an attempt to determine the boundaries of autobiographical writing, Frye identifies a series of almost imperceptible gradations (307), within which personal memory undergoes multiple transformations at the hand of the writer/narrator in order to become fiction in the making of his/her story. The presence of the writer – weaving the traces of the past into a narrative – is felt by the reader, who, however, is not able to distinguish the ways in which it has been absorbed (Hart 488).

Cosima falls into this hybrid category of autobiographical fiction, or autobiography in the form of a novel, since its formal and aesthetic qualities prevail. This could be expected in the work of a writer who is describing a life closely connected to her craft of writing which seems to have been her sole source of sustenance. *Cosima, quasi Grazia*, was published posthumously in the journal *Nuova Antologia*, during September and October 1936.[10] The ambiguous nature of the hybrid text, which falls somewhere between fiction and autobiography, is confirmed by the intentional slant given to the title, and its later return to the original title, *Cosima*, when published in book form in 1937.

Even though the material is autobiographical, the work cannot clearly be said to belong to the genre of traditional autobiography as postulated by its theorists, with its constants and conventions, range of expectations and historical origins. The first distancing between this text and the autobiographical genre can be seen at the level of the writing, that is to say, in the detachment from her referent. Deledda's capacity to step back from the material being narrated – her own story – enables her to create characters who are autonomous on a literary level, and to present a balanced relationship between diegesis and mimesis, that is, between a representation of the facts, and descriptions of things and people, which contribute to the novel-like character of the work. In *Cosima*, in fact, the realist element provided by her descriptions of the day-to-day life of her childhood, and the element of fantasy provided by her surrender to the marvels of her day dreams, constantly intertwine in descriptions of events, and analyses of the inner world, with which she transformed her reality ("si sentiva anche lei in corpo una smania di amazzone, un ardore di eroina da avventure audaci)"[11] (99-100). On the other hand, autobiography, to the extent that it is a narrative, implies a structuring that the autobiographical writer carries out in exactly the same way as the author of fiction. This starts from the moment in which he/she constructs the character, the narrated self, and organises the narrative framework in accordance with an internal, but also a structural order, compensating for the intermittent nature of memory. The writer who narrates the self therefore censors, transforms, values one episode and ignores another, uses pseudonyms or narrative masks; constructs a narrative identity, in short, which is superimposed on the biographical identity: Cosima in place of Grazia in Deledda's case.[12]

A brief digression on the use of the writer's middle name, which will be discussed more fully later, is of particular relevance here as it signifies a partial self-revelation on the part of the Sardinian writer, which can only occur on condition that her biographical identity remain hidden. It can also be connected to the larger issue of the traditional exclusion of women from the public sphere. Deledda's choice of the name Cosima is yet more evidence of the tension between the impulse to make one's personal experience public and the desire to keep one's personal experience private (Spacks *Selves In Hiding* 1980).

I have already flagged the anomalous nature of *Cosima* in relation to the autobiographical canon with my reading of its title. The text itself presents more than a few philological problems because it was published posthumously, and therefore not edited by the author (which supports the view of several critics that it is an unfinished work), and because many scholars have used it as a 'documentary' source,[13] whilst biography is generally used to confirm the authenticity of autobiography. Critical interest in *Cosima* has not focused sufficiently on the fact that it is an unfinished text, which in my opinion is crucial, in that it allows for a number of readings which would not otherwise be possible.

The first unknown we encounter concerns the genesis of the text.[14] We have absolutely no information regarding the author's plans for it, whether it was intended for publication, for example, or whether it was considered to be finished, and, therefore, intentionally covering only a specific period in Deledda's life.

From De Michelis' notes we know that the manuscript consisted of two hundred and seventy-eight pages of which five are missing (pp. 1, 211, 212, 276, 277), and that many changes were made by editors, starting with Deledda's son, Sardus Madesani. These editorial interventions were aimed at making its references to real people less explicit, at changing the narrative to the third person in places where the first person appeared in the manuscript, and in general, at tidying up the text. De Michelis tells us that in *Opere Scelte* he has restored the text to the original, removing chapter divisions which were not in the manuscript, reinstating original surnames (with the exception of one case, at the request of Deledda's son), retaining the title and making the spelling consistent throughout. But despite his efforts with the spelling, there are still some textual irregularities, such as gaps in the narrative[15] or the occasional grammatical flaw: missing or incomplete words, erratic punctuation, or the unconventional use of a tense. In these cases, the editor has cautiously intervened, signalling his changes with the use of brackets and brief footnotes.[16] These shortcomings, however, do not compromise the substantial completeness of the work, since the story, at least as far as it goes, has a clear basic structure and a sufficiently well-developed artistic form.[17]

Another problem critical analysis has to deal with relates to how Deledda handles the autobiographical self. Whether Battistini's approach is used, according to which the autobiographical persona is "a cultural and linguistic fiction" (Battistini 16), or whether it is assumed *a priori* that author, narrator and character are one and the same, as in the 'pact' theorised by Lejeune, Deledda's text invites investigation of the hermeneutic progression of the narrating self and the epistemological modes which the writer uses to construct the self-image she will leave to posterity. In this context, it is interesting to analyse the various means by which she differentiates and identifies the narrated self and the biographical self. Starting with her choice of pseudonym, albeit her middle name, as an attempt at differentiation from herself, we sense that *Cosima* does not observe the explicit pact between author and reader which according to Lejeune is the essential condition for every autobiography.

When the extradiegetic narrator appears in the text, with the use of the possessive pronoun "our" ("La casa più importante è però quella abitata dal canonico, di fronte alla nostra"[18] (19)), this does not mean a sudden admission of autobiography, with narrative fragments in which the identity of narrator/character is suddenly confirmed. If we accept the theory that this is an unfinished novel, the familiar axiom – that the use of the first person plural unmasks the writer's autobiographical persona – must remain a philologically unverifiable hypothesis, since the manuscript was never revised and corrected by the author.

If autobiography is taken to mean a text in which author, narrator and main character are one and the same, indicated by the use of the first person, and a text which recounts that person's real life from a given perspective, writing about events without ruling out imaginary elements, then we realise that *Cosima* does not fit into the traditional canon as it has been defined by scholars. Added to this is the fact that the manuscript lacked any note, preface or other information from the author that might have allowed us to identify her with Cosima. In the final analysis, it is the context which impels the identification of the main character with the author, a context which, as has already been noted, is made explicit in the editor's notes. All the verifiable details in the narrative (names, places, events, etc.), according to Baldini's useful annotations in an appendix to the text, are exact and serve to relate the events narrated in the story to real happenings, and make the book a valuable tool in retracing the beginnings of Deledda's work as a writer.

According to Lejeune, all the variants of third person narration fulfil the author's desire to distance him/herself from the past self. This may be due to modesty or to the wish to split the self in order to minimise the narcissistic identification of the writer with the autobiographical persona. However, as Starobinski notes, autobiography written in the third person can have the opposite effect, heightening the presence of the narrator, rather than reducing it, since the foregrounded events as a whole serve to present the main character in a positive light. The splitting of author and autobiographical persona, which is seen in *Cosima*, produced by an older person describing herself as a child, tends towards the reconstruction of an identity through a process of idealisation of the protagonist. Pickering-Iazzi suggests a reading of Deledda's use of the third person "as a means to subvert patriarchal authority inscribed in the history of the genre's conventions" ("The Politics" 178). She traces this particular practice to the eighteenth-century trend of autobiography, identified by Guglielminetti "un'occasione insostituibile per definire la propria funzione di uomo di cultura entro il quadro della 'repubblica letteraria'"[19] (140), thanks to which Deledda could perhaps be called 'a woman of culture' (Pickering-Iazzi, "The Politics" 189).

In Deledda's case, the use of the third person would seem more likely to be linked to the desire to depersonalise and universalise the narration in order to shift it from the sphere of autobiography to that of fiction. In this case, the decision to use the third person would be motivated more by literary considerations than by ideological, or, even less likely, political ones. We cannot ignore the fact either that the writer of an autobiography wants to pass on an image of him/herself to a real or imagined public, and that this process implies the construction of that self, the narrated self, and the taking on of a role on the part of the writer. We can deduce, therefore, as Pizzorusso does, that the relationship between author and protagonist, between the narrating self and the narrated self is not one of identity, as held by scholars in the field, but one of tension in relation to the identification of what is termed an 'autobiographical persona,' that is a construct based on a selection of historically authentic material, and which corresponds to its creator's idea of self.

As Pickering-Iazzi notes, in *Cosima* the boundaries between author, narrator and persona frequently blur ("The Politics" 189):

> Sei notti dopo la partenza di Santus, fu sentito, sul tardi, qualcuno bussare replicatamene alla porta. Dopo mezzo secolo di vita, Cosima ricorda ancora quel picchiare come di tamburo che annunzia una disgrazia: lo sente ancora rimbombare dentro il suo cuore; è il suono più terribile che abbia mai sentito, più funebre di quello che annunzia la morte (51).[20]

The use of the present tense, which signals the presence of the extradiegetic narrator, and the past tense, used for memory, alternate and intertwine during the narration, repeatedly revealing the vantage point of the writer, which is that of a privileged observer able to give meaning to events. Throughout the novel, in fact, in her use of verb tenses the writer ignores convention (the communicative and narrative tenses, according to the well-known distinction made by Genette) and mixes them to produce the interesting effect in the narrative of reducing the focal length, thus shifting the attention from the distance to the foreground. Elsewhere in the text, the alternating of present and past tenses would seem to be due to the text's lack of polish, leading once again to the hypothesis that this is an unfinished work.

Female *Bildungsroman*

Why did Deledda choose to write her memories in novel form instead of recording them in a memoir? The answer lies in the sphere of autobiographical intent, which in the case of *Cosima* is unknown. Is it apologetic or moralistic, or perhaps instructive in its intent, in order to justify the writing of the self, as was true, for example, of the autobiographical writers of the eighteenth century? According to some scholars, the autobiographer is not an historian of the self: his/her subjectivity is perceived, through the pact with the reader, not as an identity which is already fixed, but as an ongoing process in which the author constructs him/herself dynamically in an equilibrium between reality and fiction, writing the self in the relationship between the constructed text and the portrayal of reality it projects.[21] Becoming, metamorphosis and transition coexist in the autobiographical hermeneutic, so that the introspective and retrospective story of a self reveals itself as autopoietic and self-generating.

What seems to me to be the most plausible hypothesis in *Cosima*'s case is that of a writing of the self which becomes the symbolic act of bringing into the present the traces, the signs of a time, and a collective historical memory otherwise forgotten at the time of its writing.

The other unknown to reflect upon at this point is the writer's decision to narrate only part of her life, leaving out important and decisive events such as her marriage, fame, motherhood, the Nobel Prize and her illness. This choice can be interpreted in a number of ways. The first hypothesis that immediately comes to mind is that the novel is unfinished, being abruptly cut short by the death of its author, as we have no information about how the project was envisaged. But if we consider it to be the result of an intentional choice, the discussion inevitably becomes more complex, involving a range of literary and non-literary factors, including whether or not the novel can be included in the genre of *Bildungsroman*.

Hirsch defines the *Bildungsroman* as a novel of formation of an individual within a specific social context, and by means of a dialectical process of socialisation, which starts from an initial position of opposition to societal norms and culminates in the recognition of his/her destiny and, as a consequence, the successful finding of his/her place in society. The critic Moretti attributes the founding of the western tradition of novels of formation to two late eighteenth-century texts: Goethe's *Wilhelm Meister's Apprentice Years*, and Jane Austin's *Pride and Prejudice*. Austin's novel, according to Moretti, is exemplary of the distinctive character of the novel of formation, with its narrative of transition and compromise in the process of becoming adult, thanks to what Freud would later define as the 'reality principle.' Gilbert and Gubar, instead, choose Charlotte Brontë's *Jane Eyre* as a plot exemplifying the female search for her self, whilst having to overcome the enormous difficulties encountered in a thoroughly patriarchal social and cultural context.

In this sense, *Cosima* can be considered to be a novel of formation, in so much as it is the construction of a (female) identity and of a destiny fulfilled by a calling which determines the kind of contribution the protagonist can make to society. This protagonist, like the protagonists of *Bildungsroman* written by male authors, rebels against the passivity of her role in favour of action and freedom. It is important to note here that *Cosima* was published during the period of fascist dictatorship in Italy, and offers a female model which differed from that promoted by the regime, sadly referred to as that of exemplary wife and mother. Cosima presents herself to the reader as a young rebel who refuses to conform to the dominant values of her day.

In her reconstruction of Cosima's passage from childhood to maturity, Deledda uses several *topoi* typical of the novel of formation, but in place of adventure and philosophy, we find the conflict between social expectations and personal aspirations, between the very limited world which is foreseen for her, and the universe she is denied. Set in the patriarchal Sardinia of the late 1800s, the novel spans a period of seven years in the life of its protagonist, from her childhood to young adulthood – a period during which an individual's psychological make-up is determined and behaviour patterns are established. The range of experience it draws on is fairly limited to the familiar events of everyday life. It is this very day-to-day normality of things, along with their human dimension, which constitute a strong formative influence. Cosima's story does not start at birth but at an unspecified time in her childhood, most probably linked to the age at which she is capable of remembering, a moment which signals a sort of intellectual birth and thus acquires a kind of mythical status.

The novel begins with the description of a house. It is Cosima's birthplace, hence, holds a special place in her memory, and it is described with a wealth of detail. Hart, in his analysis of the role of memory in the work of Yeats, writes: "Creating a new personality is recreating one's legend in association with memorable places" (488). The paternal home, which Deledda had recalled in many of her previous novels, is the place which ties her to her past, and it is not until leaving it that she is able to recreate her identity in Rome. In the narration of *Cosima*, the house has the function of a collective actant whose role is to give the impression of authenticity and, thus, to immediately connect the main character to her natural background.

Within the narration, spatial coordinates have a narrative function: kitchen implements, for example, which are described with great accuracy, transcend their material value to take on a valuable role in the handing down of popular culture, an integral part of the novel's context. The full and detailed description at the beginning of the novel means that action is temporarily suspended, and the protagonist and the larger context become for the moment superfluous. However, the house over-looking Mount Ortobene establishes the protagonist, implicitly revealing her personality between the lines of its description.

> Di giorno era quasi sempre socchiuso, e più che il portoncino della facciata, serviva per il passaggio degli abitanti e degli amici della casa. A questo portone, una mattina di maggio, si affaccia una bambina bruna, seria, con gli occhi castanei, limpidi e grandi, le mani e i piedi minuscoli, vestita di un grembiale grigiastro con le tasche, con le calze di grosso cotone grezzo e le scarpe rustiche a lacci, più paesana che borghese, e aspetta, dondolandosi su una gamba su e giù, che passi qualcuno o qualcuno si affacci a una finestra di fronte, per comunicare una notizia importante (5).[22]

Starting with the paternal home, the writer describes the patriarchal world of her childhood, and the people around her as she grew up. She tries to analyse her young spiritual life, and fathom her secret ambitions, tracing the origins of her literary aspirations, which becomes the major theme of the novel. She describes the dramatic incident of Andrea stealing money; the stories of the love-sick goat; the unhappy fate of her other brother, Santus; the death of her sister Enza after an abortion (no trace of which is found in biographical material); her theft of wine and oil from the kitchen cupboard in order to be able to send her manuscript to a publisher; and her first publishing successes.

The themes touched upon are common to women's writing: family life, the mother, adolescence as an important period in the development of identity, sexuality, marriage as a prison for the female self; but in *Cosima* there is already a departure from this canon, since the writer speaks of marriage as an institution rather than of her marriage to Palmiro Madesani which does not come into Cosima's story. In fact, alongside mention of marriage as an unavoidable female destiny, the writer immediately introduces the idea of a literary vocation:[23]

> E la piccola sognatrice pensa che un giorno dovrà anche lei sposarsi, come la madre, come le zie, e abitare lassù, e in quei fornelli manipolare i cibi per sé e la famiglia. Per adesso le due camere, a destra e a sinistra, coi pavimenti di legno quasi ancora grezzo, sono le più povere della casa; con lettini di ferro, i pagliericci pieni di foglie crepitanti di granone, una tavola, alcune sedie; ma in quella dei ragazzi esiste pure una grande ricchezza; uno scaffale pieno di libri: libri vecchi e libri nuovi, alcuni di scuola, altri comprati da Santus nell'unica libreria della piccola città (28).[24]

Little Cosima's discovery of intellectual and literary tension, and her subsequent decision to shape her destiny around the two mirror experiences of reading and writing, make the book an important document where the history of women includes, but at the same time transcends, Deledda's personal history. *Cosima* exceeds the value of autobiographical document to become the portrait of a painstakingly reproduced social reality. Autobiographical writing and social writing blend when events in Cosima and her family's life reflect Italian society, and Sardinian society in particular, at the end of the nineteenth century.

The theme that probably is the *leit motiv* of the whole narrative is the protagonist's loneliness, due to the fact that her aspirations to intellectual freedom are not understood. The act of writing, therefore, takes on the form of a transgressive act against the dominant culture.[25] Cosima's literary vocation emerges during her adolescence, and is described by the writer as an irrepressible need, "costrettavi da una forza sotterranea, scriveva versi e novelle"(32).[26] The act of writing, though, is portrayed by the writer as being subversive, on both a personal and a social level:

> Quando si venne a sapere che la sua sorellina Cosima, quella ragazzina di quattordici anni che ne dimostrava meno e sembrava selvaggia e timida come una cerbiatta bambina, era invece una specie di ribelle a tutte le abitudini, le tradizioni, gli usi della famiglia e della razza, poiché s'era messa a scrivere versi e novelle, e tutti cominciarono a guardarla con una certa stupita diffidenza, se non pure a sbeffeggiarla e a prevedere per lei un quasi losco avvenire, Andrea prese a proteggerla (56).[27]

Deledda, too, was the victim of prejudice in her local community. In one of her letters she writes, "tutto il paese mormorò contro di me, si disse che ero male avviata, mi si scrissero lettere anonime, mi si perseguitò in tutti i modi. Per lungo tempo io scrissi di nascosto."[28]

In yet another,

anch'io mi vedo fatta segno di piccole invidie paesane, di denigrazioni, di maldicenze meschine, quando vedo che qualcuno cambia nome e cognome per abbassarmi fin dove la sua invidia vorrebbe vedermi, quando dalla Sardegna non mi arriva una parola di incoraggiamento ma solo qualche soffio di livore per le parole che io spendo in pro dell'isola e dei suoi abitanti, quando infine raccolgo perfidia dove semino amore, sogni, idealità![29]

She reacts, however, by being stubborn, by rebelling and most importantly, by realising that she must leave town.

Credevo di far piacere ai miei compatrioti, si figuri, dunque il mio dolore... allorché, comparsi alla luce quei racconti, per poco non venni lapidata.... Un altro al mio posto avrebbe spezzato la penna, maledicendola, avrebbe a furia di calzette e ricami obliato il suo ideale di ragazza fantastica purtroppo anche annoiata – io invece temperai la penna, e mentre raccoglievo la sfida del pubblico sardo tanto positivo: diventare donna di casa che sarà meglio – intromettevo un bozzetto fra l'apparecchiare la tavola e preparare il caffè, e fantasticavo versi dinanzi alla mia finestra, davanti alle montagne tinte di rosa nel crepuscolo silente, intrecciandoli ai fiori serici del mio ricamo e alle maglie della mia calzetta, ahi, quante volte bagnata da una lacrima di rancore e di sdegno![30]

Deledda recounts that Cosima wrote almost in secret: "nell'alta stanza dalla cui finestra si vede il Monte [...] scrive piegata sul suo scartafaccio, quando le sorelle tengono a bada la madre, per un bisogno fisico, come altre adolescenti corrono per i viali dei giardini" (75).[31] This image of the young writer, alone in an unused room, far from her mother's vigilant eye, reveals an uneasy relationship between women and writing, due to the fact that women were denied an education. (Cosima only went to primary school, where she had to repeat fourth grade, as there were no more. For the rest, she was self-taught).[32] If women did manage to write something, perhaps using a male pen-name to improve their very slight chance of having it published (Deledda wrote using the pen-name of Ilia di Saint-Ismael),[33] they could never, in any case, have reaped the same benefits as men in terms of recognition and financial rewards.

What is glimpsed here is a radical critique of a society steeped in patriarchal ideas, a critique which becomes clearer when retracing the stages of Deledda's professional achievement, which was constantly threatened by the systemic and atavistic exclusion of women from the social sphere.

Il libro invece ebbe un successo femminile: lo lessero le fanciulle, e vi si ritrovarono, coi loro amori più libreschi che reali [...] Ma per la scrittrice fu un disastro morale completo: non solo le zie inacidite, e i benpensanti del paese, e le donne che non sapevano leggere ma consideravano i romanzi come libri proibiti, tutti si rivoltarono contro la fanciulla: fu un rogo di malignità, di supposizioni scandalose, di profezie libertine: la voce del Battista che dalla prigione opaca della sua selvaggia castità urlava contro Erodiade, era meno inesorabile. Lo stesso Andrea era scontento: non così aveva sognato la gloria della sorella: della sorella che si vedeva minacciata dal pericolo di non trovare marito (78).[34]

The fear that this young woman might not have found a husband, and, therefore, would not have found in marriage what was considered in those days to be a woman's rightful place, worried her mother, too:

> Le ragazze sono tutte stordite: quella, poi, ha certe idee in testa. Tutte quelle scritture, quei cattivi libri, quelle lettere che riceve, e non è venuto neanche a trovarla un omaccione rosso come la volpe? Da lontano, è venuto, e poi ha scritto di lei sui giornali? La gente mormora. Cosima non troverà da maritarsi cristianamente: e anche le sorelle ne risentiranno, perché in una famiglia tutto sta a sposar bene la primogenita (109).[35]

The protagonist's solitude is reflected in her need to escape from the narrow-minded provincial environment of the island, and her desperate need to find her independence. In my opinion, it is in this binary, escape/emancipation, that Deledda's 'feminist' message lies. A message which she develops in an original way through her narrative, bringing to light the moral isolation of a female artist in a society whose cultural codes did not contemplate issues beyond motherhood, bringing up children and looking after a family.

Inspired by visions of change and wider cultural horizons beyond those of provincial Sardinia, the hope of leaving the island for the mainland, where she would finally satisfy her thirst for learning, was a precious reference point throughout her childhood:

> Pensò che bisognava almeno darle il conforto della speranza di un buon matrimonio, fra lei e un qualche bravo giovine del luogo, e passò in rassegna tutti i proprietari, i professionisti, gl'impiegati di sua conoscenza. Ma essi erano tutti imbevuti del pregiudizio che ella non potesse, con quella sua passione dei libri, diventare una buona moglie; né, d'altronde, ella voleva più umiliarsi con nessuno. E fu in quel momento che le venne l'idea di muoversi, di uscire dal ristretto ambiente della piccola città, e andare in cerca di fortuna. Per dare una consolazione alla madre (111).[36]

The letters written during Deledda's youth also confirm this impatience with the conventions of an archaic and patriarchal society which saw women confined to a role and social position which was alien to the process of emancipation and the possibility of self-determination. Furthermore, the condition of women in Sardinia was provincial and extremely limited.[37] The restrictions under which she was forced to live produced an uncontrollable urge to escape into a different world. She writes to Sofia Bisi Albini:

> mi pare – e sento che è così – che per fare qualche cosa di veramente e potentemente artistico, io debba muovermi, sentire la vita in tutta la sua modernità e realtà, vedere, toccare, studiare con gli occhi sul vero e non sui libri. E tutto ciò mi viene proibito dalla convenienza, dalle esigenze, dalle convenzioni insormontabili, di cui tocca la piaga viva certa lettera di una lettrice, pubblicata nella vostra rivista per le signorine.[38]

Her literary calling was thus the primary motivation behind all her life choices: "Di nessuno si curava, tranne delle sue scritture, illuminate dalla luce di quel sogno che era il più bello dei romanzi che ella avrebbe mai potuto scrivere" (100).[39]

She begins to be clear that her profession, and therefore her only means of support, will be that of a writer: "Decise di non aspettare più nulla che le arrivasse dall'esterno, dal mondo agitato degli uomini; ma tutto da se stessa, dal mistero della sua vita interiore" (107).[40] It is amazing, given the times in which she lived, how easily Cosima-Grazia seemed to find her bearings in the world of publishing. The ease with which she networked with publishers and men of letters is evidence of her 'masculine' attitude towards managing her work as an artist and her image as a writer. Alone, coming from one of the most backward parts of Italy, she succeeded in making a name for herself in cultural circles, and aided only by her own determination she reached the highest point in world literature. It is in this light that we must interpret Deledda's struggle for emancipation, which she carried out in a very personal way and without any political motivation. She was ahead of her times in her way of conceptualising the position of women and rejecting the over-restrictive traditions of her world. Without giving up her role as a wife and mother she succeeded in freeing herself from an inferior position.

In this sense Cosima becomes an exemplary figure whose desire to write clashed with the rules of the archaic culture of Sardinia. As Giacobbe Harder puts it:

nell'atto di scrivere assumeva dei poteri che non le competevano, di prepotenza usurpava un ruolo quanto mai contrastante con la sua condizione di donna, di donna barbaricina, che il paese ebbe difficoltà a perdonarle finché visse, almeno fino a che la gloria ufficiale, arrivatale col nobel, non affrancò anche lei dalle leggi arcaiche del villaggio che dovette finalmente accettare il fatto compiuto.[41]

Leaving aside the literary value of her work, about which literary criticism, especially at the time, was unanimous, Grazia Deledda represents an extraordinary case in Italian literature, as was stated in my introduction, considering that she had to overcome two great obstacles: being a woman, and living in a setting which was provincial, and more importantly, far from literary circles.

Alongside the theme of loneliness, there is that of inter-generational conflict, which obviously involves the whole system of family relationships, based on a faltering socio-cultural model. Deledda's family was a patriarchal family which disintegrates right before the reader's eyes. The father's authority does not prevent his sons from becoming an alcoholic and a spendthrift, respectively. The relationship with her mother, "tutta religione e austerità (all religion and sternness)," who "smorzava fin che poteva la vivacità interiore dei figli (repressed as much as she could her children's inner liveliness)," was explained by the author as a result of a marriage lacking "quel piacere e la soddisfazione sensuale dei quali tutte le donne giovani hanno bisogno" (28).[42] The character of the mother fully reflects the commonplaces of the time:

> ella non poteva procurarseli fuori del recinto domestico: non poteva, per dovere innato, per superstizione e pregiudizio, o forse anche per assoluta mancanza di occasioni. Aveva una volta amato? Si diceva che, sì, prima di sposarsi, avesse corrisposto ad un giovine povero; nessuno sapeva però chi era, e forse neppure esisteva (29).[43]

It is opposed to the figure of the father, much loved by the protagonist, which reflects the traditional role of the *pater familias*, the family man providing for the material needs of his children. Within the closed world of the family, Cosima/Grazia feels a sense of estrangement and suffocation which is relieved by a tempered rebellion against the social rules which relegated women to positions of inferiority; a silent rebellion which found support in literature and an outlet in travel, at first in her imagination, and then in reality. Her journeys become a metaphor for rebirth.

> Leggendo già di nascosto i libri del fratello maggiore, e quelli che esistevano in casa, pensava a una vita lontana, diversa dalla sua, e che pure le sembrava di aver un giorno conosciuto. Così a quell'età, lesse i primi romanzi: uno dei quali era *I Martiri di Chateaubriand*, che lasciò nella sua fantasia una traccia profonda (33).[44]

Cosima's position, and that of her mother and sisters, are totally opposite: resignation and acquiescence on their part, as opposed to rebellion on hers. In the contrast between these two positions it seems possible to see Deledda's desire to create a female model which finds its expression in her awareness of culture and work as vehicles of emancipation. Consequently *Cosima* becomes a site where personal myth is inextricably intertwined with a universal myth. Behind any individual or social implications, Deledda's process of self-determination hides a desire for transcendence and immortality to the extent that this self-examination becomes a (veiled) act of self-celebration. Deledda's *Cosima* can be seen, therefore, as an autobiography that is a strategy whereby the autobiographical writer gives his/her readers a role model: a female subjectivity is presented to the reader as an exemplum.

Notes

1. Translated from the Italian by Susi Walker.

2. Comprehensive collections of Deledda's works include: Cecchi, E. ed. *Romanzi e novelle.*; De Michelis, E. ed. *Opere scelte.*; Sapegno, N. ed. *Romanzi e Novelle.*; Scano, A. ed. *Versi e prose giovanili.*

3. It was the second Italian Nobel Prize: Carducci in 1906 preceded her. She was followed by Pirandello in 1934, Quasimodo in 1959, Montale in 1976, and Fo in 1997.

4. "the notion that women are marginalised in creative fields"

5. "I have an almost masculine spirit and I fear nothing: neither the living nor the dead, neither superstition nor criticism, whether personal or artistic, or prejudice. I fear nothing but I am an anxious person and sometimes my nerves despotically take control over my spirit and reduce me to shaking over nothing at all, and make me cry and rage like a small child." From a letter to A. Pirrodda, Nuoro, 1893.

6. Respected critics such as B. Croce, R. Serra, E. Cecchi, A. Bocelli, and L. Russo passed overall negative judgements on her work; others, such as P. Pancrazi, looked at it within a regional context; others still, like G. Debenedetti and F. Contini, simply ignored it.

7. "Frankly, one can only admire this young, self-educated woman, alone, with no literary background to draw on, who succeeded in getting her work published – as a woman, without putting a foot outside Cagliari, living amongst incomprehension in a hostile and untrusting environment – thousands and thousands of pages of prose and poetry [...] and who wrote literally hundreds of letters to men more worldly than herself [...] for this alone we feel that Deledda, as a cultural phenomenon, from the time she was a very young woman, is worthy of great respect and appreciation."

8. I refer in particular to the following works: Jelinek, E. ed. *Women's Autobiography: Essays in Criticism.*; Smith, S. *A Poetics of Women's Autobiography: Marginality and the Fictions of Self-Representation.*; Smith, S. and Watson, J. eds. *De/Colonizing the Subject: The Politics of Gender in Women's Autobiography.*; Brodzki, B. and Schenck, C. eds. *Life/Lines: Theorizing Women's Autobiography.*

9. "possible diffraction, increasing the number of situational variables which are at the intersection of neighbouring genres"

10. Grazia Deledda died on 15 August 1936 in Rome after a long illness.

11. "she, too, felt in her body the frenzy of an Amazon, the ardour of the audacious heroine of an adventure story"

12. Deledda alters the names of her family members and friends, and some of their physical characteristics. Fortunio, for example, who was lame in the novel, was really blind in one eye. She also censors some of the events in her life, like meeting Pirodda, her first love, opposed by the family who saw him as socially inferior, as her letter to Epaminonda Provaglio tells us. In July 1893, she wrote to Provaglio: "ciò che so è che sono felice e fiera del mio amore perché Andrea, il mio amato Andrea, è il giovane più buono e virtuoso che si possa dare. Io non ho guardato alla sua personalità dirò materiale, ho guardato al suo spirito, dopo averlo studiato in tutte le sue esplicazioni, e dopo quattro anni che egli mi amava senza speranza, me ne innamorai perché l'ho trovato lo spirito più buono, più leale, più onesto e retto del mondo." ("what I do know is that I am happy and proud of my love because Andrea, my beloved Andrea, is the most virtuous and good young man you could ever hope to find. I didn't look at what I call his material personality, I looked at his spirit, and after having studied it in all of its manifestations, and after four years of him loving me without hope, I fell in love with him because I found it to be the most loyal, honest, upright and good spirit in the world.")

In another letter written in November 1893 her tone changes: "Egli non sarà mai altro che un povero insegnante, e capirai bene che per me ci vuol altro, perché io, nella mia carriera, ho bisogno di essere sorretta da un uomo forte, ho bisogno di appoggio, di aiuto e consiglio ed anche di una relativa agiatezza [...] e voglio vivere; perché non si vive di solo amore, ma di tante altre cose. Si vive anche per gli affetti domestici, per la patria, per l'arte." ("He will never be anything but a poor teacher, and you'll understand how much I need something else, because in my career as a writer I need a strong man at my side. I need support, help and advice, and to live reasonably comfortably [...] and I want to live; because one doesn't live by love alone, but by lots of other things – for family affection, for one's country and for art.")

13. Several critics and writers of monographs on Deledda start from *Cosima*. See M. Miccinesi. *Deledda*; O. Lombardi. *Invito alla lettura di Grazia Deledda*; A. Piromalli. *Grazia Deledda*; N. De Giovanni. *L'Ora di Lilith*; G. Petronio. "Grazia Deledda."

14. No biographical information exists regarding the last period of Deledda's life and the circumstances surrounding the writing of *Cosima*, since the writer lived in complete isolation. In a concluding note to the collection of letters between Moretti and Deledda, Mario Moretti recalls that "specie dopo il conferimento del premio Nobel (1926), la D. non scrisse quasi più lettere, ma solo cartoline, sempre brevi e a lunghi intervalli. Era stanca e malata e non voleva farlo sapere. [...] Si sa che nell'ultimo anno soffrì atrocemente e nessuno potè più rivederla." ("especially after the conferring of the Nobel Prize (in 1926), Deledda hardly ever wrote letters anymore, but just brief postcards at long intervals apart. She was tired and ill and did not want anyone to know [...] We know that she suffered terribly in the last year of her life and that no-one was able to see her again.") In *Opere scelte*, Balducci tells us that the manuscript of *Cosima* was found after the author's death, locked in her bedside table (1018).

15. For example, there is still a note in the text between parentheses "[Intorno a quel tempo morì la nonnina]" ("[Around that time Granny died]") (37) an episode which probably was going to be expanded.

16. One sees "da qualunque parte lo si guardasse" ("whichever way one looked at it") in place of "dovunque" ("wherever") in the manuscript (16); elsewhere, "E poiché [la famiglia era] in questo cerchio d'ombra" ("And since [the family was] in this shaded circle") where the editor's corrections are in Italics (49).

17. Evidence of the text's closeness to completion can be drawn from a statement made by Deledda: "Se un testo non mi riesce bene subito, lo distruggo, perché non ho la pazienza di rifare le cose." ("If my work isn't immediately good, I destroy it, because I haven't the patience to do things again.")

18. "The most important house, though, is the one the priest lives in, opposite *our* own"

19. "as providing the perfect opportunity to declare one's status as a 'man of culture' within the 'literary republic.'"

20. "Six nights after Santus' departure, as it was getting late, someone could be heard knocking insistently on the door. Half a century later, Cosima still remembers that beating, like a drum announcing some terrible misfortune: she still feels its pounding in her heart. It is the most awful sound that she has ever heard, more mournful than the one announcing that someone has died."

21. See A. Pizzorusso. *Ai margini dell'autobiografia*, 183-197.

22. "During the day it was nearly always ajar. It was the entrance used by the household and family friends, instead of the small front door. In this big doorway, one morning in May, a little girl stood looking out. She was dark and serious, with big, clear, brown eyes, and tiny hands and feet. She was wearing a grey smock with pockets, coarse cotton socks and rough lace-up boots – looking more like a peasant girl than one of the middle classes. Rocking to and fro on one leg, she waits for someone to pass, or for a head to lean out of the window of the house opposite, with some important news to tell."

23. References to her own future are frequent in the letters to Provaglio: "Mi dici di pigliar marito!![...]Ma non sai che questo è il più brutto e prosastico augurio che tu possa farmi?" ("You tell me to find a husband!! [...]Don't you know that this is the most awful and boring thing you could ever wish on me?") Michelis 968.

24. "And the young day dreamer thought that one day she, too, would have to get married, like her mother and her aunts, and live up there and prepare the food for herself and her family on those stoves. For now, these two rooms, one on the left and the other on the right, with their rough wooden floors, are the poorest in the house; with iron bedsteads and mattresses stuffed with crackling corn leaves, a table and a few chairs. But in the boys' room there are riches to be found, a bookshelf full of books: old books and new books, a few school books, others bought by Santus in the only bookshop in the little town."

25. Deledda writes about how difficult it was for women to gain recognition in a letter to Provaglio on 15 May 1892 in which she praises the poetry of Ada Negri: "Peccato, però, che sia donna e giovine! Sì, proprio peccato! Perché ad una donna giovine non conviene cantare così: se la Negri fosse stata uomo tutti l'avrebbero levata al cielo: invece, così, la buona parte della critica l'atterra e il senso comune, il senso del pubblico, si rivolta nel leggere la poesia "Sfida," e si forma un brutto concetto della fanciulla che ha osato scriverla; mentre se fosse stata scritta da un uomo avrebbe forse avuto il successo delle più ardite e battagliere poesie di Stecchetti." 996-7

26. "driven by a hidden force, she wrote poems and novels."

27. "When it became known that his little sister Cosima – that fourteen-year-old girl who looked even younger and seemed as wild and timid as a young faun – was some sort of rebel against everything they did, their traditions, the ways of the family and of the race, because she had started to write poems and stories; and when everyone began to look at her with a sort of amazed suspicion, and even mock her, and predict a grim future, Andrea took her under his wing."

28. "the whole town talked about me behind my back, they said I would come to no good, they wrote me anonymous letters, and continually harassed me. For a long time, I kept my writing secret."

29. "I, too, see myself as the target of petty provincial envy, denigration and malicious gossip, when I see someone changing [my] name and surname to take me down to where their envy would like to see me, when not a word of encouragement arrives from Sardinia but only the occasional spiteful hiss in reaction to the words I write about the island and its people, when I reap malice where I sow love, dreams and idealism."

30. Letter to Santis Manca, 8th June, 1891, in Deledda: *Lettere inedite (1891 – 1900)*, 12. "Just think, I thought my compatriots would be pleased with me, but my pain when the stories came out […] I was nearly stoned. [. . .] Anyone else in my place would have thrown away the pen, cursing it, and by dint of knitting and sewing, would have given up the ideal of being a super-girl, sometimes bored girl – but I just sharpened my pen and whilst I took up the positive challenge of the Sardinian people – become a housewife, it will be better for you – I dashed off a draft between setting the table and making the coffee, and I thought up poems looking out of the window onto the silent mountains as they turned pink in the sunset, weaving them into the silky flowers I embroidered and the stitches of the stockings I knitted. Oh! How often I wet them with my tears of wrath and indignation!"

31. "in the high room with the window looking out on Mount [...], while her sisters keep her mother away, she bends over her notebook writing, in order to satisfy a physical need, in the same way as other adolescents run round the paths in the park."

32. In his profile of the writer, Petronio says of her education: "A dieci anni aveva letto *i martiri di Chateaubriand*, e ne aveva ricavato, disse più tardi, un'impressione duratura e profonda; poi si abbandonò alle letture più varie, senza alcun piano e senza alcun discernimento, entusiasmandosi tutt'assieme per Giovanni Prati, Giuseppe Aurelio Costanzo, Ada Negri, Lorenzo Stecchetti, and Contessa Lara, messi tutti sullo stesso piano, amati tutti con lo stesso fervore ingenuo, per cui poteva accendersi, come s'è visto per Eugenio Sue e nello stesso tempo, con la stessa passione, per Victor Hugo... E poteva più tardi subire di volta in volta, sovrapponendo le diverse esperienze, l'influsso del romanzo casalingo, per signorine, di Anna Vertua Gentile, quello del romanzo fogazzariano (in La Giustizia del 1899), quello del romanzo russo, sia di Dostoevskij, sia di Tolstoj." ("By the time she was ten, she had read Chateaubriand's *The Martyrs*, which, she later said, made a strong and lasting impression on her. She then abandoned herself to reading a wide range of books, without any discrimination or plan, being equally enthusiastic about Giovanni Prati, Giuseppe Aurelio Costanzo, Ada Negri, Lorenzo Stecchetti, and Contessa Lara, putting them all on the same plane, and loving them all with the same naïve fervour, which could be ignited by someone like Eugenio Sue, or, at the same time, and with the same intensity, Victor Hugo... And later, from time to time, she would open herself to the combined influences of texts as diverse as Anna Vertua Gentile's romantic novels for young women, Antonio Fogazzaro's novels (in *La Giustizia*, 1899), and the Russian novels of Dostoievski and Tolstoy.") (Petronio 1963).

33. Deledda's long story "Novelle d'autunno – Il palazzo dello zio" was published in instalments in *L'Ultima moda* from March 1890 to May 1891, and the novel *Stelle d'Oriente* appeared in an appendix to the Cagliari daily *L'Avvenire della Sardegna* from November to December 1890.

34. "Nevertheless, the book was very popular with women. Girls read it and saw themselves in it, with their loves – more fictional than real. […] But for the author, it was a complete moral disaster. Not just the embittered aunts, and the upright citizens of the town, but women who did not know how to read and who thought of novels as banned books all turned against her. She was at the centre of a blaze of malice, scurrilous suggestions and licentious predictions. The voice of John the Baptist, railing against Herodias from the dark prison of his fierce chastity, could not have been as relentless. Even Andrea was unhappy. It had not been like this that he had imagined his sister's glory – the sister who was now in danger of never finding a husband."

35. "The girls are all stunned: that girl's got some strange ideas in her head – all that writing, those terrible books, those letters she gets, and didn't a man even come to see her – big, and red as a fox? He'd come a long way, and didn't he write about her in the papers? People talk behind her back. Cosima will never find a good Christian husband. Her sisters will suffer, too, because in a family, everything depends on the eldest daughter marrying well."

36. "She thought that she ought to at least give her [mother] some comfort in the hope of a good marriage, between herself and one of the town's upright young men. She ran down the list of all the land owners, professional men and clerks that she could think of, but they were all steeped in the same prejudice – that with her passion for books, she was incapable of becoming a good wife. Neither did she, on her part, want to humiliate herself for anyone anymore. And it was in that moment that the idea came to her that she should move away from the confines of the small town, and set out to seek her fortune. To bring some solace to her mother."

37. An example of this is given in a letter to Provaglio in which Deledda describes the mourning on the death of her father: "Tu non puoi immaginarti con che rigidezza qui si osservi il lutto! Le nostre finestre son chiuse e io non mi posso neppure avvicinare ai vetri. Per due o tre mesi le donne dobbiamo (sic) stare ermeticamente chiuse in casa e poi ci sarà concesso di uscire sì, ma per ricambiare sole le visite o per andare in chiesa. Niente passaggio, – a meno che non sia in campagna, – nessuno svago, e un contegno sempre rigorosamente triste[…] e così per tre o quattro e magari cinque anni. Per buona fortuna io sono quasi avvezza a questa tetra esistenza, e spero di cambiarla fra due anni al più tardi; altrimenti questo lutto artificiale, unito al lutto intimo del mio cuore, mi ucciderebbe." (*Lettere inedite* 1021) ("You can't imagine how strictly mourning is observed here! Our windows are closed and I can't even go near them. For two or three months we women must stay tightly shut up in the house and then we will be allowed to go out, but only to repay visits or to go to church. No strolls – unless they are in the country – no entertainment, a strictly restrained and sad demeanour[...]and this for three or four, or even five years. Luckily I'm almost used to this grim existence, and hope to be able to change it in two years at the latest, otherwise this artificial mourning, on top of the real mourning in my heart, would kill me")

38. "It seems to me – and I really think it is true – that to produce something really and powerfully artistic, I would have to move around, experience the reality and modernity of life, see, touch, and study the real thing, not just what is written in books. And I am forbidden all of this by the demands of propriety, and insurmountable social conventions – on which point, a letter from one of your readers published in your journal for young ladies, hits a raw nerve." See http://www.danielaperniola.com/donnedeleddiane.asp

39. "She cared for no-one, only for her writing, which was illuminated by the light of that dream, which was to write the best novel she would ever be capable of." In a letter to Provaglio written in September,1892, she writes of Andrea Pirrodda: "è un giovane buono e bravo e bello che mi adora … pigliandomi questo corro il rischio di restare sempre qui." ("he's a good, honest, handsome young man who adores me […] if I accept him I run the risk of staying here for ever.") This was certainly one of the factors which made her decide not to marry him.

40. "She decided that she would no longer expect anything coming to her from outside, from the frenetic world of men; she would expect everything from herself, from the mystery of her own inner life."

41. "in the act of writing, she took on powers that were not hers by rights arrogantly seizing a role which was so much at odds with her position as a Sardinian woman, that Sardinia found it difficult to forgive her in her lifetime – or at least until official praise, which arrived in the form of the Nobel Prize, set her free too, from the archaic rules of her village which finally had to accept the *fait accompli*."

42. "that pleasure and sensual satisfaction all young women need"

43. "she was unable to get them outside the confines of the family, whether for reasons of innate duty, superstition or prejudice, or a complete lack of opportunity. Had she ever loved? She told herself, yes, before getting married, she had written to a poor young man. Nobody knew who he was, though, or whether he had ever even existed."

44. "Already secretly reading her oldest brother's books, and all the others in the house, she dreamt of a faraway life, different from her own, and which she even felt she had already known. In this way, at that age, she read her first novels, one of which was Chateaubriand's *The Martyrs*, which left a deep impression in her imagination."

Revisiting and Resisting Fascism: Gender Revisionism in Elsa Morante's *La Storia*

Dana Renga

Political ideology and gender subversion

Elsa Morante in *La Storia* (1974) refuses to consider the sexual politics of fascism a closed chapter in Italian cultural history. She is a child of the resistance, part of a generation acutely interested in unmasking the continual sway of power in contemporary Italian political life. *La Storia*'s characters chip away at rooted convictions of gender autonomy. The actions of mother and son Ida and Useppe Ramundo reaffirm the impossibility of separating the personal arena of the body from the public construction of the state apparatus. In her novel, sex and politics are intimately entwined, to the point that distinctions between the personal and the collective are often blurred, yet their interpolation is rarely, if ever, indifferent. The history of sexuality, as Michel Foucault points out, is a history of culture and politics. Such thematics are consistently apparent in Morante's novel.

In returning to the subject of fascism, Morante critiques totalitarian thought processes intrinsic to her own era. Her deconstruction is readily apparent in the title combining political systems and movements with fantastical revisions. *La Storia: Romanzo* juxtaposes official and marginal history as the classification of "*romanzo*/novel" depriviliges a linear historical approach to Italian fascism. This association is perpetuated throughout the novel as each chapter – all entitled a year between 1941 and 1947 – is introduced by an 'objective' historical chronology of the year's events that concern Europe, Asia and America, yet impersonal and 'official' history is time and again interwoven with the personal realm as the narrator recounts in minute detail how World War II and its aftermath affect the personal lives of the novel's protagonists. The dichotomy between historical chronicle and individual experience is thus made immediately clear as recorded history excludes innumerable individual experiences. Furthermore, Morante directly involves the reader in her evolving interpretation through the heading preceding her novel, "Por el analfabeto a quien escribo." *La Storia* is about re-reading history and re-positioning the individual in the process of historical signification. Through Morante's reinterpretations, would-be peripheral, marginal and forgotten characters such as Ida and Useppe reclaim positions that were at one time denied them.[1]

La Storia engages in a process of historical awakening that redefines gender identity and destabilises political power centres. Morante is profoundly interested in how the individual subject creates and interacts with 'history.' She investigates the constructions of gender identity and political ideology, ultimately unravelling biased and misrepresented historical patterns that, left unquestioned, are bound to repeat themselves. Rather than presenting history as a closed, linear system, the textual employment of tragic irony breaks down the would-be obsessive pattern of 'official' history. Irony allows for the text's characters to momentarily disengage themselves from the patriarchal/symbolic order, exploring instead that which is fragmentary, nomadic, embryonic and prophetic. La Storia demystifies cultural mythologies associated with imperialism, giving narrative voices to some of history's *vinti*.

Critical attention paid to Morante's novel focuses mainly on its historical and/or political themes. Topics of gender and the politics of sexual identity have been given little attention, however.[2] This could have resulted from the misguided classification of Morante as primarily anti-feminist,[3] a relevant observation in a decade where the Italian feminist movement was growing stronger not only in number, but also in terms of its influence on contemporary legislation. Moreover, Morante was directly criticised in terms of how she chooses to construct her principal female character: Ida is an unconfident single mother with a fear of patriarchal authority, completely uninvolved (by choice) in the political system.

Foreshadowing the work of such theorists as Judith Butler, Teresa De Lauretis, Monique Wittig and Foucault (to name a few), Morante's novel proposes that identities of gender and their subsequent interpolations into cultural and political arenas are socially constructed, perpetuated and disciplined. Through the presentation of dissonant images and narrative descriptions it is apparent that traditional representations of male dominance with female subservience – in such roles as prostitute and mother – are as superficial and inaccurate as Nietzsche's dictum "La donna è un enigma la quale soluzione si chiama la maternità (Woman is an enigma whose solution is called maternity)."[4] Morante revisits various enigmas of male and female gender identity, and in her reinterpretation challenges traditional images associated with mothers, prostitutes, children and heroes, but also, and more significantly, carves out utopian spaces of resistance. In Morante's text, the idealised image of the family unit promoted by both the historical regime and various right-wing political groups in the 1970s is highly criticised as the notion of 'sposa e madre esemplare (exemplary wife and mother)' is directly subverted.

My study looks closely at two of the novel's main protagonists: Ida and Useppe Ramundo, disclosing Morante's creation of female-engendered textual spaces. Specifically, I argue that rather than foster negative conceptions of female identity in her portrayal of polemical and marginal forms of sexuality and family structures, Morante's La Storia effectively affirms a 'feminine' component of humanity. By 'feminine' I do not necessarily imply 'feminist' as these texts do not represent exemplary models of female behaviour. In fact, Morante does not offer any sort of 'positive' fate for her female protagonist:

La Storia's Ida chooses to live out her life in silence. She is closed off from the rest of the world in a mental hospital when the death of her son Useppe results initially in the demise of her mental capacity and then her physical death some nine years later. This finality does not hermetically seal her fate and can be read in terms of Foucault's reappropriation of the politics of power and sexuality observed in the dominating and 'closed' systems of the brothel and mental hospital. In looking at areas where "illegitimate sexualities" were, as he puts it, "reintegrated," it is possible to "define the regime of power-knowledge-pleasure that sustains the discourse on human sexuality in our part of the world" (11). In line with Foucault, Morante presents alternative points-of-view on gender representation, and in doing so discloses new practices of reading sexuality and politics that feminises, and therefore dismantles and reproves, dominating patriarchal structures.

In my examination of *La Storia* I will illustrate how Morante critiques the rhetoric of virility in the following ways: (1) By constructing feminised spaces that are nostalgic and natural, poetic and oneiric, and (2) by deflecting and/ or reappropriating the male gaze or point of view by feminising Useppe and positioning him in utopian spaces. *La Storia* offers novel perspectives on the politics of gender and power so often debated and contested in the cultural arena of the 1960s and early 1970s. Like Foucault, who looks at how socio-sexual and political trends encourage and perpetuate discourses of sexual, political and economic power while simultaneously subverting and threatening the hegemony, Morante challenges traditional definitions of the sexual and political in her re-presentation of the *ventennio*.

Feminine anti-fascism: female space and gender identity

Ida refuses to appropriate the tyrannical significance of History and all of the wars, dictatorships and centres of power with which it is traditionally associated. Ida's ignorance of History throughout *La Storia* overshadows many of her narrative descriptions: "secondo gli ordini delle Autorità, essa introduceva nei temi e nei dettati i re, duci, patrie, glorie e battaglie che la Storia imponeva; però lo faceva in tutta purezza mentale e senza nessun sospetto, perché la Storia, non meno di Dio, non era mai stata argomento dei suoi pensieri"[5] (475, 534). Morante presents militarism, patriotism and heroism as ill suited to any transcendental ideal.[6] Ida's apolitical associations are of course laden with political overtones, as her rape by a Nazi soldier and feelings of anxiety towards patriarchal authority situate her within the public realm.

This section is interested in how Ida's oneiric roving unveils the consequences of patriarchal violence and subordination – both in the 'private' sphere of her rape and the 'public' arena of the workplace – as momentarily liberated from entrenched associations of a dynamic male voyeur. In *Nomadic Subjects*, Rosi Braidotti discusses female subjectivity as mutable and inconstant, positioning 'woman' as in control of her own transformations: "The starting point, for my scheme of feminist nomadism [...] is [...] the positive affirmation of women's desire to affirm and enact different forms of subjectivity" (158). Ida can be read as nomadic in nature in that readings of her transmigrations unveil alternative points of view on gender relations. As the point of view is destabilised and multiple, *La Storia* problematicises notions of interiority/exteriority and historical account/mythical revisionism.

I will now look at the construction of gender identities in the novel, demonstrating that Ida's battered consciousness becomes emancipated through her dreams and interior monologues, as she possesses a prophetic wisdom. Morante's presentation of Ida is a case study in alternative histories, offering a privileged vision into the world of a would-be 'marginal' character. Apart from the narrator and her sons, Ida is ignored by practically everyone in the text. The narrator, in fact, describes her as not belonging to traditional society: "Né fra tali ricchi, né fra tali poveri, aveva posto Iduzza Ramundo, la quale apparteneva, invero, a una terza specie. È una specie che esiste (forse, in via di estinzione?) e passa, né se ne dà notizia, se non a volte, eventualmente, nella cronaca near"[7] (481, 540). Throughout the text, Ida's rejection by the symbolic order is continually reinforced as she is described as plain looking, not incredibly intelligent and lacking of social bonds. Her epileptic attacks could be read as an interruption of thought and memory, and thereby of her own place within a historical/social/political environment. Ironically, this textual attitude is introduced early on in the novel through the eyes of Gunther, her rapist and the father of Useppe who describes her as "d'apparenza dimessa ma civile (humble-looking but decent)" (20, 19). This abrupt and not too flattering portrait is quickly revisited and elaborated on by the narrator, as the next 40 pages go on to develop the particulars of Ida's youth, maladies and familial/marital relations. The text often engages in this process of recreation, proffering profound counterparts to characters such as Gunther's abbreviated and limited interpretation.

The narration of Ida's personal history, however, is laden with political implications as the reader soon discovers that her horrified reaction to Gunther's greeting is founded on a lifetime of humiliation based on the perception of difference. Ida's childhood was clouded with silence as her parents consistently attempted to keep the family's political, medical and racial 'anomalies' from entering the social sphere: her parents were unrelenting about concealing her epileptic seizures from friends and relatives, her mother Nora was insistent in concealing her own racial identity and Ida's father Giuseppe's alcoholism and anarchist beliefs. As a child, Ida learnt to associate social, racial, political and medical diversities with shame and the realm of the unsaid. It is no surprise then that the presence of the Nazi soldier stimulates Ida's longstanding fear of racial persecution, as she is convinced that the only reason Gunther would address her is to arrest and deport her and her son. The textual diversion narrating Ida's personal history functions to connect linear history to individual, nomadic subjecthood, this intersection obviously being a central argument of

Morante's text. As Ida's categorisation as sickly becomes linked to the political realm through its association with other 'deviant' – at least in the eyes of Nora – classifications of anarchist or Jew, Morante proposes the impossibility of separating the personal and political realms.

Ida, then, belongs not directly to the temporal and linear progression of masculinist history, as her dreams, visions and aforementioned ignorance of official history position her within Julia Kristeva's notion of "women's time." Kristeva distinguishes masculine and feminine times and spaces in order to propose a radically new generation of feminist thought where, like in Braidotti's *Nomadic Subjects*,[8] "sexual identity" is no longer the primary basis of difference. Women's time is repetitive, intuitive, eternal and rhythmical while simultaneously monumental in that it links individual subjectivity to the timeless world of myth and fable (862).[9] Ida's textual identity exemplifies Kristeva's notion of "women's time" as her actions and choices are almost entirely governed by her maternal instinct, therefore associating her with a world influenced by cycles and rhythms. Ida belongs more to the innocent world of children than to the corrupt, threatening realm of her peers. Her vocation as teacher allows her to regularly reconnect with her youthful nature, simultaneously granting her a limited amount of control over a contained social milieu that is somewhat sheltered from authoritarian influence.

Her prescient wisdom so often evidenced in her dreams reveals her intuition and vision, also demonstrating that she is highly (and unwillingly) engaged in the process of historical signification. Ida, in fact, is endowed early on in the text with divination, as the narrator explains that the strangeness of her eyes evokes: "l'idiozia misteriosa degli animali, i quali non con la mente, ma con un senso dei loro colpi vulnerabili, 'sanno' il passato e il futuro di ogni destino. Chiamerei quel senso […] *il senso del sacro*: intendendosi […] per *sacro*, il potere universale che può mangiarli e annientarli, per la loro colpa di essere nati" (21, 21).[10] Ida is connected to a realm of the senses that transcends the temporal historical moment. Like Useppe and his dog Bella, who are both linked to interminable spaces, times and populations, Ida's enhanced visionary sensitivity connects her to past, present and future life cycles. Her dreamt premonitions of apocalyptic visions of mass murder, the Holocaust and bombed out buildings connect her to the public arena while her images of the birth and death of her second son insinuate a strong connection to the private domain.

As Freud originally illustrates in *The Interpretation of Dreams*, in dreaming the individual expresses unconscious desires and fears, allowing transitory glimpses into habitually repressed emotions. Ida's dreams and nightmares specifically express her fear of subjugation in terms of sexuality and race. Her dreams of blossoming gardens and streams of blood simultaneously allude to the cycle of life, her pregnancy and her rape: "Dal canestro usciva una pianta verde, che in un attimo si ramificava nella stanza, e fuori della casa, per tutti i muri del cortile […] Lei si trova bambina piccola sola […] perdendo rivoletti di sangue dalla vagina" (84-86, 92-93).[11] Her nightmarish visions of blank and gaunt staring faces of naked bodies and piles of old, dusty and forgotten shoes, however, intimate her connection to the plight of the Italian Jews sent to the camps: "Lei è la sola vestita in mezzo a una folla di gente nuda, tutta in piedi, coi corpi ammassati uno all'altro senza spazio di respiro … Tutta quella gente pare abbacinata, coi volti gessosi e fissi in un'assenza degli sguardi e delle voci, come se ogni mezzo di comunicare con loro fosse scaduto" (128, 140-141).[12] "Le pareva di trovarsi all'esterno di un recinto, qualcosa come un terreno di rifiuti in abbandono. Altro non c'era che delle scarpe ammucchiate, malridotte e polverose, che parevano smesse da anni" (342, 382).[13]

Early on in the text, shortly after discovering that she is pregnant, Ida expresses her fears for her unborn son through a telling dream of Polish children: "Tanti ragazzettucci polacchi, stracciati, giocano a rotolare degli anelli d'oro, Anellini consacrati, e loro non lo sanno. Questo gioco è proibito, in Polonia. Punito con la pena di morte!!!" (86, 95).[14] In Ida's dream, although the dreidel is metamorphosed into gold rings, its overall significance as foreboding of the death of most of Poland's Jewish children is clear. Ida's dreams tragically evoke her attachment to a collective historical moment, regardless of her self-declared naivety of contemporary 'history.' Throughout the text Ida unconsciously searches out the Jewish roots that she consistently attempts to cover up. She journeys both physically in her daily travels and mentally in her night-time dreams and nightmares. Before the Jews are deported, she finds herself drawn to the commotion of the ghetto, choosing to shop there on a regular basis. Even during the mass deportation in the Tiburtina station, when danger to her and Useppe would be at its highest, she feels compelled to follow Signora Di Segni who searches for her family amongst the boxcars. After the incident at the train station, Ida returns to the ghetto only once to deliver a message to the Efrati family which has been dropped from a man on one of the cattle cars on the train. The uncanny silence of the ghetto confirms her fears of certain death of most of Rome's Jewish population.[15] Ida's nocturnal wanderings connect an outwardly ahistorical character to a decisive historical moment as her anxiety over her racial constitution foreshadows familiar images of documentary footage of racial persecution during the Holocaust not released until after the conclusion of World War II.

Ida's chimerical discourses imply textual breaks from the hegemonic cultural order, as her persistent dreaming expresses an intensified – and recurrent – rupture of linear history with its phallogocentric slant. In creating her own subconscious language, Ida inserts herself into a tenuous space hovering between the real and the imaginary, where constituted subjectivity and regressive longing might quite possibly coexist. Ida's dreams of racial persecution and sacrifice/mothering serve to habitually reinforce her place both inside and outside of the symbolic cultural order. Her dreaming also effectively contrasts with Mussolini and Hitler's dreaming. Early in the text, the narrator discusses the historic milieu of pre-World War II Europe, addressing both Mussolini and

Hitler as "dreamers" – "Mussolini e Hitler, a loro modo, erano due sognatori (Mussolini and Hitler, in their way, were two dreamers)" (45, 47). Mussolini's dreams are described as life loving and parade-like yet nonetheless focused on totalitarian manipulation. Hitler's prophecies, however, are positioned in the nihilistic realm of death and sadism. Whereas the goal of Mussolini and Hitler's 'dreaming' is to dominate and exploit, Ida's reveries disorder their expectations through blending personal lore and civic attachment, and assimilating nostalgia with the consequences of fascist violence.

In the last lines of the text, the narrator explains that the final nine years of Ida's life were spent according to another time, as after the death of her second child Useppe she detached herself from the realm of historical materialisation: "Lei pure, come il famoso Panda Minore della leggenda, stava sospesa in cima a un albero dove le carte temporali non avevano più corso" (649, 726).[16] Ida becomes an ahistorical and atemporal subject, as the final years of her life pass in a fleeting moment. In reinventing her own system of expression associated with silence and myth, Ida offers a privileged (re)vision into historical processes associated with racial, sexual and political persecution. Ida's gradual descent into madness and subsequent lack of language discloses an unconventional viewpoint on the politics of racial and gender persecution in twentieth-century Italy. In re-reading Ida's dreamscapes it is clear that traditionally 'passive' character associations such as madness, submissiveness and silence can successfully unveil visionary enclaves able to subtly resist forms of totalitarianism and patriarchal violence.

Feminised male space and expression

This section is primarily concerned with looking at narrative moments where Useppe's actions and utterances untangle the logos of masculinist behaviour desired by the fascist regime. La Storia revisits the ventennio and re-presents this cultural moment through oneiric narrative situations. Useppe, a character that is continually feminised and intimately bound to the natural world, opposes integration into the symbolic order, preferring a world of dreams, poetry and silence to that of the oppressive fascist body politic. Useppe's visionary spaces – often connected with such pre-symbolic elements as reverie, lyrical expression and reticence – represent traditional historiography as mythic possibility.

Useppe renounces social systems as he consistently rebels at school, refusing to speak with authoritarian figures such as teachers and doctors. Conceived out of a rape by a Nazi soldier, Useppe does not inherit any of the prototypical 'masculine' attributes associated with patriarchal violence and aggression. Instead, he is presented as the classic scapegoat, a weak character described as undernourished and small for his age, and like his mother and grandmother before him, he suffers from epileptic seizures. Useppe's eyes are consistently referred to as "tristi/sad" by his brother Nino, his mother, the anarchist Davide Segre, his doctor and the narrator, and Davide comments that Useppe is too beautiful for this world. Useppe's sad and beautiful face is a living metaphor for the effects of brutality performed on the innocent through both rape and war. Useppe's "occhi tristi" are reminiscent of the narrative description of Davide's photograph on his identity card. In comparing the card, whose photo was taken a few years before the war, with his current appearance, he is described as physically changed: transformations that are "prodotti non da una maturazione graduale; ma da una violenza fulminea, simile a uno stupor (produced not by a gradual development, but by a lightening violence, like a rape)" (199, 219). A parallel could be drawn between Useppe and Davide and Ida as well – all victims of the ravages of war – whose rape ages her, forever marking her as a victim of violence.

Useppe rarely speaks. Rather, he spends his time "thinking," dreaming and composing mental poetry. Useppe is most at ease either with the women of his life, in the natural world or with his dog Bella, and as he grows older he spends more and more time outside of the confines of his small set of rooms. Useppe resists integration into all too familiar systems of language, power and violence. Instead, he creates his own world of poetry, play and imagination. Morante's novel privileges silence and contemplation, as is markedly clear in her portrayal of Ida and Useppe. Useppe's first experience with linguistic expression is indicative of his resistance to its signifying power. In 1942, when he is a little over a year old, Useppe's brother Nino takes him outside of the house for the first time. The reader interprets Useppe's world as a defamiliarised landscape of colour, light and sound. Such objects as "field," "leaf" and "person" all become reinterpreted through a magical vocabulary suited more to a poet than a one-year-old child. The narrator explains:

> Era la prima volta in vita sua che vedeva un prato; e ogni stelo d'erba gli appariva illuminato dal di dentro, quasi contenesse un filo di luce verde. Cosí le foglie degli alberi erano centinaia di lampade, in cui si accendeva non solo il verde ... ma ancora altri colori sconosciuti ... e la gente vestita di colori era mossa intorno, per lo spiazzo, dello stesso vento ritmico e grandioso che muove i cerchi celesti, con le loro nubi, i loro soli e le loro lune."[17] (123, 135)

The Dantean reference – "dello stesso vento ritmico e grandioso che muove i cerchi celesti" from "l'Amor che muove il sole e l'altre stelle (love which moves the sun and the other stars)" (Paradiso XXXIII 145) – is clear here. Useppe's paradise, however, is earthly and temporal rather than heavenly and eternal. La Storia's "vento ritmico e grandioso" connects regular passers-by to a non-hierarchical order obtained through contemplation and intuition. Useppe presents a defamiliarised world in which blades of grass and leaves glow like fireflies in the sunlight. Appropriation is questioned as the possessive adjective "loro" could give tenancy of the clouds, suns and moons to either the people in the street or the "cerchi celesti," creating a relationship between individual and ideal that is fluid, and not regimented.

Useppe is drawn to things that fly, attracted to their lightness and ability to render trivial the weight of a social order governed by authoritarian principles.

Through identifying the light and fluid within the war-torn landscape of the urban environment, Useppe overcomes, albeit temporarily, the weight of historical materialisation. He follows such creatures as butterflies and swallows, and succeeds in teaching himself the expression "vola via/fly away."

Useppe's grasp on language is remarkably insightful, approximating Vico's "age of the poets" where language developed out of intuition and wonder rather than masculine reason and instruction. When asked by brother Nino to correctly name a white butterfly, Useppe vocalises a word that he has never before uttered or been taught: "lampàna," a variation of "lampada/light." Useppe identifies the insect by a word that previously appears in the narrative description of his first adventure outside of the house: "Cosí le foglie degli alberi erano centinaia di *lampade*" (123, italics mine). Rather than repeat what he has been told, Useppe creates his own world of poetic representation where meaning is not weighed down by the heaviness of the temporal world/word. Useppe names things, yet in naming them offers fresh approaches to perceiving familiar phenomena. Nino – an aspiring fascist *camicia nera* – attempts to socialise Useppe through teaching him the patriotic phrase "bandiera tricolore/tricolor flag" which Useppe repeats as "addèla ole." Obviously, Useppe's repetition differs greatly from the original, and as Useppe moves on to study swallows and butterflies, the fascist emblem of *patria* is pushed aside as well, as its signifying power as icon of authority has no place in the unconfined thought processes of a young boy.

The birth of Useppe's name is also telling of how his is not a typical story of social integration. Shortly after his outing with Nino, Useppe – birth name Giuseppe, like his anarchist grandfather – is described as standing in front of a mirror: "Davanti a uno specchio, ravvisandosi diceva: 'Useppe' [...] Il quale, poi gli rimase per tutti, sempre. E anch'io qua d'ora in poi lo chiamerò Useppe, giacché questo è il nome che sempre gli ho conosciuto" (131, 144).[18] Useppe, now just over one year old, is precisely in the middle of Lacan's "mirror stage," whose proper surmounting inaugurates the individual into the symbolic, and synthesises him/her with the social environment. Rather than adapting the self to the world, Useppe creates his own language of self-identification, which then not only becomes adopted by his mother and brother, but by the narrator as well. At only one year of age, Useppe resists social integration, and instead carves out his own language resisting the violence of his contemporary world. The thematics of Useppe's non-integration are continued in his sexual maturation as well. The narrator describes him as "una vivente smentita (ovvero forse eccezione?) alla scienza del Professor Freud. Per essere maschietto, difatti, lo era senz'altro ... ma per ora ... del proprio organo virile non se ne interessava affatto" (405, 455-6).[19] Re reads this passage in terms of Useppe's unconscious resistance to sexual difference, therefore signifying his reluctance to give up his innocence, grow up and subsequently enter the symbolic order. She rightly concludes that Morante positions Useppe as a "figure of what humanity itself could be were it to be free (or freed) of its obsession with the regimentation of difference" (368).

Unfortunately, Useppe must encounter tyrannical violence at a young age. In two of the most poignant moments of the text, Useppe comes across images so horrible that he remains paralysed with a mixture of fear and bewilderment. In the first instance, Ida is drawn to the train station after hearing rumors that the Roman Jews are being deported to the concentration camps. As she surveys the rows of cattle cars all full of people yelling to be freed and begging for help, she is shocked and terrified. Useppe's heartbeat reminds her of his presence against her chest, and when she turns to examine him, she finds him staring at the train with an indescribable gaze of horror. The second instance is more traumatic for both the reader and Useppe: He peruses an old magazine depicting a series of photographs of the atrocities of the concentration camps including mass graves, various tortures, death and human experiments. The most disquieting aspect of this description is that it is retold through the point of view of how an illiterate might interpret these stills, someone who understands neither the images nor their significance. For Useppe then, a pile of bodies becomes "un cumolo chaotico di materie biancastre e stecchite (a chaotic heap of whitish, sticklike objects)" (372, 417) and starving inmates resemble puppets wearing agonising smiles. His reaction is exactly the same as it was at the Tiburtina station: his face is marked by the same accepting horror, as if these images were intrinsic to the human experience. As dehumanising violence is introduced to Useppe, it becomes defamiliarised for the reader, who is forced to re-examine the repercussions of fascist regimes.

It is not surprising then that Useppe chooses to reject written and visual signifiers. He has learned that the symbolic order is hurtful and brutal. He destroys his drawings upon completing them and avoids learning to read and write, choosing instead to create mental poetry that he memorises and only repeats to his most trusted companions: his faithful dog Bella and the anarchist Davide. Useppe's poetry bespeaks a world of universal connection, and posits a way out of the snare of the symbolic order. When asked by Davide to "think" up some poetry, Useppe voices a stream of similes in a state of mystic abstraction:

> Le stelle come gli alberi e fruscolano come gli alberi.
> Il sole per terra come una manata di catanelle e anelli.
> Il sole tutto come tante piume cento piume mila piume.
> Il sole su per l'aria come tante scale di palazzi.
> La luna come una scala e su in cima s'affaccia Bella che s'annisconne.
> Dormite canarini arinchiusi come due rose.
> Le 'ttelle come tante rondini che si salutano. E negli alberi.
> Il fiume come i belli capelli. E i belli capelli.
> I pesci come canarini. E volano via.
> E le foie come ali. E volano via.
> E il cavallo come una bandiera.
> E vola via.[20] (523, 588)

Useppe's twelve-line spoken poem is replete with similes, internal rhyme, anaphora and repetition, as his is an integrated world where all can be connected with a simple "come." He relates such natural elements as the stars, the sun, the moon, two canaries, a river, a fish, some leaves and a horse to things that either he looks up at – trees, staircases, his mother's hair – or things that fly – feathers, canaries, swallows, wings, a flag – and as the poem gradually builds towards the visually guided epistrophe "E vola via," such disparate elements as horses and canaries, a flag and long hair all drift into the child's mythical world of otherness, of lightness. Ironically, the world of lightness for Useppe is also the realm of death, as he soundly believes that there is no heaven or hell, all things just "fly away."[21] Relative elements of flight and lightness within the poem intimate Morante's belief in a utopian existence where dissimilar particulars can coexist without hierarchical categorisation – a theme elsewhere addressed in her collection of poems and short plays appropriately entitled *Il mondo salvato dai ragazzini*.

Useppe's repudiation of the symbolic and discreet reaction through poetry and reticence to his brutal milieu locates him, like his mother, within Kristeva's concept of "women's time." Through his tacit and instinctual rapport with his world, he resists "the break indispensable to the advent of the symbolic" (Kristeva 867). Sexual difference and identification have no bearing on his life, rather, Useppe expresses the uncanny primitive belief of the possibility of infinite connections between self and world. As such, Morante's novel challenges the strict symbolism of language as the written word can produce infinite echoes into boundless temporal spaces. Useppe himself demonstrates this possibility as he lies down in a field and listens to the silence speaking to him, hearing "tutte le voci e le frasi e i discorsi [...] e le canzonette, e i belati, e il mare, e le sirene d'allarme, e gli spari, e le tossi, e i motori, e i covogli per Auschwitz, e i grilli, e le bombe dirompenti, e il grugnito minimo dell'animaluccio senza coda [...] e 'che me lo dài, un bacetto, a' Usè?'" (510, 574).[22] In a seemingly ironic contradiction, Useppe connects songs and the ocean to concentration camps and exploding bombs, fusing monumental and cyclical temporalities.

In many respects, Useppe, albeit a fictional character, fits in with Kristeva's "third attitude" of males and females categorised by the "demassification" of "sexual identity" and "*difference*" (875). Throughout the novel, he actively resists gender cataloguing and searches out organic textual spaces. Useppe's repudiation of the symbolic, his non-violent outlook and his non-gender specific traits all challenge the very notion of gender identity vital to authoritarian regimes. The little boys' utopian sensibilities, however, are discordant with fascism's rhetoric of virility. Subsequently, his death from an epileptic attack positions Useppe as a sacrificial character, Girard's scapegoat, and Morante's novel can be read as an attempt to represent a "counter society" as explained by Kristeva: "The new generation of women is showing that its major social concern has become the sociosymbolic contract as a sacrificial contract [...] women are today affirming [...] that they are forced to experience this sacrificial contract against their will" (869). Written five years before the publication of Kristeva's *Women's Time*, *La Storia* clearly exposes the compulsory sacrificial nature of a collective resistance to fascism.

Nomadic visions: "e la Storia continua"

Morante's characters travel within textual landscapes plagued by the ubiquitous presence of authoritarian politics. Ida and Useppe offer alternative interpretations of and perspectives on female and male gender identity, problematising the relationship between society and the production of gender. Throughout their journeys, they offer alternative "nomadic" – in the words of Braidotti, and Deleuze and Guattari – points of view on the patterns of linear history. Although Braidotti's and Deleuze and Guattaris' overall theses differ – Braidotti uses the concept of nomadism in relation to feminist theory while Deleuze and Guattari discuss nomadism and schizophrenia as that which disinvests binary systems of power such as psychoanalysis and neofascism – they all celebrate the nomadic individual or act as resistance to forms or centres of power.[23] *La Storia* presents nomadic characters that, through their textual wanderings, upset traditionally passive points of view associated with linear history. Through privileging that which is non-hierarchical, ahistorical and anti-establishment, the point of view within *La Storia* becomes multiplied, non-objectified and dis-empowered.

The last line of Morante's text reads: "e la Storia continua (and History continues)" (656, 734), and this concluding impression does not signify the continuation of 'official' recorded history with all of its accompanying wars, debates and political controversies. Instead, Morante's conclusion is a testimonial to all of those who live on the fringes of society, yet whose actions and interfaces reflect utopian/visionary connections at odds with conventional historical and gender chronicle. Different as the character attributes of Morante's Ida and Useppe might be, each assists in exposing the weaknesses of a historical tradition based on patriarchal imperialism. My investigation of *La Storia*'s characters attests to the unviability of binary oppositions inherent in any totalitarian system.

Notes

1. Walter Benjamin, in "Theses on the Philosophy of History" proposes a new approach to 'history' that approximates what is at work in Morante's text. He believes in the dialectical nature of historical awakening, as the past is intimately bound to the present. Benjamin explains that no past moment, however insignificant to the traditional historian, should go unexplored. Maurizia Boscagli in "Brushing Benjamin Against the Grain" treats the function of Benjamin's notion of *Jetztzeit*, or the historical flash, in Morante's novel.

2. Some critical attention has been paid to such issues in Lucia Re's "Utopian Longing" and Cristina Della Coletta's chapter on Morante in *Plotting the Past*

3. Robyn Pickering-Iazzi writes: "*La storia* does not belong to the tradition of Italian feminist authorship, whose discourses customarily manifest a commitment to shared socio-political objectives." ("Images" 329)

4. As cited in Elisabetta Mondello (13).

5. "obeying the dictates of the Authorities, she introduced into their themes and dictation the Kings, Duces, Fatherland, glory, battles that History imposed; however, she did it in all mental innocence, unsuspecting, because History, no more than God, had never been an object of her thoughts."

6. *La Storia* clearly disputes the significance of militarism as many of the novel's characters are devoid of any ideology whatsoever. Ida's first son Nino turns from fascist to resistance fighter seemingly overnight and the German soldier who rapes Ida is caught between heroic idealism and nihilistic individualism.

7. "But neither among those rich, nor among those poor was the place of Iduzza Raimondo, who belonged, truly, to a third species. It is a species that lives (perhaps endangered?) and dies, and gives no news of itself, except at times, perhaps, in the crime reports."

8. Braidotti revisits the idea of "sexual difference," asserting that feminist theory is "the positive affirmation of women's desire to affirm and enact different forms of subjectivity." (158)

9. Della Colletta discusses "women's time" in terms of Useppe's interaction (or lack thereof) with the historical process.

10. "the mysterious idiocy of animals, who, not with their mind, but with a sense of their vulnerable bodies, 'know' the past and the future of every destiny. I would call that sense [...] the *sense of the sacred*: meaning by *sacred* [...] the universal power that can devour them and annihilate them, for their guilt of being born."

11. "From the basket a green plant sprouted, and, in an instant, it ramified through the room, and outside the house, over all the walls of the courtyard [...] She finds herself a tiny girl again, alone [...] losing little trickles of blood from her vagina."

12. "She is the only one wearing clothes in the midst of a crowd of naked people, all standing, their bodies huddled one against the other with no breathing space [...] All those people look dazed, with chalky, staring faces, absent eyes, and without voice, as if every means of communication among them had vanished."

13. "She seemed to be outside of an enclosure, something like an abandoned refuse dump. There was nothing but piles of shoes, worn and dusty, which seemed to have been thrown away years ago."

14. "Lots of little Polish children, in rags, are playing, rolling some tiny golden rings. Blessed rings, and they don't know it. This game is forbidden, in Poland. Punished by death!!!"

15. Re treats Ida's relation to her Jewish roots, the Roman ghetto and her fear of racial persecution, discussing how Ida's attraction to the ghetto is at its strongest during her pregnancy, as the ghetto represents a womb-like space of the pre-symbolic. ("Utopian" 364-5)

16. "She too, like the famous Lesser Panda of legend, was suspended at the top of a tree where temporal charters were no longer in effect."

17. "It was the first time in his life he had seen a field; and every blade of grass seemed to him illuminated from within, as if it contained a thread of green light. And so the leaves of the trees were hundreds of light bulbs, where not only the green glowed [...] but also, other, unknown colors [...] and the people, dressed in colors, were moved around through the square by the same rhythmic and grandiose wind that moves the celestial circles, with their clouds, their suns, and their moons."

18. "In front of a mirror, seeing himself, he would say: 'Useppe' [...] Which then remained his for everybody, always. And I, too, from now on will call him Useppe, because this is the name by which I always know him."

19. "a living refutation of the science of Professor Freud (or perhaps the exception to it?). He was a male, no doubt about it [...] but for the present [...] he took absolutely no interest in his own virile organ."

20. Stars like trees and rustle like trees.
The sun on the ground like a handful of little chains and rings.
The sun all like lots of feathers and a hundred a thousand feathers.
The sun up in the air like lots of steps of buildings.
The moon like a stairway and at the top Bella looks out and hides.
Sleep canaries folded up like two roses.
The stars like swallows saying hello to each other. And in the trees.
The river like pretty hair. And the pretty hair.
The fish like canaries. And they fly away.
And the leaves like wings. And they fly away.
And the horse like a flag.
And he flies away.

21. Concetta D'Angeli discusses the novel's temporal dimensions, treating Morante's interest in Simone Weil, Plato and Dante, concluding that images of flight and the inclusion of Useppe's poetry overcome the severity of the human condition. (234)

22. "all voices and phrases and speeches […] and songs, and bleatings, and the sea and the alarm sirens, and shots, and coughs, and the engines, and the trains for Auschwitz, and crickets, and the exploding bombs, and the tiniest grunt of the tailless animal […] and 'Hey, how about giving me a little kiss Usè?'"

23. Braidotti's *Nomadic Subjects* defines the nomadic individual as a subversive entity continually in process, a mythical composition of class, racial, linguistic and sexual difference whose itinerant roamings disrupt established orders. In *A Thousand Plateaus*, Deleuze and Guattari discuss the rhizome as an emblem for nonsignifying, fluid, acentered, abstract systems that contrast hierarchical, linear, territorialised political/historical/cultural/sexual centres. They sustain the need to divest "History" of its autarchic, imperialist slant, replacing the term with the arbitrary and contingent "Nomadology."

Gender and Patriotism in Carla Capponi's *Con cuore di donna*

Maja Mikula

Introduction

Carla Capponi (known also by her wartime names of *inglesina*, the "little English girl," Elena, and Silvia) was born in Rome on 7 December 1918, as the firstborn of Giuseppe Capponi, a mining engineer, and Maria Tamburri, a schoolteacher and union activist. Carla and her sister Flora, sixteen months her junior, received their primary education at home from their parents, who wanted to protect them from fascist indoctrination characteristically imparted through the public education system. The two sisters developed a close bond, central during Carla's formative years. The third sibling, Piero, was much younger (born in 1928) and thus could not take part in their youthful exploits. The economic hardship the family endured after the death of Carla's father in a mining accident in 1940 forced both sisters to forego further studies and enter the workforce in their early twenties. Carla joined the Communist Party in the same year (Slaughter 46).

Soon after the fall of fascism and the ensuing German occupation of Rome, Carla's home in the Foro di Traiano became a distribution centre for the Communist Party newspaper, *L'Unità,* and the newspaper of the Catholic left, *Voce Operaia*; safehaven for partisans and runaway Italian soldiers; and a venue for meetings of various antifascist groups, including Patriotic Action Groups (*Gruppi di Azione Patriottica*, or GAP) – the urban antifascist guerilla engaging in acts of sabotage and attacks on German strongholds – of which Carla later became an active member. She participated in numerous actions against the Germans, including bomb strikes and armed attacks against prominent individuals and the key establishments run by the occupying forces. She was also a vice-commander of a partisan unit on the outskirts of Rome, at Palestrina and Monti Prenestini.

In the postwar period, she was a Member of Parliament for the Communist Party on two occasions (1953 and 1972), a member of the Justice Commission in the early 1970s, and of the Presidential Committee of the National Association of Italian Partisans (ANPI) until her death in 2000. As a woman who was actively involved in the armed resistance, one of only sixteen Italian women decorated with a gold medal for military bravery in World War II, Capponi is a legendary figure who bends the traditional perceptions of patriotism and gendered agency.

Together with other organisers and executors of the controversial Via Rasella attack on a division of SS military police in Nazi-occupied Rome in March 1944, Capponi has been held responsible by some for the subsequent German reprisal, in which 335 persons were brutally killed in the Ardeatine caves near Rome. The prompt reprisal was announced by the Germans *post facto*, three days after the attack, on the front page of the Roman daily *Il Giornale d'Italia*. The announcement read as follows:

> "Nel pomeriggio del 23 marzo 1944, elementi criminali hanno eseguito un attentato con lancio di bomba contro una colonna tedesca di Polizia in transito per Via Rasella. In seguito a questa imboscata, 32 uomini della Polizia tedesca sono stati uccisi e parecchi feriti ... Il Comando Tedesco, perciò, ha ordinato che per ogni Tedesco ammazzato dieci criminali comunisti-badogliani saranno fucilati. Quest'ordine è già stato eseguito."[1]

However, the myth that the Germans first publicly pledged to forego the reprisal if the partisans responsible for the attack turned themselves in has been present for decades in the popular imagination.[2] In 1948, a group of relatives of the Ardeatine victims initiated a legal suit against the perpetrators of the Via Rasella attack. Notwithstanding the court's decision, which exonerated the partisans from any responsibility for the reprisal and declared the Via Rasella attack a legitimate act of war, public condemnation has persisted until the present. For decades, Capponi was the target of threatening phone calls and abusive graffiti. Interviewed in the 1980s by the Canadian documentary film-maker Shelley Saywell, she described this persistent exposure to public abuse as "personally very upsetting." She also felt that most of the attacks targeted her in particular (Saywell 100), perhaps taking advantage of her assumed greater vulnerability as a woman. In 1954, the case was taken to the Roman Court of Appeal, but it was dismissed again, only to be resurrected in the 1990s, with yet another judicial inquiry (1996-99) seeking to classify the Via Rasella attack as a crime. For a second time, the case was concluded in favour of the accused, and the attack was sanctioned by the court as a legitimate act of war.

A bequest to posterity

In her book *Con cuore di donna* (With the Heart of a Woman), Carla Capponi constructs her identity through the moral dilemmas and choices she had to work through in a crucial moment in the history of contemporary Italy, namely during the two decades of the consolidation of fascist dictatorship (1922-43) and the resistance period (1943-44). Although her decision to fight in antifascist resistance seems to challenge the conventional gender expectations of her time, she interprets it as the only natural response in the given historical circumstances. Moreover, the text displays a particular version of patriotism, associated with antifascist resistance and the first post-World War II constitution, based on ostensibly universal values, yet firmly rooted in the specific Italian historical and socio-cultural context. This study examines Capponi's construction of her gendered and national identity, interpreting it as a politically charged act of resistance by someone whose version of truth has been under attack, and as a master narrative with a therapeutic potential for the author.

Capponi's book is not easily classifiable in terms of genre. Published by Il Saggiatore (Milan) as part of the *Collana storica* (History Series), it is simultaneously an autobiography in which the author's life is interpreted as an intersection of verifiable historical circumstances, and a history in which the historian herself was one of the participants. In this history, the author's own recollections serve as the key primary sources, at times reinforced by other material, such as official documents, newspaper articles and oral history. Reading Hobsbawm's *A Short Century*, Capponi becomes aware of the extent to which the public affairs recorded in his book have made an impact on her own life, making her a valuable witness of the events which shaped her country's recent history (Capponi 11-12). She sets out to take her memories out of the private sphere, motivated by a desire to claim a place in history for the numerous fellow resistance fighters whose names would otherwise be forgotten (12).

It is evident that Capponi, like many women autobiographers before her, goes to great lengths to explain the motives that prompted her to produce a text intended for public consumption, to "justify [her] entry into the realm of public (thus, male) discourse" (Morgan 8). In the Preface, she offers a number of interesting thoughts on the relationship between personal and social memory, autobiography and history. The reader is told that *Con cuore di donna* was commissioned by the publisher and that the author's immediate response was one of "panic," "torment" and "profound depression." Memory, says Capponi, follows a logic all of its own: "[u]na memoria ha molte altre memorie, attaccate al tronco di un albero come rami scomposti ma pure armoniosi" (7).[3] Once fixed in the narrative form, thought is reduced to a lifeless skeleton, "come se perdesse interesse, divenisse noioso (7, as if it lost interest and became boring)." Writing is further perceived as a kind of life mapping, which forces the author "a considerare gli spazi entro i quali si è svolta la [sua] vita, a misurarne il valore (to consider the spaces within which [her] life has unfolded and measure their worth)." (8) It also conjures up thoughts of death, as the author comes to terms with her advanced age and the limited time left for new experiences (8).[4]

Published in late 2000, and officially launched a week before the author's death at the age of eighty-two, *Con cuore di donna* may be read as Capponi's bequest to posterity, in which her memory of personal experience is offered to validate the truthfulness of historical interpretation. The detailed account of the events that unfolded immediately after the Via Rasella attack, in which the author implicitly addresses the accusations she was exposed to day after day throughout the postwar period,[5] opens up the possibility of reading the entire text as a therapeutic endeavour, that is, an undertaking by the author to exculpate herself before the judgment of history.

With the heart of a woman: a gendered perspective

The title of the text, as well as its discursive framework, reveal the author's subjectivity as highly gendered. The title itself captures the ambiguity of a gendered war experience by inviting different readings of the word "heart," with its overlapping semantic fields – as the locus of both love/compassion and spirit/audacity. With the "heart of a woman," Capponi does not engage in acts of violence lightly, seeing them first and foremost as forced upon her by historical circumstances. Time after time, taking life presents moral dilemmas, which can only be resolved by calling to mind the remedial intent of each action, to prevent further violence by the Germans. In particular, immediately before the Via Rasella bombing, Capponi has to find strength to perform the attack by reminding herself of all the atrocities committed by the Germans, of the devastation of Rome caused by allied bombing, of the torture and executions of her comrades, of deportations, concentration camps and the numerous Italian soldiers who perished on the Russian, Greek or Yugoslav fronts (Capponi 229).

By joining the armed struggle against the occupying forces, Capponi and other female combatants in the Italian Resistance transgressed the popular expectations that permitted women a limited range of stereotypically female duties, such as care for the wounded; assistance with food, clothes and sanitary equipment; sabotage of enemy supplies; organisation of strikes, demonstrations and various cultural and educational activities; and engagement in the production and distribution of an underground press. Capponi's choice would have been considered unusual, if not emphatically improper, by many of her contemporaries. In fact, even her mother considered it downright madness. When, in the growing turmoil upon the announcement of the armistice on 8 September 1943, Capponi declared that she wanted to join a group of armed civilians inviting Romans to resist the impending German occupation, her mother's immediate response was: "Ma sei matta! Ma che ci va a fare una donna? Quell'invito è rivolto agli uomini" (96).[6] Capponi herself explains her decision as a natural, commonsensical response to the "orrore delle aberranti teorie nazifasciste (horror of aberrant Nazi-fascist theories)" (13).

However, the entire first chapter of her autobiography, entitled "The garden and the world" ("Il giardino e il mondo"), seems to be an endeavour by the author to 'justify' her decision by constructing a well-matched identity through an account of her family background and early childhood. Indeed, when asked by a co-fighter, Lucia Ottobrini (wartime name Maria), what motivated her to participate actively in the war, she realises that her choice was determined by the isolation of her family, which had a "culture" of its own, different and far removed from fascist reality (142).

If such a socially unsanctioned decision came to her as the only natural course of action, this has to be explicable in terms of who she was, of what stock, and how she spent her formative years. The story of her family over several generations conveys the rootedness and the Italianness of her male ancestors (with origins traceable to the sixteenth century, in Tuscany and the Marche region), as well as their open-minded spirit, demonstrated by their marriage choices: "le consorti dei miei avi sono inglesi, tedesche, polacche, protestanti, ebree, cattoliche: segno che i Capponi non erano per il detto 'moglie e buoi dei paesi tuoi' e avevano quantomeno una visione europea del loro mondo di interessi" (15).[7] The family's nobility and considerable fortunes in land and mansions derived from the ownership of a number of paper-mills in the Marche region, which were supplying paper to the Vatican State until the annexation of Rome to the Italian Kingdom in 1870.

Thus, the narrative structure of Capponi's text reflects a tendency, characteristically female according to some critics (Hooton), to accord a significant role to childhood experiences. The memoir covers two main periods: the author's childhood and early adulthood during the two decades of fascism (1922-43), and the occupation of Rome (September 1943 to June 1944) when she actively participated in the armed resistance.

> Women's narratives [...] seem characteristically bent on cherishing the past for its own sake, recreating its sensuous flavor, rediscovering the nuances of relationships or the sensations of old familiar rhythms. The patterns that women perceive in their lives tend to converge around the central early experience; childhood is the heart of the later story, which frequently attempts to explain itself in terms of the early life, to perceive itself as an elaboration on a given pattern, or a reconstitution of given ingredients. (Hooton 35)

The early years spent in the isolation of her parental home, away from society and protected as much as possible from fascist propaganda, are seen by Capponi as a period of primeval innocence, lived as a "simulation of reality" enclosed in an "eden" inside the walls of their garden (27).

Furthermore, the subject of Capponi's autobiography is not a self-contained, unified, 'specular' self. Rather, the speaking voices, both individual and collective, are many. In the preface, the author identifies this multi-vocality as an essential part of her authorial intention:

> Vorrei poter scrivere veramente per gli altri, degli "altri," [sic!] di tutte le persone, i fatti, gli avvenimenti che hanno attraversato la mia vita. Non dire di me come soggetto che si mostra e si fa riconoscere e indagare, ma di me come tramite per far conoscere personaggi, paesaggi, situazioni, abitudini di vita e tutto il mondo che ha popolato la mia esistenza e quella delle persone del mio tempo.[8] (8)

The child Carla, the Resistance fighter Elena, and Carla the author, are engaged in a perpetual dialogue with one another and with a number of 'significant others:' family, friends, acquaintances, political allies and opponents. This multiplicity of voices may be interpreted as a mark of what Hélène Cixous has called *ecriture féminine* (feminine writing), or Luce Irigaray *le parler femme* (womanspeak). Notably, Irigaray's womanspeak is interpreted as arising naturally when women speak among themselves, but vanishing again in the presence of men (Moi 144). Capponi likewise dedicates her text to the schoolgirl Betta, thus framing it as a dialogue between two women of different generations, in a stereotypically 'women's business' gesture of handing down tradition.

Feminist literary theorists have identified a "primal connection to significant others" and a "sense of the self as plural" as crucial elements of female autobiographical tradition: "from at least as early as the Renaissance [...] women have been aware of their roles/identities as multiple – and, given societal constraints on women's aspirations, frequently in conflict with one another" (Morgan 8). Capponi's account of her childhood during the Fascist *ventennio* focuses on family relationships, primarily with her sister Flora and mother Maria, as well as her father Giuseppe, whose quiet, yet unswerving antifascism has an indelible impact on Carla's development. Three carefully selected episodes substantiate Giuseppe's political stance: his refusal to remove his hat and stand during the playing of the Fascist anthem in the late 1920s (30); his indignation at Carla's participation in a swimming contest organised by fascist youth in the early 1930s (44-46); and finally, his straight refusal to join the National Fascist Party in 1935, which resulted in his forced four-year working sojourn in Albania, only to be revoked after his wife's pragmatic acceptance of fascist Party membership. (64-65)

Yet, Giuseppe does not actively resist the fascist regime, perhaps for a lack of courage to oppose the dictatorship more decisively, "come avevano fatto altri, ora costretti nelle carceri, relegati al confine politico, emigrati all'estero o ridotti ai margini della società nelle borgate, perseguitati e ributtati in carcere ogni qual volta si svolgevano le manifestazioni 'patriottiche' del PNF" (54).[9] Carla's father thus performs an important narrative function in the text: he is the key for interpreting her motivations and moral choices later in life. His compelling adherence to his political persuasion in fact reaches its full potential only through his daughter's audacious, unconditional resistance.

On the other hand, the female 'significant others' of her early life, her mother and sister, despite their assumed or demonstrated sharing of Giuseppe's basic ideological standpoint, appear to be more clearly existentially driven by the vicissitudes of daily life than by a clear political vision. Flora thus participates in Carla's early "acts of resistance" against Fascism: together, the two girls steal a copy of a pamphlet about the Matteotti murder, make five copies of it by hand and distribute it among their friends at school (48-52); together, they play a practical joke on a young fascist soldier, by dropping into the sea his precious gold ring, part of his booty from the Spanish Civil War (63). Throughout their childhood, Capponi notes, the two sisters would always talk about themselves in the plural, so strong was the oneness of the spirit with which they engaged in their youthful adventures.

However, Flora's marriage to an army officer, Giulio Calenti, signifies a rupture of the relationship between the two sisters. Capponi does not tell us much about Giulio, apart from a hint about his possible pro-fascist stance.

We are told that the moment he proposed, in the year following Giuseppe Capponi's death, and while Flora was still under age, he expected his future wife to discontinue her office job (71). The young couple soon moved to the provincial town of Pesaro, where Flora was isolated from her family, friends and the vibrant Roman atmosphere (89-90). After a brief reunion with Flora in the summer of 1943, Carla left her sister's house in Pesaro, saddened by Flora's pervasive melancholy and her inability or unwillingness to talk about it. After this emotional episode, which conveys a feeling of mourning for a Flora as she had been in their childhood and as she could have been had she not been repressed by an unhappy marriage, Flora does not appear at all in the remaining text.

Carla's mother Maria is portrayed as a woman with a primary allegiance to her husband and children, and a charitable spirit sensitive to people's suffering. When Giuseppe is sent to Albania, following his refusal to join the National Fascist Party, she cannot "sopportare la solitudine nella grande casa e la lontananza del suo uomo (bear the solitude of the big house and the absence of her man)" (64-65). Following her friends' advice, she takes the opportunity of enrolling in the Fascist Party and using her connections to bring him back (65). However, listening to the radio announcement of the armistice on 8 September 1943, she is convinced that the Italians have to contribute to the liberation of their country, as the "unica soluzione che può restituirci dignità e onore (only solution that can restore our dignity and honour)" (94). Initially, her own activities are limited to offering shelter and assistance in food and clothing to the homeless and the wounded through a women's charitable organisation (*le dame di San Vincenzo*).

Later, at Carla's initiative, she consents to opening her house in Foro Traiano for the political meetings of various women's organisations, the Communist Party and the Patriotic Action Groups. She takes this decision aware of the risks associated with it. Indeed, in early 1944, she is forced to leave the flat with her teenage son and hide at a friend's house for several days to avoid arrest by the Germans (175). Later, with the help of the concierge, they re-enter their own flat, which has been sealed by the Germans, via the service staircase, and remain there until the end of the occupation of Rome, hidden behind closed windows and with blinds fully drawn (176).

Thus the microcosm of the Capponi family encapsulates the wide range of responses to the fascist dictatorship – with the exception of wholesale support – that were present during that period in Italian society as a whole: from pragmatic adherence and the "wait and see" attitude (*attendismo*), to passive resistance and, finally, active opposition. Yet, in her text, Capponi carefully avoids any moral judgement, which would privilege one response over another and thus 'silence' the voices of those whose choices were different from her own. This is a refreshing strategy, as the author seems to be aware that only a more inclusive narrative can demythologise the resistance rhetoric, to reinstate it as a true foundation stone of national consciousness.[10]

While the first two chapters of Capponi's autobiography, focusing respectively on the author's childhood and adolescence, reflect a characteristic authorial perception of self in an intricate network of relationships, the rest of the text, covering the period of the occupation of Rome, places more emphasis on the collective agency of Roman antifascists. Even Rosario Bentivegna, whom she married soon after the war, is portrayed as one of many comrades united by a common political vision and a determination to take an active part in the resistance. There are only sporadic intimations of the "sentimenti di solidarietà, di lealtà, di coraggio nella paura (sentiments of solidarity, loyalty, courage in fear)" (259), which inspired the romantic liaison between the two through the many actions they performed together; hints at the shared love of poetry and music (135-36); and a brief account of their first kiss, in the midst of a burst of machine-gun fire on the way to join the partisans in the countryside (269).

In addition to a "definition of the self in a context of relationship," critics have identified a "judgment of the self in terms of ability to care" (Hooton 34) as another common characteristic of women's autobiographies. In *Con cuore di donna*, Capponi's "ability to care" emerges as an instinctive need to protect others – even those on the enemy side – and spare lives whenever possible. This is particularly true when children are concerned; one of Carla's most pressing preoccupations before an attack is to make sure that there are no children around (207; 233). The occupying forces, on the other hand, are defined in terms of their "inability to care," that is, their disregard for human life, including the life of children. Accordingly, the period of the German occupation of Rome is symbolically circumscribed by two tragic events in which innocent children were killed by the occupying forces – at the beginning of the occupation, two brothers, aged nine and eleven, are brutally murdered by a German soldier while rummaging through a garbage heap to find some food; a day after the liberation, a twelve-year old boy is killed while trying to prevent the retreating German soldiers from blowing up an iron bridge (307-9).

In line with her judgment of the self in terms of ability to care, death emerges as one of the central themes of the book, both in the story of her childhood and in her account of the resistance period, when it was part and parcel of her daily existence. This fixation with death can be interpreted at several levels, encapsulating the multiplicity and interplay of speaking subjects in the text: as a reflection of the moral dilemmas which accompanied her war-time activities in which taking life was a *sine qua non*; of her advanced age at the moment of writing; and finally and most importantly, of her assumed gendered predisposition towards giving life, rather than taking it.

Saving the honour of the fatherland: reclaiming the *italianità* of the resistance movement

> "Do you know what they call you here? They call you the little English girl, but you are more Roman than I am!" (Saywell 88)

So far, the focus of this paper has been on an analysis of Capponi's text from the perspective of gender. In this section, I look at the national sentiment emerging from the book, in relation to the current debate surrounding the elusive notion of *italianità*. Since the early 1990s, which saw the collapse of Italy's postwar party system and the growing impetus of European integration, Italian national identity has been at the centre of heated debates. In this context, *italianità* came to be seen as both a potential unifying force above party politics and a safeguard against the would-be assimilation into the European melting pot. During the latter half of the twentieth century, the country's two major parties – the Christian Democrats and the Communists – espoused a rather cautious attitude to nationalism, which had acquired a negative aura through fascist propagandist manipulation. Ostensibly, the universalising aspirations of both parties and their allegiance to their 'ideological homelands' – the United States and the Soviet Union, respectively – also undermined the possibility of creating an integrative national discourse for Italy's so-called First Republic. When this weak model of identification lost its *raison d'être* at the end of the Cold War period, laments over the apparent lack of an alternative nation-centred model entered public discourse from across the political spectrum.

Despite the complexities of this discourse, it is possible to distinguish two general trends within it: an emphasis on 'loyalty to the nation,' based on an essentially ethno-cultural identification,[11] which is commonly advocated by the cultures of the political right; and a focus on 'love of country,' or republican patriotism, championed by the cultures of the left.[12] Maurizio Viroli, for example, insists on a clear distinction between nationalism and patriotism and on a dialectical relationship between the two discourses, which, according to him, compete "on the same terrain of passions and particularity" (Viroli 8). Patriotism, in fact, may be interpreted as a continuation of the national discourse prevalent during the First Republic, albeit more clearly entrenched in the specific Italian historical and socio-cultural milieu. According to Viroli, republican patriotism has always been linked to an identifiable 'homeland,' despite its universalising rhetoric:

> Even the theorists who wanted to make the distance between the political values of the republic and the sphere of ethnicity and culture as wide as possible, always meant the republic as it was expressed by the common liberty of a particular people with its particular background and its particular culture. The crucial distinction lies in the priority or the emphasis: for the patriots, the primary value is the republic and the free way of life that the republic permits; for the nationalists, the primary values are the spiritual and cultural unity of the people. (Viroli 2)

This emphasis on the embedded nature of patriotism, which may have become more manifest in the last decade or so, is not without precedents in recent Italian history. In his masterful account of liberal socialism, written in exile in 1929, antifascist intellectual Carlo Rosselli urged the socialists not to ignore the "valori più alti della vita nazionale," because by ignoring them they could only facilitate the "gioco delle altre correnti che nello sfruttamento del mito nazionale basano le loro fortune" (Rosselli 135).[13] Thus, in order to compete with exclusivist nationalism and possibly serve as its "antidote" (Viroli 8), republican patriotism has to call attention to its own version of *italianità*, with which a large proportion of Italians could identify. I would like to suggest that Capponi's book does precisely that, through a number of strategies outlined below.

The period of antifascist resistance and the first republican constitution (1948) would appear to be the natural foundation stones of the republican patriotic national narrative. However, the Italian memories of the two decades of fascism and the early years of the republic are markedly disharmonious, contributing to what historians have called the "most serious lacuna in contemporary Italian culture," that is, an "incapacity to recount the nation's history in a convincing way" (Rusconi, "Will Italy Remain a Nation?" 316). According to Gian Enrico Rusconi,

> "[rimangono] reticenze e cautele che impediscono che la Resistenza reale, non la sua trasfigurazione retorica, sia riconosciuta come l'evento fondante della democrazia italiana – come dovrebbe essere. Attorno ad esso persistono memorie divise, inconciliate, antagoniste che nella nuova congiuntura politica sono alla ricerca di un riconoscimento se non di una rivincita."[14] (Rusconi, *Resistenza*, 7)

Indeed, since the early 1990s, historians such as Renzo De Felice (*Rosso e nero*) and Ernesto Galli della Loggia (*La morte della patria*) have challenged the assumptions, rooted in the national rhetoric of the First Republic, of an overwhelming dissatisfaction with and opposition to the fascist rule among the Italians of the time; of the substantial role of the resistance movement in the country's liberation; and, finally, of the moral righteousness of the violent acts committed by the Italian partisans.

Rather than being considered a period of national awakening, or, as it was called by some, a "second Risorgimento" (Adams and Barile; Traniello), for these historians the resistance in fact marked a demise of the Italian sense of national identity. De Felice called for its thorough re-evaluation, "per capire il danno alla moralità nazionale consumato in quel biennio e le ragioni della mancata ricostituzione di quel tessuto morale andato perduto" (De Felice 61).[15] A scholar who has devoted years of painstaking research to recording oral testimonies of the Italian resistance, Alessandro Portelli, has endeavoured to reconcile the discordant memories by shifting his focus away from any moral judgment:

C'è chi ha chiamato queste giornate la "morte della patria," e chi le ha chiamate "secondo Risorgimento." Hanno ragione tutti e due, ma l'uno non si capisce senza l'altro: muore una patria che non era di tutti, e un'altra – per iniziativa e coscienza di molti, se non per consenso e partecipazione di tutti – sta provando a nascere.[16] (Portelli 126)

There is no doubt that Capponi's text seeks to address the contemporary polemic surrounding the role of the resistance in Italian nation building. She interprets the debate in terms of historical revisionism and negationism, used by the right to mask the return of "vecchie ideologie infauste" (old dismal ideologies) (12). Although the target audience of Capponi's book is not limited to a particular age group, the text is meant to carry a message of major consequence for younger generations. In some way, it is dedicated to the schoolgirl Betta, whose letter of admiration inspired Carla to talk about her generation "as it really was" and dissociate it from the many myths that have formed about it in popular imagination. In the preface, Capponi writes: "mi sono determinata a scrivere minutamente di quel tempo ormai 'mitico' o 'mitizzato' perché sento che occorre convincere i giovani di oggi che ognuno di noi fu esattamente un giovane come loro, stretto fra dubbi e paure, convinto di non fare nulla di così eccezionale, di 'storico'" (9).[17] Passing an exam at school, or escaping from the SS by jumping from a window and disappearing into the night, may give us the same feeling of fulfilment, and "[è] solo la spettacolarità della vicenda che ci illude sul valore di quella prova" (10).[18] By dedicating her memoirs to the younger generations, Capponi constructs the resistance as a process that continues in the future, based on a perception of democracy "come sbocco naturale della partecipazione (as a natural outlet for participation)" (10). She structures her version of *italianità* first and foremost on moral grounds. It is an *italianità* based on a belief in tolerance, freedom, and an imagined better future for the country.

Capponi sees the resistance movement as primarily motivated by a desire to "salvare l'onore della patria (save the honour of the fatherland)" (12). This desire resonates with what Rusconi has termed the "expiative patriotism of a part of the Italian population [...] diffused among the people with the disastrous course of the war" (Rusconi, "Will Italy," 317), a "spontaneous feeling of national solidarity developed through a common suffering perceived as not wholly undeserved" (Rusconi, "Will Italy" 318). Although based on the author's reading of universal values, which goes hand in hand with communist internationalism and the rhetoric of inclusion, Capponi's patriotism – with its declared expiative intent – has a uniquely Italian flavour. In the previously mentioned interview with Shelley Saywell, Capponi noted that she and her fellow resistance fighters "wanted to change Italy into a more civilised, freer, more democratic nation where there would be greater social justice. We were young, and young people are affected by injustice. They possess qualities, such as generosity, and feel sympathy towards their fellow men. That is what drove us to organise against Fascism – and later to fight" (Saywell 75-76). *Con cuore di donna* thus reaffirms Maurizio Viroli's thesis that republican patriotism does not say to the Italians [...] that they should think and act as [...] lovers of an anonymous liberty and justice; it tells them that they should become Italian ... citizens committed to defend and improve their own republic [...] and it says so by using poignant images that refer to shared memories and by telling meaningful stories that give color and warmth to the ideal of the republic. (Viroli 8-9)

Indeed, *Con cuore di donna* abounds with images drawn from a pool of shared memories at the heart of Italian national sentiment. They emerge first and foremost from the topography of the text, in which Rome and its surroundings provide an unambiguous epicentre. The two focal sites, staging the events described in Capponi's book, are the districts of Porta Fabrica,[19] adjacent to the Vatican walls, where she spent most of her early childhood, and Foro Traiano, one of the imperial forums at the heart of Mussolini's monumental Rome, to which her family moved in 1929 and where she lived during her formative years, including most of the period of the armed resistance.

The Rome of Carla Capponi's childhood was undergoing profound transformations during the fascist period, as palingenetic nationalism called for interventions in urban development, which would reinforce the rhetoric of a revival of past greatness. The Duce wanted Rome to "appear marvelous to all the peoples of the world – vast, orderly, powerful, as in the time of the empire of Augustus" (Mussolini, quoted in Fried 31). In order to achieve this, he had to demolish the medieval and Renaissance residential districts, such as those described by Capponi, and relocate their residents to the outer Roman suburbs. When the offices of the prime minister were moved to Piazza Venezia, in the immediate neighbourhood of the Foro Traiano district, many locals were turned out of their homes and shops in order to provide space for enlarging the square and opening up access routes, to make it the focal point for fascist rallies and ceremonies. Interviewed by Alessandro Portelli, Capponi recalls the story of a distinguished local restorer, who, evicted from his little shop in one of the narrow lanes of Foro Traiano and forced to live in a desolate hut in a distant suburb, had to go to the center of Rome on a daily basis to look for families to whom he could offer his services (Portelli 84). On the other hand, Mussolini's oceanic rallies provided an occasion for the Capponi family to seek refuge in the countryside, given their aversion to the show of force of the fascist regime (Capponi 59-60). Thus, while the public, monumental Rome was expanding at the expense of the private, intimate world of local residents and small shop owners, Capponi's sympathy stayed decidedly on the side of the latter.[20]

Capponi's topography, zoomed in on the districts of Porta Fabrica and Foro Traiano, emblematises two important elements of the Italian national narrative, namely a strong influence of Catholicism and the continuity with the traditions of ancient Rome. Capponi divests the two historical districts of their ceremonial grandeur and presents them from an insider's point of view, as intimate spaces where ordinary people live their daily lives, increasingly afflicted by the exigencies of modernisation and fascist interventions in urban development. She considers herself privileged for spending her childhood "in quelle strade, in quella Roma antica dove ogni pietra ha una storia (in those streets […] where every stone has a story to tell)," where the everyday life of the residents unfolds " sulla strada, davanti alle botteghe, sulle sedie poste avanti casa con le donne quiete, intente a lavorare la maglia o a mondare i piselli per la cena" (31).[21] She describes the still bustling activity of the kilns of Porta Fabrica, producing everything from bricks, vases and earthenware to terracotta saints, nativity cherubs, babies in cradles, and even a particular brand of terracotta whistles shaped like figures of contemporary policemen, for which the resourceful street vendors invented the irreverent advertising slogan of "Il carabiniere! Il carabiniere con il fischio nel sedere! (Policeman, policeman, with a whistle in his back side!)" (21). Capponi's nostalgic memories of the yet un-sanitised central Rome, with scents of roast chestnuts, fritters and milk emanating from carts, shops and taverns seem to 'resemanticise' the images of the same spaces exploited in the nationalist narrative, by 'contaminating' them through a lens of intimacy and familiarity.

In a similar fashion, Michelangelo's magnificent dome of St Peter's, illuminated during the celebrations to mark the end of the first Jubilee year of the fascist period (1925),[22] is seen by Carla at the age of seven as a fairytale spectacle, with hundreds of acrobats hurling themselves from incredible heights to light the myriad of oil lanterns adorning the vault-ribs of the basilica (29-30). The Palatine Hill, the mythical birthplace of the city of Rome, where, according to the legend, Romulus and Remus were found by the she-wolf that kept them alive, becomes a playground for Carla and her sister Flora, who enjoy roaming in the midst of marble pedestals, columns and porticoes, searching for relics of the times gone by (33).

In her account of the period of the occupation of Rome, pivotal for the understanding of the text as a whole,[23] Capponi continues to view the city through a lens of intimacy, now underscored by her awareness of the devastation the war causes to monuments of national heritage. In this section, Rome emerges as a national museum, with "tutti quei preziosi monumenti antichi di duemila anni (all those precious two-thousand-year old monuments)" (102) threatened by allied bombing and continuous gunfire. In one instance, machine-gun fire is described as coming from the Temple of Venus, the "luogo che i romani avevano destinato al tempio della dea della bellezza, dell'amore e della romanità (place the Romans assigned to the goddess of beauty, love and the Roman spirit)" (102). Capponi thus foregrounds a reading of the symbolic value of ancient Rome for a national narrative quite different from that espoused by the fascists, in that it purports to be primarily based on harmony and tolerance. Monuments associated with fascist power have no part in this narrative. They conceal "la vista dei bei tetti di Roma (the view of the beautiful roofs of Rome)," and the *Gappisti* vindicate themselves by covering them with the graffiti of the hammer and sickle and communist slogans (Capponi 127-8).

Conclusion

From the observations outlined above, it is evident that *Con cuore di donna* aligns itself with the tradition of female life writing at several levels. The text speaks in a multiplicity of voices, rather than constructing a 'seamless', specular self. The author perpetuates another *locus comuni* of female autobiography by going to great lengths to justify her writing endeavour. Throughout the narrative, she questions and implicitly refutes patriarchal constraints. She defines herself in the context of the relationships she has with her significant others, especially when recounting her childhood experiences. She judges herself primarily in terms of an ability to preserve and nurture life, developing a complex moral argument whereby taking life by the resistance fighters is seen as abominable but necessary to prevent further injustice and devastation.

The therapeutic intent of the text is particularly evident from the author's expression of her national sentiment, which emerges in the form of "expiative patriotism," informed by a declared desire to "protect the honour of the fatherland." Furthermore, she positions herself at the heart of the Italian national narrative, by claiming an intimate relationship with the places figuring prominently in its symbolic geography. By emphasising the feminine, caring aspects of her identity, as well as her quintessential *romanità* and *italianità*, Capponi implicitly addresses the revisionist debate and the accusations she was exposed to in later life and offers a definite account, as far as she is concerned, of a controversial episode in recent Italian history.

Notes

1. "In the afternoon of the 23rd March 1944, criminal elements have executed a bomb attack against a German police column in transit through Via Rasella. Following this ambush, 32 German policemen were killed and several were wounded [...] The German command has therefore ordered that for each killed German, ten communist-Badoglian criminals will be shot. This order has already been executed."

2. It was recently exposed as a myth by the literary historian Alessandro Portelli (1999).

3. "[e]ach memory has many other memories attached to it just like branches are joined to a tree trunk, disarranged, yet harmonious."

4. "allora più chiaro mi è apparso il margine di tempo che mi resta in essa [la vita] e le ultime pochissime speranze."

5. For example, she emphasises that, for the resistance movements throughout Europe, surrendering oneself to the enemy meant "treason." Not knowing the exact time and place of the execution, it was impossible for the partisans to prevent it by, for example, attacking the convoys carrying the condemned to the Ardeatine caves. No ultimatum was issued, but, had there been one, *"avrebbero certamente messo in crisi la nostra coscienza, ma non avrebbero incrinato le leggi che regolavano il comportamento di fronte al nemico."* ("this would certainly have provoked a crisis in our conscience, but it would not have undermined the rules regulating our behaviour towards the enemy.") (Capponi 240)

6. "Are you mad? What can a woman do there? That invitation was addressed to men."

7. "the spouses of my ancestors are English, German, Polish, Protestant, Jewish, Catholic: a sign that the Capponi did not agree with the saying 'choose women and oxen from your own village', but had no less than a European vision of their sphere of interest."

8. "I would like to be able to write truly for others, about 'others' [sic!], about all the people, facts and events which have crossed my life. Not to talk about myself as a subject revealing itself, making itself acknowledged and examined, but about myself as a medium for bringing into the light the characters, landscapes, situations, everyday practices and the whole world which has inhabited my own existence and that of the people of my time."

9. "like others have done, those who are now confined to prisons, sent to political exile, emigrated abroad or reduced to the margins of society in villages, persecuted and thrown into prison every time a 'patriotic' manifestation of the Fascist National Party [is] taking place."

10. Capponi's non-judgemental attitude extends beyond family boundaries. A case in point are her reflections on the volunteers in Mussolini's Abyssinian campaign (1935-36): "I finally understood what impelled them to go so far as to risk their lives: they had the dignity of a uniform, of some money to feed their starving children; they felt they were 'legionaries in the conquest of an empire;' the fatherland needed them and did not forget them." (58) "Capii finalmente che cosa li aveva spinti a rischiare anche la vita: avevano avuto la dignità di una divisa, di un 'soldo' con cui sfamare i figli; si erano sentiti 'legionari alla conquista di un impero', la patria aveva avuto bisogno di loro e non li aveva dimenticati."

11. See Galli della Loggia *L'identità italiana* and Veneziani.

12. See Rusconi "Will Italy Remain a Nation?," and *Patria e Repubblica, Se cessiamo di essere una nazione*; and Viroli.

13. "highest value of national life" "facilitate the game of other currents which base their fortunes precisely on the exploitation of the national myth."

14. "[r]eticence and caution remain, which impede the real resistance, not its rhetorical transfiguration, from being recognised as the founding event of Italian democracy – as it should be. Around this issue, divided, recalcitrant, antagonistic memories persist, which in the new political constellation demand recognition, or even vindication."

15. "in order to understand the damage inflicted on national morality during those two years and the reasons behind the subsequent failure to reconstitute the lost moral fabric."

16. "Someone has called those days the 'death of the fatherland', someone has called them the 'second Risorgimento'. Both are right, but one cannot be understood without the other: a fatherland not shared by everyone dies, and another one is endeavouring to emerge, through the initiative and conscience of many, if not through a consensus and participation of all."

17. "I have decided to write in minute detail about that time that has now become 'mythical', or 'mythologised', because I feel that the youth of today need to be convinced that every one of us was exactly a youth like they are now, afflicted by doubts and fears, convinced not to be doing anything exceptional or 'historical.'"

18. "[it] is only the spectacular nature of the event that gives us the wrong impression about the value of the trial."

19. 'Kilns' Gate', named after the many kilns producing bricks for the building of St Peter's Basilica. The gate itself, which used to provide thoroughfare for the building material for St Peter's, was closed after the annexation of Rome to the Italian Kingdom in 1870.

20. For example, her aunts who have to discontinue their regular visits to a café in Piazza Venezia, as all the cafés are relocated from the square, which becomes dedicated solely to fascist rallies (Capponi 27).

21. "in the streets …, on the chairs placed in front of the houses, with quiet women absorbed in knitting or shelling peas for dinner."

22. The Holy Year was inaugurated by Pius XI, the same Pope who later became one of the signatories of the controversial Concordat with the Italian state (1929), which recognised Catholicism as the only official religion in Italy. The Jubilee of 1925 was in some way the first public occasion to inaugurate the new bond between the state and the church, and the Fascist authorities marked it by introducing a number of measures foreshadowing the future rapprochement. In the same year, a number of old houses adjoining the colonnade of St Peter's were demolished by the Commune, to make the Basilica more visible, and a considerable part of the Borgo Sant'Angelo was pulled down to make way for the new Via della Conciliazione, connecting St Peter's to Castel Sant'Angelo and the Tiber river.

23. This section is reminiscent of Roberto Rossellini's neorealist classic *Rome Open City* (*Roma città aperta*, 1944), which deals with the same historical period and incorporates references to the same real-life personages of the Roman resistance. Rossellini's Don Pietro is thus modelled on the priest Don Giuseppe Morosini, who was executed by the Gestapo in April 1944 (see Capponi 155); Pina, the heroine of Rossellini's film, is based on another victim of Nazi terror, Teresa Gullace. (Capponi 220)

"Better Losers Than Lost:" Self, Other and Irony in Clara Sereni's Autobiographical Macrotext

Mirna Cicioni

[Questi sono] i quattro spicchi dei quali, con continui sconfinamenti, mi sembra di compormi: ebrea per scelta piú che per destino, donna non solo per l'anagrafe, esperta di handicap e debolezze come chiunque ne faccia l'esperienza, utopista come chi, radicandosi in quanto esiste qui e oggi, senza esimersi dall'intervenire sulla realtà quotidiana, coltiva il bisogno di darsi un respiro e una passione agganciati al domani.[1] (Sereni, *Taccuino di un'ultimista* 12)

Clara Sereni's life writing, from her first personal narrative (*Casalinghitudine*, 1987) to her latest autobiographical novel (*Passami il sale*, 2002), has situated itself at the intersection of a number of discourses. Her narrated self moves through and across several interconnected subject positions: a woman, a writer, a Jew, a public intellectual, a participant in various political activities of the Italian left, a wife, and a "handicapped mother" (her term to define herself as the mother of a son who has a serious psychological illness). This narrated self is at the centre of several texts linked by numerous cross-references, each presupposing some acquaintance with the previous ones. Besides *Casalinghitudine* and *Passami il sale,* Sereni's autobiographical macrotext contains the family narrative *Il gioco dei regni* (1993), the essay "Diario" in *Mi riguarda* (1994; a collection of autobiographical texts by public figures who had direct knowledge of serious disabilities), *Taccuino di un'ultimista* (1998), a selection of articles written for Italian periodicals, especially the left-wing daily *L'Unità*, and *Da un grigio all'altro* (1998), a long interview interspersed with passages from her writings.

The macrotext constructs a persona who engages in a variety of political and personal projects in the context of developments in Italian society from the 1970s to the beginning of the new century. At the centre of some of these projects, and of some texts, is a process of defining, and redefining, possible meanings of Jewishness; other texts and projects deal with the politics of difference in relation to disability; still others are connected with the power struggles of party politics. Critical attention so far has focused mostly on *Casalinghitudine*, whose unexpected success launched Sereni publicly. Giuliana Menozzi looks at the way this text uses recipes to construct the narrated self's negotiations between the need for dependence and the need for autonomy. Stephen Kolsky analyses the way *Casalinghitudine* represents power relations within the family, focusing on its intertextual references and particularly on its relationship with another autobiographical text by an Italian Jewish writer, Primo Levi's *Il sistema periodico*. Mirna Cicioni and Susan Walker look at the fragmentation of *Casalinghitudine* both as gendered self-representation and as a technique for dismantling the notion of identity, whether in relation to social groups or to social roles. In two different essays, Giovanna Miceli Jeffries and Elisabetta Properzi Nelsen examine *Il gioco dei regni*, mapping out its connections between male and female genealogies, Jewishness and political choices.

Sereni's macrotext maps her subjectivity by using a variety of narrative techniques: interweaving recipes and memories, diary writing, quoting family letters and *midrashim*, biblical interpretations through legends and parables. The central feature, however, is always an awareness of tensions and contradictions arising out of culturally marked differences. The narrated self is constructed as constantly wanting to 'belong.' At different stages of her life, she seeks acceptance from family members or various cultural and political groups; she hopes to find her identity (in terms both of *sameness* and of *sense of self*) with them, only to find herself defined as other and pushed to the margins.[2] At other times, her gender, origins, class, generation and politics lead her narrated self to define individuals or discourses as other; the consequences are unease and self-consciousness, but also attempts to find points of contact. The narrating self accepts these uncertainties and foregrounds them through verbal and situational irony. My study focuses on this irony, defining its forms and functions.

Although irony eludes classifications and categorisations, most of its theorists agree that it focuses on the gap between expectations and actual events,[3] and that it leads to knowledge, if only of ambiguities and contradictions.[4] In Sereni's macrotext, irony often foregrounds a gap between emotions and reason, and is consequently self-deprecating: the narrated self 'should have known better.' This is especially evident in the representation of the narrated self's relations with some 'significant others,'[5] particularly her son and her father, Emilio Sereni, a rigidly Stalinist leader of the Italian Communist Party until the 'historic compromise' of the 1970s. In *Casalinghitudine*, Emilio Sereni is constructed as an embodiment of patriarchal control within the private sphere of his family, incapable of genuine exchanges or spontaneous affection with the narrated self, Clara, who desperately tries again and again to win his approval.[6] Twenty-year-old Clara, having left home, shares a flat with her friend Paola, who is on quite good terms with *her* father.

Un giorno squillò il telefono, stavo dormendo:

"Ciao, tesoro mio, sono papà, come stai?"

Intontita dal sonno ebbi un attimo di illusione felice, poi mi alzai e andai a chiamarla.[7] (81)

In Linda Hutcheon's terms,[8] the irony here "happens" in the space between what the narrating self says and what she implies: the narrated self should have known better than to expect tender effusions from her father. However, the experience of defeat ironically produces knowledge, since it makes Clara more aware of the gap between expectations and experience, and therefore less likely to delude herself in the future.

Longing and disappointment recur throughout *Casalinghitudine*. Clara tends to seek recognition from her father, based on the fact of their common interest in politics and food; he, however, does nothing but point out her shortcomings in both areas, denying her a subject position and viewing her as a trespasser on the vast territories of his experience. Eventually Clara realises that her survival depends on detaching herself from him and claiming knowledge on her own terms:

> ogni mio atto di autonomia, di libertà, di intellettualità si scontrava con il suo furore, o con un sorriso di sufficienza. In età piú verde aveva sempre già fatto, e meglio, qualunque cosa io tentassi di fare: gli studi, i rapporti sentimentali, la politica, perfino la cucina. [...] Evitare di sconfinare nei suoi territori non era facile: aveva fatto e sapeva tante di quelle cose. E allora non mi restava che sconfinare, sconfinare in continuazione: nella scelta degli esami universitari, nel fare politica con altri occhi, nel preparare le zucchine di mammà.[9] (72)

Parallel connections between food, self and otherness are made in Sereni's recollections of the left-wing group to which she belonged in the 1970s. The "group," called simply that in the text,[10] is represented as being dogmatic and patriarchal, just like the traditional left whose policies it opposes. Clara understands that in order to become like them (and to be liked by them) she must suppress her love of cooking, because enjoyment of good food and wine is condemned as not only bourgeois, but also dangerously individualistic. Aldo, the leader, defines and dismisses her as inadequate, just as her father did:

> A casa di Aldo e Maria il menu era fisso, pastasciutta scotta e ascetiche frittate insapori: il massimo di economicità, il minimo tempo in cucina, servire il popolo era adeguarsi ai suoi standards piú bassi e incolti [...]
>
> Feci sparire i formaggi francesi, il vino buono, il pane ricercato; il bollito costa poco, pensai che fosse accettabile. I colori dei sottaceti, i ricami di maionese lo rendevano tollerabile per me.
>
> Aldo disse: "Devi averci perso tutta la giornata."[11] (83)

Slogans and judgements are quoted ironically to distance the narrating self's evaluation and the narrated self's hard-won subjectivity from the group's discourse. Much greater distance, and bitterer irony, are at the centre of another recollection, where Clara encounters people who are other to the point of alienness. In 1973, with feminism and different kinds of 'counter-cultures' thriving in Italian cities, Clara – politically distant from her father's party, but eager for a new experience – agrees to sing in a *festa dell'Unità*[12] in a remote village in Calabria. She arrives with an hour of challenging songs on oppressive institutions and women's estate, and finds herself in a square full of others: party faithfuls, all men, who speak an incomprehensible dialect and are rowdily hostile to women singers. When her turn comes, she is all too aware that her language, gender, and culture make her hopelessly other to her audience, and resorts to a desperate measure:

> Attaccai a pieni polmoni *Bandiera rossa*: il sindaco, continuando a distribuire urtoni, cominciò a farmi coro, seguito quasi immediatamente dai piú anziani, che l'inno richiamava a un ordine non suscettibile di discussione. Prima che la canzone finisse la piazza era calma, anche i giovani cantavano. Benedicevo per la prima volta la "disciplina rivoluzionaria" contro cui mi ero piú volte battuta. L'applauso finale fu compatto.
>
> Snocciolai l'intero repertorio degli inni piú popolari e alla fine potei permettermi qualche canzone piú "difficile": evitai accuratamente tutte quelle sulla condizione femminile.[13] (97)

The irony here is situational: the member of the new revolutionary movement is saved by her appeal to the culture and "revolutionary discipline" of the old party. However, the ambiguity of "ordine non suscettibile di discussione" and "potei permettermi," and the bitterness of "evitai accuratamente," foreground the power of the two totalising discourses, patriarchy and party politics. In a confrontation with them, the price Clara must pay for survival is her own self-erasure.

By the end of *Casalinghitudine*, totalising discourses are declared dead. The group's vision died in the crisis of the political hopes of the period between 1968 and the early 1980s; Emilio Sereni died first metaphorically and then literally when he withdrew from active life after his party veered towards the politics of compromise. In both cases Sereni foregrounds the aspect of defeat and loss, to which she opposes the notion of survival, "vivere" and "sopravvivere," which is not a resigned withdrawal from politics, but rather an acceptance that the time of absolute truths is over. After the demise of "the group," the narrating self reflects that Aldo, no longer an autocratic leader, "ha accettato che ormai si può solo vivere" (135) (has accepted that at this point we can only get on with living), while her father's "scientific approach" to politics and life is summed up as a deathly defeat:

> Le mie improvvisazioni la mia fatica a vivere e la sua scientificità, il suo suicidarsi di silenzio, una guerra senza quartiere fino all'ultimo.
>
> Lui non ha vinto; io, mi limito a vivere.[14] (162)

The fact that Sereni's autobiographical writings are a macrotext – in Booth's terms, they provide a "relevant context" (99): each text positions itself against the background of the previous ones, and there is constant interplay between the fragments of autobiography in the various texts – is significant for reading the ironies of *Il gioco dei regni*. Clara speaks in the first person only in the last chapters of the multi-voiced, multi-genre family narrative and becomes central in the afterword, "Dopo la storia: perché" (After the story: why). This final chapter traces Clara's physical and emotional journey of discovery of several silenced strands of her family's past. Clara, approaching middle age, is beginning to retrieve her own Jewishness, and this process is problematised by her knowledge that her father had broken contact with his Zionist brother Enzo in the 1940s, and at the time of the 1967 Six-Day War had formally withdrawn from Rome's Jewish community and broken all ties with his relatives in Israel. The narrative of her tentative journey to Israel and of her renewal of family connections is pervaded by irony: she gradually unveils lies and omissions, finally realising that most of her family history does not correspond to what she had always believed. Emilio Sereni, before becoming a passionate, rigid Marxist, had been an equally passionate, and equally rigid, orthodox Jew and Zionist: a past he and his family had buried after he had chosen total allegiance to Stalinism. Her mother's mother – someone peripheral to the Sereni family, and dismissed as a bourgeois housewife in her daughter's published account of her marriage – is revealed, when Clara begins probing in an Israeli archive, to have been not only a fully-fledged revolutionary, but a very productive intellectual:

> [D]i nonna Xenia pensavo di sapere già tutto, che era scappata dalla Russia zarista con mia madre nella pancia, dopo la morte del marito congiurato [...] Priva di parenti, e non avendo nient'altro da fare, ad un certo punto era andata in Palestina, e lí era morta. [...] [M]i aspettavo una cartellina, mi aspettavano ventotto scatoloni.[15] (435-36)

The preceding narrative had already told that Xenia had been declared "counter-revolutionary" and rejected by both Clara's Stalinist parents: the shock of this discovery establishes that Clara's other is, rather than her grandmother, the political orthodoxy that had led to this estrangement. Here, however, the irony is also self-deprecating. The narrating self, by parodying the casually dismissive tone of what Clara already 'knows', stresses that she should have 'known' better. This is further emphasised by the contrast between "una cartellina" and "ventotto scatoloni" and underlined by the anaphoric antithesis between "mi aspettavo" and "mi aspettavano."

As Clara learns to reconceptualise her 'significant others', she also learns to reconceptualise herself. She explains her father's adherence to religious orthodoxy first and Marxism later in terms of a need for the certainty of what in Italy is known as *pensiero forte*, an all-embracing discourse which would explain and subsume all contradictions: "un obiettivo assoluto, totale. Una rete che lo aiuti a tenere insieme i suoi pezzi" (166).[16] Her autobiographical self, on the other hand, no longer relies on a totalising ideology, and accepts instead that her subjectivity is fragmented, whether in relation to social groups (women, Jews, left-wing intellectuals), roles (daughter, wife, mother, writer, deputy mayor) or political discourses. The "pezzettini dentro di me" (443) (little pieces inside me) cannot be held together: they can, at best, be shaped into a pattern, but with the awareness that patterns may change at any time ("c'è un ordine, benché lo sappia precario e suscettibile di modificazioni infinite,"[17]

(447)) and that therefore her 'self' needs to be constantly created, recreated, retrieved and reinvented.

By the 1990s, international politics and economics had brought about the disintegration of the traditional left. Its all-embracing ideologies and principles of authority had been abandoned, and in their place was growing something the philosopher Gianni Vattimo defined as *pensiero debole*: a diversity of contingent social and political projects, recognised as limited by those involved in them, but based on the conviction that certain values and virtues still do matter.[18] Sereni, who had already published a volume of stories dealing with moments when the dark side of every human being comes to the surface (*Manicomio primavera*, 1989) and was working on another volume dealing with different kinds of marginalisation (*Eppure*, 1995), became increasingly visible as a public intellectual who spoke and wrote on issues of social justice. She also acknowledged publicly her status as "madre handicappata," with a personal stake in campaigning for the integration of people with physical and psychological handicaps into school and the workplace; she made it clear that, for all its difficulties and uncertainties, her situation gave her useful insights into processes of marginalisation. The interview *Da un grigio all'altro* and the articles reprinted in *Taccuino di un'ultimista* – written mainly during the two years (1995-97) when Sereni was deputy mayor of the city of Perugia – connect the four 'segments' of her life to her perspectives on politics and the future of Italian society. The title *Da un grigio all'altro* indirectly recalls the analyses of *pensiero debole*:

> Le contraddizioni su cui ho riflettuto di più non sono [...] le scelte epocali tra il bene ed il male, che sono paradossalmente facili e che nella realtà non capitano quasi mai, ma come si 'saltabecca' tra due grigi. Viviamo in un mondo sostanzialmente grigio, non abbiamo per esempio la guerra e la pace, ma la pace guerreggiata. M'interessa allora la scelta che uno fa ogni mattina fra un grigio e l'altro, fra l'essere fedele a un'identità priva di smalto e il compiere un tradimento piccolo piccolo: è quella la contraddizione.[19] (20-21)

The self-definition *ultimista* chosen for the title of her collection of opinion pieces is apparently incongruous for Sereni, since it is derived from the discourse of socially radical Catholics who are on the side of the *ultimi*, society's rejects (12). In Sereni's discourse, the label is deliberately ambiguous and ironic: for those who no longer can believe in global projects and do not want to slide into self-centred individualism, the last possible hope is "di ancorarsi a progetti concreti, tangibili, che abbiano però dietro di sé un'idea complessiva di modificazione della realtà" (125). (to anchor themselves to concrete, tangible projects, but which need to be backed by an overall vision of how reality can be changed). The central concern of the projects she describes in her articles is the integration of diversities: alternative living arrangements which may allow the housebound elderly, the sick and the handicapped to receive, but also to give, companionship and care. The focus of several pieces is the plight of the mentally ill, who are still dramatically other, since the 1978 law which deinstitutionalised them was not followed by the creation of the infrastructures necessary for their integration into the community and the workplace.

Sereni situates her autobiographical self at the centre of the tangle of contradictions between the private and the public spheres, and uses irony to foreground these contradictions as well as to distance the narrating from the narrated self and both from all generalising discourses. At the heart of her reflections on Otherness is her son, whose difference had been only hinted at in *Casalinghitudine* and represented indirectly, through other characters, in *Il gioco dei regni* and in the stories of *Manicomio primavera*. "Non è solo questione di 'matti,' ma di tutti" (*Taccuino* 76) (It doesn't just concern 'crazy' people, it concerns us all), she states uncompromisingly, explicitly connecting her political commitments and the demands of her daily experiences. One article represents the way multiple alterities intersect for a few months, when she agrees to a group of teenage rapists spending some leisure time with her son as part of their sentence to undertake "community service." The narrating self ironises about the first response of the narrated self, which was all in terms of stereotypes:

> Quando li accolsi sulla porta di casa, la prima volta, non dico che mi aspettassi occhi iniettati di sangue, ma poco ci mancava.[20] (73)

At the end of her account, she quotes an expression of pride by the father of one of the young men, and comments:

> Quella frase ... è il segno che l'informazione originaria e pregiudiziale ("i violentatori" o "gli handicappati") si è integrata con altre informazioni trasformandosi in sentimento, interesse, partecipazione. ... [N]on possiamo discriminare fra gravissimi "buoni" (per esempio gli handicappati) e gravissimi "cattivi" (per esempio i violentatori).[21] (75)

The irony is in the inverted commas,[22] which is Sereni's way of distancing herself from generalising labels and of suggesting that the preferable response to diversity is neither unthinking rejection nor unthinking acceptance, but rather more flexible, context-dependent approaches.

As well as the Catholic definition *ultimista*, Sereni, a Jewish atheist, ironically appropriates the motto "meglio perdenti che perduti" (better losers than lost), first formulated by the radical poet and Catholic friar David Maria Turoldo,[23] to stress the need for minorities and 'others' to articulate their differences and argue for their places in civil society. She first quotes this motto in an article written in the aftermath of the first electoral victory of the right-wing coalition led by Silvio Berlusconi in May 1994; she ironises about the far left who rejoiced in the defeat and expresses the hope that defeat may be used as a starting point for new strategies:

> una cosa è accettare, senza rassegnazione, di essere minoranza ("Meglio perdenti che perduti," diceva padre Turoldo), e altro è volersi eternamente minoranza, con l'alibi di poter scaricare sempre sugli altri – il Pci, i progressisti, il destino cinico e baro – ogni responsabilità.[24] (*Taccuino* 126)

Passami il sale, written several years later, is a fictionalised account (in seventy vignettes) of Sereni's experience of hands-on local politics, in her two years as deputy mayor of Perugia. It is an ironic *Bildungsroman*, where the narrated self is represented as initially naive, and where irony emphasises the gap between her expectations (to be able to make small but significant changes, and to make compromises while retaining her integrity) and the reality of power relations and behind-the-scenes bargains and negotiations. Sometimes the irony is self-deprecating and foregrounds the narrated self's status as an outsider, with the recurrent implication that she 'should have known better.' At the beginning of her term in office, after a meeting in another part of town, a council officer asks her if she "ha la macchina" (has got the car). She helpfully, and proudly because she obtained her driver's license fairly recently, offers him a lift in her small car, and they both get drenched walking from the car park to the town hall in driving rain. A little later, in her office, her (male) secretary mentions another engagement:

> "A che ora ti faccio venire la macchina?" chiede [...] con il suo tono piú neutro. E finalmente mi sento un'imbecille: un'imbecille inzuppata.

> Un attimo di esitazione, per maturare il passaggio da un'autonomia conquistata tardi a un potere concreto. Poi cercando il tono che avrei se l'avessi sempre fatto, indico il luogo e l'ora in cui l'auto di servizio mi preleverà.[25] (41)

Throughout the text Sereni presents a variety of small but pertinent details that represent her narrated self's outsider status. These details become metaphors and metonyms of a political culture which is, in spite of her family history, still completely alien to her. This culture pays lip service to women's rights, but is still uncompromisingly masculine: men have authority and behave authoritatively, and the few women with a public profile are constantly reminded of their otherness, implicitly or explicitly. While smoking in a corridor of the town hall, Clara observes her male colleagues putting out cigarette stubs on the floor and throwing rubbish into corners, and reflects that they are "forti della certezza che qualcun altro, prima o poi, pulirà: donne di servizio, qualcuno che ha abilità, attenzioni, premure che fra di loro non hanno corso, non hanno valore. Non contano"[26] (30). Irony distances the narrating self not only from the narrated self's otherness, but also from her pain and exclusion. When Clara tries to establish gender-based alliances around proposed anti-sexual harassment regulations, the women involved in politics keep their distance, and the men refuse to take the proposal seriously:

> [È] un grande sbandieramento di proclami di gentilezza, e le donne non si colpiscono neanche con un fiore, e le donne sono cosí forti da non avere bisogno di nessuno che le difenda, e le donne sono Madonne. Insomma, non c'è certo bisogno di una come me, scrittrice malata di fantasia, per dettare nuove regole di comportamento.[27] (122)

The tensions and overwork caused by politics flow over into Clara's private life: her growing son is an other whose difference is unpredictable and usually beyond rational negotiation, her husband's loving cooperation is occasionally fractured by moments of impatience, and Clara feels constantly guilty for serving them frozen food, for leaving them alone, for washing whites and coloureds together:

> [N]on ho pazienza con me stessa, e non smetto di sentirmi in colpa. Con Tommaso, con Giovanni: per tutti i pensieri di cui li privo, per le attenzioni che non ho piú, per le piante secche del balcone, per i cibi che non preparo.[28] (49)

Conversely, some of the private tensions spill over into Clara's public life. Her son's violent outbursts in streets and supermarkets add to her anxieties and fears, contributing to a sense of embarrassment in her public role as deputy mayor. One afternoon Clara and her husband are summoned to the school where her son's integration progresses slowly and unevenly, and are informed that his disruptive presence is holding back the other children in his class. One of the teachers suggests that a partial solution could be for the council to award the school some money for additional excursions and support staff:

> Un gran rimescolamento dentro, una grande confusione: mamma di Tommaso, vicesindaco, i miei ruoli in un frullatore di richieste tutte improprie.
>
> Non ricordo come uscimmo dalla riunione. So che da allora in poi non andai piú agli incontri con la scuola, e Giovanni dovette affrontarli da solo. Senza sua moglie, senza la mamma di Tommaso.
>
> Esaminata la situazione di bilancio, e su parere contrario del funzionario addetto, la vicesindaco non concesse, alla scuola, finanziamenti aggiuntivi.[29] (125)

Here the situational irony is bitter, foregrounded by a narrative shift. The paragraphs in the first person are full of contradictory emotions (guilt, anger at the attempted blackmail, confusion). The shift to the third person indicates the narrated self's attempt to reassert reason and authoritativeness, and ultimately foregrounds her contradictions: her emotions are silenced but not eliminated, and the confrontation ends with everyone's defeat.

The only way Clara can find a sense of continuity for her identity is through the concrete gestures of her daily life: sorting out her clothes and her son's, planning meals, shopping for them, and above all preparing food. In nearly every one of the vignettes in *Passami il sale* there is – skilfully integrated in the middle of other private and public activities and concerns – a brief description of the preparation of one or more dishes for the family meal: Clara, often with her son, chops, mixes, sautés, bakes, adds her own creative touches to recipes. Food is a central theme, which establishes continuity between this text and *Casalinghitudine*; there are, however, significant variations. In the earlier text, cooking was the site where the narrated self inscribed her subjectivity and reappropriated various kinds of knowledge, adapting them to her own needs.[30] Here, Clara's cooking is an assertion of her own identity in moments snatched from phone calls, meetings, demands on her time and energies by colleagues, allies, opponents, citizens, friends and family; it is a survival strategy as well as a way to nurture the 'significant others' in her life. One unusually trouble-free evening sees Clara cooking for her husband, her son and Zattera, a local behind-the-scenes power broker.

> Tutti a tavola: Tommaso, che stasera è tranquillo e disponibile; Zattera, che ora racconta storielle divertenti; Giovanni, che amo. Li guardo, e mi viene da pensare che è finito il tempo di essere figlia, la mia famiglia adesso sono loro. Sí, anche Zattera, forse soltanto per adozione, perché siamo cosí soli.[31] (136)

In the book, Zattera is identified only by the nickname the narrating self gives him: he is a life raft for the narrated self in times of need, and his name also recalls that of *zatterino*, an ice-cream which Clara and their generation ate when they were children, growing up in relative prosperity, with many hopes of social and political change.

Other than Zattera, Clara's only ally is – ironically – the bishop. Although both the left-wing power broker and the Catholic ecclesiastic silently acknowledge that Clara is not really part of either of their worlds, they nevertheless accept and respect her as a complex human being with multiple responsibilities, and focus on small shared projects rather than ideological positions. Theirs is the kind of solidarity Richard Rorty attributes to his "ironists:" a "solidarity constructed out of little pieces, rather than found already waiting" (Rorty 94).

Most of Clara's projects – an attempt to make a group of adults with Down's syndrome more independent by moving them out of a sheltered workshop; opposition to a substantial contract being awarded by the council to the city's biggest confectionery industry (thinly disguised as "Pannapiú" in the text) – end up in partial or total defeats. Each time, Clara's initiatives encounter schemes and alliances of which she knows little; each time, she manages to preserve most of her personal integrity, but ends up tired and disillusioned, if a little wiser.

> [Zattera] mi afferra per un lembo della manica, mi fa fermare:
>
> "E che, pensi che il mondo sia *da già* finito?"
>
> Ha ragione, il mondo non finirà né oggi né domani: finisce soltanto una fiaba, l'idea infantile di poter dare forma alle speranze con poco piú di un colpo di bacchetta magica.[32] (244)

The salt in the title is an encompassing metaphor for several key elements in the text. It stands for attempts to communicate across differences and for essential humanity, which is often the other in contexts of political wheelings and dealings; Clara and another woman of the left, who is almost, but not quite, an ally and a friend, pass the salt to each other as they attempt to swallow flavourless food and indigestible political compromises simultaneously.

In the last scene, salt has been defeated by the whipped cream with which the triumphant confectioners, who have won the council contract, fill the central square of the city. The narrated self has resigned her office, and is feeling both defeated and free. She has a coffee with Zattera, who refuses to let her pay:

"Quando vincerai" promette estraendo una manciata di spiccioli dalla tasca. E non so se è una minaccia, una speranza, o soltanto il modo per inchiodarmi in via definitiva alla mia pochezza.

"Meglio perdenti che perduti" gli dico citando, e non spero piú che mi ascolti, che trovi al mio stesso modo la via per salvare la faccia e la speranza.[33] (264)

The irony is complex and ambiguous. Clara's response is partly assertive and partly – given the situation – self-deprecating. Just as she quotes Turoldo, she distances herself from him, since the Catholic conviction of his statement is only partly reassuring in the context of present and future prospects of powerlessness and defeats.

"[L'ironia] è la mia risorsa, mi permette di rivoltare il melodramma che in realtà mi verrebbe automatico,"[34] Sereni said in a 1989 interview.[35] Throughout her autobiographical macrotext the narrated self finds herself, in different contexts, other and confronted by a variety of others; her irony comes from the interplay of the notions of 'self' and 'other' with several political discourses, none of which ultimately prevails. Sereni represents her autobiographical self as a 'loser,' and at the same time implies that "losers" are more able than 'winners' to grasp the contradictions of human interactions. In a world where, as she wrote in 1993, clear-cut categories are no longer applicable,

le antinomie si affollano in primo piano, laceranti e innovative: leggerle, scavarci dentro, cercare con il cuore e con la testa un primo bandolo [...] significa mettere in discussione ogni passo compiuto, da sé e dagli altri.[36] (*Taccuino* 52)

In Linda Hutcheon's words, irony "can only 'complexify;' it can never 'disambiguate'" (13). Sereni's irony is "lacerante e innovativa," harrowing and innovative, affirmative and destructive. It leads to new knowledge and simultaneously to new uncertainties. It undermines totalising discourses and visions, and also shows the provisional nature of all projects, hopes and alliances.

Notes

1. "I think of myself as being made up of four segments whose boundaries constantly blur: a Jew because I chose rather than happened to be; a woman not only because my birth certificate says so; an expert on disabilities and shortcomings, like anyone who has direct experience of them; a utopian like anyone who is firmly rooted in the here and now, and who, without refusing to get involved in day-to-day issues, cultivates the need to have a vision and a passion which draws them towards to the future." All translations of the quotations from Sereni's works are mine.

2. Sereni sums this up in *Da un grigio all'altro* as "Nel bene e nel male sono sempre stata una fuori-gregge, ma lo dico senza orgoglio perché è anche molto scomodo, infatti ho spesso desiderato – soprattutto quando ero molto giovane – di far parte anch'io di un insieme di eguali" (8) (For better or for worse I have always been an outsider, and I am saying this without any pride, because it can also be very uncomfortable. I have often wished – especially when I was very young – that I belonged to a group of people who were alike). In *Passami il sale* she adds "Ho cercato amore, affetto, le gentilezze da tutti e per tutta la vita; pronta per ottenerli a compromessi anche umilianti" (123) (I have sought love, affection and kindness from everyone and for the whole of my life – being ready even to make some humiliating compromises to get them).

3. Booth 91-99 and 274-75.

4. See Hutcheon, especially 14 and 60-64. For Almansi, "l'ironia concede all'uomo lo spazio vitale della contraddizione" (37) (irony gives us the essential space of contradiction). For Mizzau ("La qualità dell'ironia"), "l'ambiguità degli indici fa parte del progetto comunicativo del parlante (192) (the ambiguity of markers is part of the speaker's communicative intention). For Lang, irony "serves to preclude any possibility of reducing a text to a single voice or final meaning." (59) See also Mizzau, *L'ironia. La contraddizione consentita.*

5. The term comes from Sidonie Smith and Julia Watson's overview *Reading Autobiography – A Guide for Interpreting Life Narratives.* "Significant others" are people "through which the narrator understands his or her own self-formation." (64-66)

6. See Cicioni and Walker 38-40.

7. "One day the phone rang. I was asleep:
"Hello, my darling, this is Dad, how are you?"
Befuddled by sleep, for one deluded moment I was happy, then I got up and went to get her."

8. According to Hutcheon, irony "'happens' in the space *between* (and including) the said and the unsaid." (12, her emphasis)

9. "any attempt on my part to exercise my will, my freedom, or my intellectual skills would meet with fury, or a condescending smile on his part. In his youth, he had already done anything that I might attempt, and better: study, love, politics, and even cooking. […] It was not easy to avoid trespassing on his territories: he had done, and he knew, so many things. So there was nothing to do but to trespass, and to keep trespassing: in the subjects I studied at university, in the political choices I made that were different from his, and in cooking zucchini like his mother did."

10. In a personal interview (22 May 2000), Sereni revealed that "the group" was Lotta Continua, one of the extra-parliamentary left's leading movements.

11. "At Aldo and Maria's the Spartan menu was always the same, overcooked pasta and insipid omelettes: the cheapest possible meals, cooked in the shortest possible time. Serving the people meant adapting to its lowest and most unsophisticated standards. […]

I hid the French cheeses, the good wine, and the gourmet bread; mixed boiled meats are cheap, I thought, so they shouldn't mind that. The colours of the pickled vegetables and the swirls of mayonnaise cheered it up for me.

Aldo said: "You must have been messing around in the kitchen all day.""

12. The *feste dell'Unità* were Communist Party festivals, with food, drink, music, speeches by Party leaders, and various cultural and community initiatives.

13. "I started belting out the Italian Communist Party anthem; the mayor, still elbowing his way through the crowd, started singing along, followed almost immediately by the older comrades, recalled by the anthem to an order beyond argument. Before the song came to an end the square was peaceful; young people were singing too. For the first time I blessed the "revolutionary discipline" against which I had fought on several occasions. The whole crowd applauded at the end.

I worked my way through the whole repertoire of working-class anthems and at the end I managed to sneak in a few more "difficult" songs; I carefully avoided any song I had about women's estate."

14. "My improvising, my painful struggle with life, and his scientific approach, his suicide by silence, a war without quarter to the last.

He did not win; as for me, I just aim at living."

15. "I thought I already knew everything about my grandmother Xenia: after the death of her conspirator husband she had escaped from Tsarist Russia pregnant with my mother […]. Having no relatives, and having nothing else to do, one day she had gone to Palestine, and there she had died. […] I was expecting to find one slim folder; I found twenty-eight cartons waiting for me."

16. "a total, all-encompassing objective. A net which may help him to keep all his pieces together."

17. "there is an order, although I know that it is a precarious one, subject to endless changes"

18. See Vattimo and Rovatti. Similar views are developed in Rorty.

19. "The contradictions I have thought about the most are not [...] the world-changing choices between good and evil, which, paradoxically, are easy and which hardly ever occur in real life; they are, rather, the ways people swing back and forth between two shades of grey. We live in a predominantly grey world: we have neither war nor peace, for instance, what we have is a warring peace. That is why I am interested in the choice we make every morning between one shade of grey and another, being faithful to a worn-out identity or committing a very small act of betrayal – that is the contradiction I'm talking about."

20. "The first time I greeted them at my front door, I wasn't quite expecting bloodshot eyes, but I wasn't far from it."

21. "That expression [...] is a signal that the original, prejudiced information ("the rapists" or "the handicapped") has become integrated with other information, turning into compassion, interest, interaction [...] We cannot discriminate between "good" problem people (such as the handicapped) and "bad" problem people (such as rapists)."

22. On the ironic use of quotation marks, see Mizzau, *L'ironia* 47-50 and Lang 58-60.

23. David Maria Turoldo (1916-1992) was a consistently radical friar, who wrote and preached about the *ultimi* and wrote poetry with many biblical echoes.

24. "there is a difference between accepting, without being resigned to it, that we are in the minority ("Better losers than lost," as Father Turoldo put it), and wanting to be in the minority for ever, absolving ourselves from any responsibility by blaming someone else, be it the Communist Party, radicals, or cruel, cheating destiny."

25. ""What time shall I book the car for you?" he asks [...] in his most neutral tone. And then it dawns on me and I feel an idiot: a soaking wet idiot.

A moment's hesitation, to complete the passage from late-won autonomy to tangible power. Then, looking for the tone I would have used if I had been in the habit of doing it, I state the time and place I want to be picked up by the official car."

26. "secure in the knowledge that sooner or later someone will clean up after them: some woman at their service, someone who has skills, consideration for others, and sensitivity, things which for them have no currency or value. Things which don't count."

27. "Everyone starts proclaiming their goodwill towards women: women shouldn't be hit with as much as a flower, and women are so strong that they don't need anyone to protect them, and women are goddesses. In short, there's no need for a writer with an over-active imagination, like me, to dictate new rules of behaviour."

28. "I get impatient with myself and I can't stop feeling guilty. About Tommaso, about Giovanni: for all the care I'm depriving them of, for the little things I'm no longer doing for them, the dried up plants on the balcony, the meals I don't cook."

29. "A great turmoil, a great confusion inside me: Tommaso's mother, deputy mayor, my roles tied in a knot by these improper requests.

I don't remember how we left the meeting. I know that from then on I no longer went to school meetings, and Giovanni had to face them by himself. Without his wife, without Tommaso's mother.

After investigating the current financial situation, and against the advice of the official responsible, the deputy mayor did not grant any additional funding to the school."

30. This point is made, from different perspectives, in Menozzi, Kolsky, and Cicioni and Walker.

31. "Everyone sits down to the meal: Tommaso, who is being well-behaved and sociable tonight; Zattera, who is telling funny anecdotes; Giovanni whom I love. I look at them, and I am hit by the thought that the time to be a daughter is over, they are my family now. Including Zattera, who is perhaps just an adopted member, because we are so alone."

32. "[Zattera] grabs my sleeve, makes me stop:
"What, you think the world is over, eh?"

He's right, the world isn't going to end today or tomorrow. What is ending is only a fairytale, the childish notion that we can make wishes come true with little more than the touch of a magic wand."

33. ""When you win," he promises, pulling a handful of loose change out of his pocket. And I don't know if it's a threat, a hope, or just his way of forcing me to face my inadequacy once and for all.

"Better losers than lost," I say, quoting, and I no longer hope that he'll listen to me, that he'll find, as I did, a way of saving face and keeping up his hope."

34. "[Irony] is my most useful resource – it means I can turn the high drama, which is my automatic response, on its head."

35. Clara Sereni, interview with Bia Sarasini, "Primavera anche all'inferno." 76.

36. "contradictions crowd the foreground, harrowing and innovative. To read them, to dig deep into them, to look for the first lead, with our hearts and our minds […] means to question every step we or others may take."

Across Generations

Dialoguing with Mothers in the Twenty-First Century: Three Generations of Italian Women Writers

Bernadette Luciano

In the past twenty years Italian feminists have theorised the need for women to (re)discover and/or (re)create their history in search of a female genealogy.[1] This need has inspired many contemporary women authors to write about female experiences and to explore and construct their identities, often foregrounding the relationship with the maternal, both biological and symbolic. While many female authored texts can be classified within the boundaries of traditional literary genres such as the novel, short story, drama and poetry, others fall between the cracks spilling into the territory of what Caren Kaplan calls "out-law genres" which cross the boundaries of traditional genres.[2] In her article "Nuovi percorsi tra esperienza e scrittura," Marisa Rusconi discusses the engagement of a number of Italian contemporary women writers in such an 'out-law' genre located between the critical essay and fictional prose. Rusconi defines this style of writing as a dangerous and risky hybridisation which "contaminates" the traditionally objective genre with a subjective and personal voice.[3] Speculating on the oblique autobiographical nature of such writing, Rusconi suggests that these writers:

> scegliendo la forma apparentemente obiettiva e distaccata del saggio, biografia, o libro-inchiesta, lasciano poi affiorare frammenti, piccoli o grandi, nascosti o trasparenti, isolati o multipli, di se stesse e la fra le storie degli altri.[4] (164)

Rusconi proposes that these autobiographical/critical essays represent an exciting new style of writing through which women piece themselves together discreetly and indirectly via accounts of other people. However, such life-narratives are not entirely new. Italian women writers from the beginning of the twentieth century have exploited their talents as journalists, critics, narrators and poets to engage in the production of compendia of fragmented personal writings which provide a personal and cultural mosaic of their lives and their times.[5] Michel Beaujour attributes the term self-portrait to this style of narrative to distinguish its orientation located in the present from the retrospectively oriented autobiographical narrative. The notion of self-portrait is clearly useful in locating the subject in a present that can never be fixed and in suggesting the multiple and shifting nature of the subject.

The term I would like to assign to these texts, however, is one appropriated from the title of one of the works to be examined in this chapter, Gina Lagorio's *Inventario*. While the notion of inventory implies taking stock of one's life, its etymology is also linked to the idea of invention or creation. Hence the term is particularly appropriate; for while taking stock of their lives, these writers are also reconstructing them, reinventing them from a moment of reflection, in a traditional autobiographical sense of looking back, reordering, saving and discarding. While these inventories allude to geographical and domestic landscapes, cultural figures, friends and relations and literary ideologies, this chapter will focus primarily on the way each author invents her life via a dialogue or debate with her literary mother(s), at times reflecting herself in her image, at times resisting her, at times assisting her, always reinventing her. The dialogue within the works and between the works of the three writers examined herein reveals a principle of literary *maternage*[6] that emerges from direct references to literary mothers and to the complexity and tension of these relationships and, more obliquely, from themes and experiences echoed and recast across generations of women.

I will explore works by three writers from three distinct generations: Sibilla Aleramo's *Andando e stando* (1940*)*, Lalla Romano's *Un sogno del nord* (1989), and Gina Lagorio's *Inventario* (1997). The generational distinction is based on both an obvious biological age difference and on an experiential difference that explains the generational hierarchy of Italian women writers devised by Marina Zancan. Zancan identifies the first generation as those women whose writing straddled the decades between the nineteenth and twentieth centuries and who were greatly influenced by the emancipationist movement: Sibilla Aleramo. The writers born at the beginning of the century who reached adulthood under fascism, benefited from a formal education, and identified with intellectual communities belong to the second generation: Lalla Romano. The third generation includes women who grew up under fascism and under the First Republic and were influenced by mass culture and by the feminist movement and feminist culture: Gina Lagorio.[7]

First generation: Sibilla Aleramo, 1876-1960

Sibilla Aleramo is often considered the mother of Italian feminist writing because of her groundbreaking 1906 novel, *Una donna*. Her works promote a theory of feminist writing and genealogy. From a generation with few accessible female models and lacking a formal education, Aleramo is a sort of self-made woman, and comes to her definition of feminist writing through personal experience and theorising which has been interpreted as both innovative and naive.

Feminist philospher Adriana Cavarero warns that the female subject does not emerge from history by simply investigating her existence but must rather actively decide to be her own subject, to take herself as her starting point (Bono and Kemp 185). Aleramo, in anticipation of such a concept of female discourse, maintained that a woman writer should express her own distinct experience of life rather than feeling obligated to write like a man (*Orsa Minore*

14-15). Writing became for her a form of *autocoscienza*, a continuous process of discovery and of construction and reconstruction of the self as female subject.[8] That women should in essence write themselves is the overarching moral standard that explains the autobiographical nature of Aleramo's entire body of work. For Aleramo, such a poetic construct allows for virtually no dichotomy between life and art, causing many critics to question the literariness of her works. The blatantly autobiographical nature of her writing embarrassed a literary culture that saw in her books only base matter that did not transcend human nature to rise to the level of art in the classical male tradition.[9]

In her preface to *Andando e stando,* Aleramo claimed to be responding to a challenge, the challenge that she was unable to write about anything other than herself. Ironically, this book is no less autobiographical than her other works. *Andando e stando* is one of Aleramo's three books of prose pieces, essays and articles that have been re-edited, reprinted, collected and combined in various forms during her own lifetime and since her death. The title of the collection, *Andando e stando,* derives from Saint Francis' dying words to Saint Bernard: "Benedetto sii te, andando e stando vegliando e dormento, vivendo e morendo" (*Orsa minore* 105) ("Blessed art thou, leaving and staying, awake and sleeping, living and dying"). The title refers to the author's own errant lifestyle often resulting from her pursuing or running away from a difficult amorous relationship, another noted trademark of Aleramo's life. Included in the collection, written between 1911 and 1940, are a number of important essays reflecting her philosophy of women's writing as well as her search for appropriate female literary models. Her oft referenced essay "Apologia dello spirito femminile" ("Defence of the Female Spirit") celebrates female creativity. In this essay Aleramo maintains that what is lacking in women's books is the sign of a female personality or what she calls an *impronta,* the imprint or impression which, much like a fingerprint, differentiates, characterises and legitimises female nature.

Her "Defence of the Female Spirit" is a call to arms for women to write differently; it is not an attempt to recover female voices but to invent something new. In a subsequent essay, "La pensierosa" ("The Pensive One"), Aleramo personally accepts the blame for what other women writers have been guilty of and for her own style of writing, which imitated the style of her male models and distanced her from a more authentic representation of herself:

> Per conquistare questa necessaria stima dei miei fratelli, io ho dovuto adattare la mia intelligenza alla loro, con sforzo di decenni: capire l'uomo, imparare il suo linguaggio, è stato allontanarmi da me stessa [...] io non mi esprimo, non mi traduco neppure: rifletto la vostra rappresentazione del mondo.[10] (194)

In "Defence," Aleramo goes on to lament that women have not yet found a form of authentic expression – a spiritual difference demands an expressive difference, a language with triggers, shivers, pauses, transitions with vortices unknown to masculine poetry. Aleramo identifies her own highly triggered, emotional voice with the voice she is calling upon women writers to create.

Autobiographical citation is obviously at work in this collection. The women she cites raise their voices to reflect the new distinctly feminine voice which clearly references her own. Aleramo is in pursuit of women writers who serve as symbolic writers who might legitimise her own style of writing and who might pave the way for new distinctly female modes of expression. Such citation is obvious in the piece she dedicates to Colette Willy. Her defence of Colette's protagonist in *La vagabonda* is a defence of Aleramo's own autobiographical characters and indeed of the autobiographical genre itself. Aleramo defends the rebellious bourgeois protagonist who breaks free from an oppressive lifestyle, follows her passions and comes to realise that all she needs is her own freedom.

> Realtà o favola, che importa saperlo? Vita tradotta in arte, per magica virtù, questo sì[. . .] Credo di non aver mai trovato in un libro moderno, certo mai in un libro di donna, una rispondenza così costantemente perfetta dello stile collo spirito dello scrittore.[11] (170-71)

Aleramo's enthusiasm for this novel is a defence of her own autobiographical text, *Una donna*, of its liberated protagonist and of Aleramo's own predilection for crossing the boundaries between life and art.

In her essay "The Pensive One," Aleramo praises the French writer, Aurel, a woman "che già più non inceppano le formule virili, e che cerca in sé e si esprime, non per somigliare all'uomo ma per differenziarvisi e integrarlo" (195).[12] It is in Aurel that Aleramo finally finds the ideal woman writer advocated by "Defence," a woman able to express herself authentically and in her own voice. Similar praise is accorded to Virginia Woolf's *Orlando*, a book whose greatness lies in a character who breaks with the laws of nature, who transforms from man to woman and acknowledges the profound difference between the sexes that Aleramo claims to have been exploring for some time ("Orlando inglese" 231). In"Orlando inglese," Aleramo praises Woolf, calling her the new Sappho and certainly the greatest European woman writer of her times (229).

Finally, Katherine Mansfield, again via affinity and identification, gains a position of prominence in this collection. Spawned by a recent reading of Mansfield's letters, Aleramo nostalgically describes the solitary nature of Mansfied's adult life occupied with reading and writing about the "poor humanity" that surround her so distant from the free and healthy lifestyle she enjoyed in New Zealand as a child. The words echo the opening lines of *Una donna* : "La mia fanciullezza fu libera e gagliarda" (1) ("My childhood was carefree and vigorous") in which Aleramo nostalgically recalls her own childhood far from the pain and hardships that came with gendered adolescence and adulthood. Geographically and symbolically distant from the open places of her childhood, Aleramo finds herself immersed, like Mansfield, in a politically engaged vocation which requires contact with sometimes harsh social realities. Aleramo ultimately describes Mansfield as she often describes herself in her diaries: a woman for whom life reigned above all else. It is in essence the intensity of life, and the inextricable relationship between life and art which prevails in Aleramo's own self-construction, a passion which searches out in others a verification of herself, and a work which clearly displays what Susan Friedman would call "a sense of shared identity with other women, an aspect of identification that exists in tension with a sense of their own uniqueness" (44).

Second generation: Lalla Romano, 1906-2001

Lalla Romano, a prominent and prolific Italian writer and cultural figure whose life spanned almost a century postdates Aleramo by a generation and expresses an attitude to women's writing which, superficially at least, is almost antithetical to Aleramo's feminism. Raised in a pre-feminist era before the literary canon began to reflect the benefits of the feminist movement, Romano and many of her contemporaries aspired to a position of narrative authority which was decidedly male.[13] They were reluctant to operate outside the canon of Italian literature for fear that their works would be relegated to the sub-category of 'women's writing.'

Lalla Romano's *Un sogno del nord* (A Dream of the North) (1989) is a collection of what Romano calls "brevi prose" (1325) – brief pieces of prose writing written primarily between the mid 1970s and the mid 1980s with a few dating back to the immediate postwar period. Most had previously appeared in Italian newspapers. In Romano's words each piece is "databile ma non datato" (1325) ("datable but not dated") in the sense that, like Aleramo's essays, they can be attributed to a particular historical time, place and event, but they are also associated with details, images and emotions whose meaning and relevance do not diminish with time and hence remain contemporary. Romano further rejects the attribution of dates to these pieces because dates impose a diachronic order which she rejects. The fragments are ordered in a different way, Romano claims, by affinity rather than chronology, but even that grouping is not rigorously adhered to. Each fragment can stand on its own, but may also be linked to others in the same section, and the ordering could be easily rearranged. Thus in her preface, Romano both challenges and invites the reader to participate in the construction of this book, to look for the links, to imagine an alternative order to suture this very seamless text. In its lack of linearity, in its fragmentation, in its construction of what she claims can only be history in the lower case, that is her personal history, Romano creates in this work what she claimed she had never before attempted: an unsuspected self-portrait (*Un sogno del nord* 1326).

The book is ordered in twelve thematic divisions which include sections on specific geographical locations, people, writing, painting and personal history. *Un sogno del nord* is a repository of memories, images and sensory perceptions. The essays explore Romano's relationship to painting, to music, to her city (Tule) and to her mother's cities, to domestic spaces such as the kitchen, to the foods that are produced there, and to her mother who inhabits that realm. In *Un sogno del nord* she writes about travels, particularly travels in northern Europe, and recounts her love for the north. The name "Baltic" itself evokes indefinite distances, deserted and cold seas, long sunsets and stories about aristocratic and secret people, Romano recalls how her reading brought her to an identification with Nora, Hedda and the mysterious Ellida, the woman of the sea. While the collection begins by exploring exotic and faraway places, it ends by coming home – home to her city of origin, the city square, the hotel, the streets, the buildings, the town hall, her dead sister. All these episodes represent a present that slips into a past that is always present.

Notably, Romana writes herself as the descendent of an Italian male literary culture. In a section entitled "Ombre," Romana focuses on her relationship with and memories of significant literary figures of the twentieth century: Vittorio Sereni, Cesare Pavese, Pierpaolo Pasolini, Elio Vittorini, Carlo Levi, Arnaldo Momigliano and, in the section "Incontri," Alberto Moravia and Mario Soldati. These writers and friends are her literary fathers and their influence is clearly visible in her writing where they emerge almost spontaneously and effortlessly. This is visible, for example, in the way she appears to have subsumed Pavese:

quello che è per me Pavese, è quello che compare di lui nei miei stessi libri. Senza che io mi proponga in nessun modo di ricordarlo, nei libri in cui parlo a fondo di me stessa, che sono un po' tutti, viene fuori ogni tanto una sentenza di Pavese. Io non lo cerco: è il lato arguto ma anche sapienziale di Pavese, che è rimasto dentro di me."[14] (1412)

In a similar vein her references to Moravia suggest a sense of intimacy and equality: "Eppure io ho sempre sentito Moravia in qualche modo fraterno, anzi uguale" (1453) ("I have always considered Moravia a sort of brother, indeed an equal"). By writing herself through her literary fathers and brothers, Romano gives herself the clout unattainable via her literary mothers.

Indeed the gaps with regard to women writers are conspicuous and limited to Simone de Beauvoir, Sibilla Aleramo, and Marguerite Duras. The portrait of Simone de Beauvoir in "Il coraggio di una donna" ("A Woman's Courage"), is curiously ambivalent. While Romano praises her female intellectual curiosity and creativity, she is nonetheless reserved in her description:

[...] se c'è una figura femminile di spicco e fama mondiale, che potrebbe rappresentare un caso eminente di curiosità intelletuale, è proprio lei.

La Beauvoir è stata – lo è ancora – mai sazia di conoscere, di imparare, e anche di creare (a suo modo).[15] (1517)

Romano's choice of a conditional verb tense, "potrebbe rappresentare" ("could represent"), rather than an indicative "rappresenta" ("represents") is an example of her guarded enthusiasm. In fact, her essay descends into the derogatory when she attributes Beauvoir's "ideas" to Sartre. Romano creates out of Simone de Beauvoir a reflection of herself, an intellectual artistic woman indebted to her male models.

A piece entitled "La donna che scrive" ("The woman who writes") focuses on Marguerite Duras and Sibilla Aleramo. The event that spawns this textual encounter is Romano's reading of a new book by Marguerite Duras, *La vita materiale* (*Material life*) in which Duras sustains that writers throughout their lives must maintain "una carica erotica" (1518) ("an erotic charge"). In a direct denial of sexed language, Romano claims that such a statement negatively affirms life over art. While such "spudoratezza" (1518) ("impudence") is a characteristic of other modern women writers, such as Anaïs Nin and Colette, Romano blatantly denies an association with her contemporaries and with feminine language, opting instead to define her own writing as displaiying "spietatezza" (1518) ("ruthlessness").

On the surface, Duras' association with Aleramo results from the fact that Romano had discovered Duras' latest book in Milan at a conference celebrating Sibilla Aleramo's life and art. The strange coupling, Romano claims, is due to the fact that both Aleramo and Duras are women who write, but it is also clearly linked to Sibilla's own "erotic charge." Romano claims that what has endured of Sibilla's image are her beauty, the sincerity of her ideological engagement, and her ingenuity. But ingenuity is not, Romano warns, an artistic gift. Romano struggles with the life/art binomial warning against the lack of control often attributed to women's writing while at the same time praising Duras' commitment to a profession which takes over her life. This is a curious and contradictory piece, which illustrates Romano's strange and difficult relationship with avowedly 'women' writers. As in the piece on Beauvoir, Romano is cautious in her appraisal, yet cannot resist calling Duras' *The Lover* an almost perfect book. Unlike Aleramo, who is searching for women models, and when she finds them, exalts their courage, Romano seems dubious and indeed critical of women writers who celebrate their sexuality as well as their sexual difference. While recognising their contribution, Romano excludes her gender identification with them. Indeed if there is one thing that Romano categorically rejects it is the very notion of an essentialist *scrittura femminile* while not completely denying a gendered signature. In addition, Romano feels the need to protect her writing from being labelled autobiographical and being relegated to a less legitimate genre. She insists that autobiography is an inappropriate descriptor for her work, recalling how "Anni fa mio figlio, interrogato pubblicamente sui miei libri, disse: – So che mia madre scrive storie di famiglia penso che siano libri noiosi e non li leggo-" (1563).[16]

While many of her works are obliquely autobiographical, they only become avowedly so with her 1979 novel *Una giovinezza inventata* (An invented youth). Lanser explains narrative choices by women such as Romano to sidestep the personal voice:

Given the precarious position of women in patriarchal societies, women novelists may have avoided personal voice when they feared their work would be taken for autobiography. The use of personal voice also risks reinforcing the convenient ideology of women's writing as "self-expression," the product of "intuition" rather than of art. (20)

In fact, we find in Romano's earlier work practices common among modernist women writers she admired (such as Virginia Woolf) who retained a certain distance in their writing, a distance which as Mary Gordon suggests gave "grandeur" to otherwise "trivial" female subjects (29).

Third generation: Gina Lagorio, 1930-

Gina Lagorio, born in 1930, journalist, public figure and winner of several major literary awards, displays a fervently feminine signature. Her works are populated by primarily female protagonists and deal with themes of maternity, self-actualisation, infancy and the often thwarted search for an idealised love. Rusconi calls her a creator of stories in which being woman and the mother/daughter relationship are represented successfully and authentically (162). But Lagorio has endured her own share of criticism and has often featured in the debate regarding the merits of gendered writing. In the 1960s the critic Giancarlo Vigorellli called her work "too feminine" and shaken by cyclonic excess (Rusconi 162). In contrast, Walter Mauro described her work as being "forte e concreta […] tutt'altro che femminile" (Rusconi 162) ("strong and concrete: anything but feminine") and her own reputed maestro, the poet Camillo Sbarbaro, called one of her portraits "così asciutta […], non parrebbe disegnato da una donna" (Rusconi 162) ("so lean, that it could not have been designed by a woman").

Lagorio's autobiographical *Inventario* is a retrospective reconstruction composed of 34 chapters drawing on various personal and political themes and painting a geo-cultural landscape of her life. Clearly dated at the beginning of the very first chapter, 29 October 1995, and at the very end of the book, 4 October 1997, Lagorio encloses her work within a well-defined period. Unlike the other two works examined, and unlike Lagorio's own *Penelope senza tela* (1984), this text is not a compilation of pieces written at different points in the author's life but a more coherent, self-contained work written over the span of two years. The book is introduced by a quote from Ezra Pound's *Cantos*: "What thou lovest well remains,/the rest is dross/What thou lov'st well shall not be reft from thee/What thou lov'st well is thy true heritage" (5). The final words of her text are an Italian translation of those same words. Enclosed within this arc is, as its title suggests, an inventory of the people, places, and things that Lagorio loves most: from her grand-daughter to her night-time reading, to her favourite writers, musicians, artists, film-makers and teachers, to her favourite places and to significant events in her life. Like Romano in *Un sogno del nord*, Lagorio pays homage to her literary fathers, Dante, Alessandro Manzoni and

Cesare Pavese, and more directly to Beppe Fenoglio, Camillo Sbarbaro and Angelo Barile whose geographies are also hers:

> Barile fu il mio primo lettore, Sbarbaro diede il suo avallo subito dopo. "Paragone" mi pubblicò un racconto, poi "L'approdo letterario." La provincia poteva essere anche una culla protettiva, dove lavorare in silenzio e poter sperare vero quello in cui credevo.[17] (136)

In *Inventorio* Lagorio creates a sensual link between geographical place and writing, between the rosemary on the balcony and the words of the poets and ultimately Lagorio, like Romano, demonstrates a strong need to eventually return home. As in Romano's *Un sogno del nord*, foreign places, Jerusalem, Paris, Brazil and the United States, eventually lead her back to her homeland where her identity is entrenched:

> [...] Io ho bisogno per essere io, della mia cara vecchia Europa, dei suoi monumenti che parlano la mia lingua, e più ho bisogno dell'Italia e più ancora del mio paese, dove anche le pietre mi rispondono se le interrogo.[18] (158)

From country to region to city, Lagorio ultimately returns home to the memories of her many houses, which reside within her, keeping her past forever present (220).

The book, whose avowed inspiration is the birth of her grand-daughter, is structured by what Lagorio identifies as a rigorously omni-comprehensive outline which does not follow any particular theme or adhere to the unities of space and time but spans the arc of her life (140). Central to this structure is the dialogue with the many important female figures highlighted in this book. This life-story is woven at least in part by a very prominent feminist thread suggesting a sort of genealogy that is both biological and cultural and that, in its shifting temporal perspective, is neither chronological nor spatial but reciprocal. She learns just as much from her granddaughter as she does from her grandmother, as she does from her female friends, teachers and literary mothers. There is a sort of democratic love and respect which suggests a utopian dialogue across the generations. Missing is the mother-daughter tension that often prevails in literature by women writers. Her mother in fact seems to provide the same mentoring often reserved for symbolic mothers, and it is through the reading of her mother's books that she encounters her ninenteenth-century literary predecessors, Neera, Matilde Serao, Anna Vertua Gentile and Annie Vivanti. Lagorio claims that her mother is present in all her stories and novels, in her writings of music and domestic life; Lagorio's writing is a celebration of a maternal bond which for her is unquestionably positive and free of tension.

Lagorio's work exalts her other mothers as well, for example, her teachers who introduced her to yet other female literary ancestors such as Katherine Mansfield, Elizabeth Browning and Virginia Woolf. The mothers of Aleramo echo in Lagorio's work, as exemplars for Italian feminists. Her gratitude extends ultimately to her own literary mothers: to Anna Banti and Elsa Morante, two "non-mothers" whose novels *Le mosche d'oro* and *La storia* are, according to Lagorio, the most intense accounts of the maternal relationship (123).

One of the most powerful and emotionally charged chapters of *Inventorio* is dedicated to Elsa Morante. Maintaining a central position halfway through the book, the chapter recalls the meeting between Lagorio and Morante in a hospital clinic where an elderly and humble Elsa Morante resides. Lagorio exalts the physical beauty of Morante's youth and seeks vehemently to amend the misrepresentation of Elsa as a difficult, scornful woman, describing her rather as a sick, sweet woman open to a "dialogo fraterno," (122) a fraternal dialogue. Lagorio elevates Morante to the heights of Aleramo's exceptional women, misunderstood for her genius, a genius that when female is doubly misunderstood (125). Lagorio's eulogy pre-empts the description of Morante's funeral and suggests the sense of protection of the strong daughter alongside her weakened mother, of a daughter suddenly more empowered than the mother, of a mother who soon will no longer be able to speak for herself.

Emerging from a decidedly feminist formation, Lagorio's piece on Morante is an example of the Italian feminist concept of *affidamento* or entrustment come full circle.[19] While *affidamento* originally implies the mediation of the symbolic naive daughter into the public realm by an empowered mother, the case of Lagorio/Morante implies the symbiotic nature of the relationship with the empowered daughter able to be called upon to assist the aging mother, to appropriate her voice. While Lagorio is effusive, Morante is grateful both for Lagorio's favourable review of an unpopular book and for befriending a woman who has no women friends.

But if Lagorio's work is on the one hand a utopian inventory of gratitude toward a genealogy of women, it also warns of challenges still ahead despite of or indeed because of feminist gains. Lagorio highlights the ailments, old and new, of her generation of writers:

> Ero al Salone del libro [...] Si parlava di donne, femminismo e no, differenza e no [...] Era chiaro: nessuno di loro aveva letto i libri delle autrici delle quali parlava con rotonde e ben lucidate parole. Dissi la mia convinzione ad alta voce. Fu come se nella polvere della sala fosse passata una raffica di vento: mormorii del pubblico, proteste, infide e confuse degli uomini presente toccati sul vivo.[20] (50-51)

This incident leads Lagorio to recall a reflection by the poet Dario Bellezza on Elsa Morante:

> Le donne è difficile che riescano a predominare, l'Italia è un paese troppo maschilista; è inutile fingere anche di essere scrittori, restava donna e questo per i professori universitari era grave.[21] (51)

But Lagorio suggests that the problem in Italy extends beyond the limitations and obstacles imposed by a male-dominated society. More threatening than the patriarchal institutions that die hard are women themselves. While in her work Lagorio praises many literary mothers, elevating the likes of Banti,

Morante, and Ginzburg onto a pedestal, she also acknowledges and silently mourns the tensions that exist between them. Morante fears a friendship with Lagorio because her friendship with Ginzburg did not work out: "Poi se tu mi conoscessi, non mi vorresti più bene [...] le donne con me fanno tutte così; anche Natalia Ginzburg ama i miei libri, ma non ama me" (121).[22] Banti also has difficulty with her literary sisters, and Lagorio herself fears the neglect and oblivion that her contemporaries have demonstrated in light of their literary mothers. The symbolic maternal relationship among women writers of different generations must replace relationships based on competition and inexplicable lack of respect:

> Mi chiedo anche se tra loro le donne siano poi così generose. In gioventù, quando percorrevo con il batticuore i primi passi nella scrittura narrativa, so cosa significò per me ricevere l'incoraggiamento di Gianna Manzini e Anna Banti, e ne ho reso testimonianza in ogni occasione. [...] Le studiose del femminismo hanno parlato spesso, con finezze, delle "madri" molto lodate da vive e poi presto dimenticate.[23] (52-53)

To not forget them means to continue writing them as Lagorio has in this text, using words that come from deep within herself. Lagorio's words remind us of the ideas explored by Aleramo in "Defence" and echo the French feminists so fundamental to Italian feminist thought. Like Hélène Cixous who links text and body, in a maternal metaphor of white ink (Cixous 251), Lagorio represents feminine writing as inscribed on the body and born from the feminine unconscious:

> Ci sono parole che pronunciamo senza averle presente, che vengono da molto lontano, dalle stagioni del sangue che ci ha generato e da quelle del sangue che abbiamo a nostra volta generato. Le parole senza logica e senza regole della vita ancestrale, naturale, spontanea. [...] Poi le leggiamo e le sentiamo parte di noi.[24] (227-228)

In this book wich Lagorio dedicates to her grand-daughter, she proposes a female genealogy linked to language, a cycle that allows for dialogue between generations, a linguistic genealogy that will be passed on to her daughter's daughter.

Dialoguing with our mothers

Paul Eakin, when analysing the autobiography of Roland Barthes, notes that Barthes' disavowal of any connection between the 'I' of his text and the extratextual "I" is anchored in an interpersonal discourse with his mother that fosters the emergence of the extended self and its store of autobiographical memories (139). The life narratives or inventories are similarly anchored in the maternal fibre. The ever shifting narrating 'I' entwines the writer's personal story with the stories of others in an ever shifting temporal and geographical landscape in which the mother always surfaces, ultimately proposing a female genealogy that either gives voice to the past or that offers a new paradigm for female writing. In their autobiographical inventories, each of the women writers explored in this chapter confronts her literary mothers and does so as part of the 'unsuspected' construction of her self.

While these inventories clearly highlight, promote, and at times even question literary mothers, they also elucidate a problematic relationship with writing in and against a dominant patriarchal tradition and within feminist discourses. I deliberately chose to focus on three writers with distinct temporal and ideological relationships to feminism: an emancipationist, Aleramo, who exalts and constructs clearly radical female models with whom to align herself; an avowedly non-feminist, Romano, who treats her mothers with ambivalence, aiming instead to being accepted by the dominant literary tradition; and a feminist, Lagorio, who exalts her literary mothers and poses a challenge to women writers of the new generation to carry on the responsibility of acknowledging the literary model. The position these writers assume is linked to the cultural contexts in which they write: "Autobiographical subjects know themselves as subjects of particular kinds of experience attached to their social status and identity" (Smith, *Reading Autobiography* 25).

Aleramo searches exuberantly for difficult to find literary models and praises them for their courage to write differently. Her early works, such as *Orsa minore*, serve to acknowledge female writers excluded from the canon and give authority to female voices. Romano responds with reservation to Aleramo and to her other literary mothers, wary of the cost of aligning herself with a tradition still secondary and marginalised through much of her life. Lagorio's *Inventario* utilises feminist tools to both acknowledge a female genealogy and to validate and promote women's writing as a process to be carried into the future. Lagorio applies the notion of *affidamento* in reverse, placing herself as mother to her own mother, Elsa Morante, as the balance of power and authority enables her to empower a generation of women writers no longer able to speak for themselves. As the names of women writers from both Italy and abroad echo in these works by different generations of women, they provide women of present and future generations the opportunity to recognise a literary tradition of their own, to engage in a generational debate, and to devise new ways to rediscover and reinvent their mothers and models. When juxtaposed, these inventories speak to each other across generations and suggest the potential for dialogue between women in their multiple positions as authors, characters and readers, for dialogue within and without the text. Finally, all three texts display how in exploring the literary mother, the female author acquires the authority to pass on the matrix of female strength, to write from the past into the future and to propagate a female genealogy, with all the problems and tensions that this trajectory implies. As Teresa de Lauretis suggests (in *Sui generic*), female genealogy:

> non è né una tradizione, né un legame di sangue tra madri e figlie diseredate, ma è piuttosto la traccia di un percorso, di un desiderio: una geneologia femminista discontinua ed elusive, giorno per giorno. In queste condizioni il

viaggio non è facile e la metta non è ben chiara. Ci sono momenti in cui, per la
verità, il passato mi appare più ospitale del futuro e le storie passate danno più
conforto delle nuove.[25] (35)

The new stories by the new generation of women's writers raise new issues
and new debates appropriate to that generation. In search of their own
distinct identities, these rebellious daughters, these sometimes 'bad girls,' etch
graffiti on the wall that blasphemes the language of the biological mother and
challenges the language of the symbolic (Fortini 195-209). In a similar fashion,
young feminist theorists of today reassess their relationship with their feminist
mothers and with a feminist genealogy. In 2001, an entire issue of the feminist
periodical *DWF* was dedicated to the current understanding of genealogies. In
this issue, a number of young women feminist scholars and writers adopt the
literary genre of fictional letter to dialogue with their mothers and question the
validity of past feminisms in an era of changing social contexts and changing
politics. They identify the difficulty of their relationships with the women
who came before them, a difficulty due in part to new political practices, to a
resistance to their feminist mothers, to a tension between wanting to distance
themselves from, while at the same time acknowledging their debt to, their
symbolic mothers. In these fictive letters, thirteen young women discuss many
problems and propose some solutions; propagating within these critical texts
the same tensions, debates, and dialogues witnessed in the texts of Romano
and Lagorio. What resonates in these works is a call and a need for new words,
new rhythms and new music relevant to the new experiences and contexts of
the new generation. Yet the mother is always present. The abstract of one of
these essays, entitled "Il posto dei libri" ("The place of books"), reads:

> "I want to tell you about my books and their order [...] I thought that the
> order of things wasn't predetermined, it depended on each single point of view.
> Nonsense." In moving in a new house, placing the books on the shelves is a
> way to discover that their order tells a story, the story of a relationship with
> a woman, and all her political engagement. This is the point in inheriting:
> a principle of order, can discover and deal with in every new situation and
> experience. (95)

Just as a female genealogy is undeniable, so the dialogue with the mother
is ceaseless and cyclical and will continue as new generations of writers
chronicle their lives through an exploration of their time, justifying their own
perceptions, challenging those of others, and engaging in the construction of
multiple identities in a process which is never complete.

Notes

1. Diotima and the Libreria delle Donne (Milan Women's Bookshop) have produced numerous significant works in this area. Fundamental theoretical works of Italian feminist theory exploring notions of a female genealogy and the symbolic mother include Muraro, *L'ordine simbolico della madre*; Cavarero, *Nonostante Platone*; Centro Documentazione Donna di Firenze. For a relevant discussion in English see: Bono and Kemp; Kemp and Bono; Holub "For the Record: The Non-Language of Italian Feminist Philosophy," and "The Politics of Diotima"; Lazzaro-Weis; de Lauretis, "The Essence of the Triangle"; Muraro "The Narrow Door." For a discussion in English on the Luisa Muraro-Lea Melandri debate on the symbolic order and genealogy see Parati 12-15.

2. This term is coined by Caren Kaplan in "Resisting Autobiography: Out-Law Genres and Transnational Feminist Subjects." Kaplan focuses in particular on *testimonios,* prison memoirs, ethnographies, biomythographies, cultural autobiographies, and regulative psychobiographies, but her definition of out-law genres could be extended to include all genres that "mix conventionally unmixable elements" (208).

3. Rusconi, 164, refers specifically to the following cases: Grazia Livi, *Da una stanza all'altra*; Nadia Fusini, *Nomi*; Lea Melandri, *Come nasce il sogno d'amore*; Lella Ravasi Bellocchio, *Di madre in figlia*; Ginvera Bompiani, *L'attesa*; Giuliana Mastrangeli, *Passioni,* Luisa Passerini, *Autoritratto di gruppo,* as well as more generally to the works of Armanda Guiducci and Dacia Maraini.

4. "by choosing an apparently objective and detached form of the biographical essay or investigative book, allow for the surfacing of fragments of themselves, small or large, hidden or transparent, isolated or multiple, [fragments] that break out from the stories of others."

5. In addition to the works examined in this chapter, see also: Anna Banti; Ginzburg; Lagorio, *Penelope senza tela argomenti e testi*; Livi; Manzini, *Ritratti e pretesti* and *Album di ritratti*; and Neera.

6. See de Giovanni 30, "il '*maternage*' letterario, cioè il riconoscimento di una autorità stilistica anche in scrittrici 'prima di noi'"("a literary *maternage,* that is the recognition of a stylistic authority in women writers 'before us'").

7. Zancan proposes generational divisions in *La donna.* She expands her generational categories from two to three and provides an extensive list of writers in each category in her online text *Le scrittrici e i loro testi in Memoria del 900 letterario italiano: scritture, immagini, voci.* Zancan is not the only writer to categorise Italian women writers by generations. See also Neera de Giovanni's introduction.

8. *Autocoscienza,* a key term of the Italian feminist movement, and first introduced by Carla Lonzi of Rivolta Femminile, refers to "a process of the discovery and (re-)construction of the self, both the self of the individual woman and a collective sense of self: the search for the subject-woman." See Bono and Kemp 9.

9. An extensive list of articles published in the Italian press critical of Sibilla Aleramo's writing and lifestyle are provided by Adriana Chemello in "Lo specchio opaco. Sibilla nella critica del suo tempo," in Buttafuoco and Zancan. See in particular 255-56 notes 6 and 7.

10. "In order to win the respect of my brothers I have adapted my intelligence to theirs with an effort that has taken decades to understand. To learn their language meant distancing myself from myself [...] I don't reflect myself, I don't even translate myself, I reflect your representation of the world."

11. "Who cares whether it's reality or a story? Life translated into art, by magical virtue[...] I don't think I have ever found in a modern book, certainly not in a book by a woman, such a perfect balance between the style and the spirit of the writer."

12. "who is no longer hampered by virile formulae but who rather searches within herself and tries to express herself in a way which is not like him but differentiates herself from him and integrates him."

13. Sandra Petrignani, in her introduction to *Le signore della scrittura,* describes Lalla Romano and women writers of her generation as non-feminists adamantly opposing an association with feminism notwithstanding their awareness of the fact that being women had disadvantaged them and indeed excluded them from consideration as great writers. (7)

14. "What Pavese is for me is the part of him that appears in my books. In the books in which I talk about myself in depth, which is just about all of them, a bit of Pavese always manages to emerge. I don't look for it. It is the quick-witted and knowledgeable side of Pavese."

15. "If there is a prominent female figure who has acquired international fame, who could represent a case of eminent intellectual curiousity it is certainly her [...] Beauvoir was and still is never tired of knowing, learning and even of creating (in her own way)."

16. "Years ago my son, asked about my books, said: 'I know mum writes family stories. I think they are boring books and I don't read them.'"

17. "Barile was my first reader. Sbarbaro endorsed me shortly thereafter. *Paragone* published one of my stories, and then "L'approdo letterario." The country could also be a protective cradle, where it was possible to work in silence and to hope in what I really believed in."

18. "to be myself, I need my old, dear Europe, its monuments that speak my language, and I need Italy even more, and above all, my hometown where even the stones answer me if I address them."

19. The idea of *affidamento*, generally translated as "entrustment," was put forth by the Milan's Women's Bookshop and also practiced and discussed by Diotima as a tool which can be used to examine the relationships between women. The idea of entrustment implies a practice of relationships between women whereby a woman of lesser power entrusts herself to a woman in position of power to mediate her access to the world. See Libreria delle donne di Milano, *Non credere di avere dei diritti* (translated as *Sexual Difference: a Theory of Social-Symbolic Practice*). Much debate has arisen regarding the hierarchical and power-based dynamic of *affidamento*. For a discussion in English of *affidamento* and the debate surrounding it see Paola Bono "Introduction: Without a Leg to Stand" in Kemp and Bono; Renate Holub, "Between the United States and Italy," and Lazzaro-Weis 54. For a discussion in English of *affidamento* in the context of the mother-daughter relationship and the reconstruction of the symbolic order, see Giorgio 16-18.

20. "I was at the Salone del libro, there was talk of women and feminism and it was clear that none of the male critics had read the books of the female authors about whom they were speaking with rounded and polished words. I expressed my opinion and it was as if a gust of wind had stirred up the dust in the room: murmuring among the audience, treacherous and confused protest from the men under attack."

21. "It's difficult for women to dominate in Italy, the country is too macho, and it is useless to pretend to be a writer, she remains female and this for university professors is serious."

22. "If you knew me you wouldn't like me very much [...] that's what always happens between myself and other women; even Natalia Ginzburg loves my books but doesn't love me."

23. "I ask myself if women are actually generous with themselves. In my youth when I was experimenting with narrative writing I knew what it meant to me, to be encouraged by Gianna Manzini and Anna Banti, and I have acknowledged it whenever possible [...] Feminist scholars have often talked shrewdly about their very esteemed 'mothers' when they were alive and then all too soon forgotten them."

24. "There are words that we utter without knowing it, words that come from far away, from the seasons of the blood that generated us and the blood that we have generated. Words without logic and without rules, from our ancestral, natural and spontaneous lives."

25. "[...] is neither a tradition nor a blood-bond between mothers and disinherited daughters, but rather the tracing of a route, of a desire: a feminist genealogy which is discontinuous and elusive, day after day. Under these conditions the journey is not easy and the destination is not always clear. There are moments when the past appears more hospitable than the future, and when the stories from the past provide greater comfort than new ones."

Writing Home to Her Mother: Fabrizia Ramondino's *Althénopis*

Paula Green

Ritorno dal Nord[1] This mother would be the real mother over and against the gelid domain, all gooseflesh and teeth chattering, her occlusion the repressed mother of patriarchal love. Oh ice-bound lips. Oh congealed tongue. In this writerly account, where the body her body was a mute character, a warm breath is now gathering together love and hate, desire and anger. Returned daughter.

Writing home the mother

A desire to write versions of the mother, embedded in a desire to write versions of home, relies upon invention *and* memory, transformation *and* mourning, transcendence *and* description. In this chapter, I am proposing that writing home can be interpreted as a form of writing the mother; and that similarly, writing the mother can be interpreted as a form of writing home. In part, such writing is driven by a need to represent origins inside a need to recreate traces of one's own subjectivity or, to put it otherwise, to articulate a subjective, maternal position inside and against the locus of home. However, such writing, leading through entwined levels of the maternal and the domestic, courts dispute as much current feminist theory will testify. Marianne Hirsch, in *The Mother/Daughter Plot*, suggests that the difficulty of defining "mother" or "maternal" becomes "an object of sometimes radical division within feminist analysis" (163). A question, then, that I bring to my analysis of the mother-writing-home triad is: when writing a version of 'home' that includes the mother, or even depends upon the mother, how can we represent her in a way that allows maternal subjectivity, maternal voice, and that will include body and experience without imprisoning her in essentialising or debilitating representations or discourse?

Fabrizia Ramondino's *Althénopis* builds a compelling example of a woman beginning to come to terms with her maternal origins. In writing a version of home, Ramondino implicates the mother; the figure of the mother, both absent and present, propels a narrative that in seeking home is seeking the mother herself. Ramondino's novel functions as a process of both recuperation and reconception: she writes the novel upon the death of her own mother and shortly after the birth of her own daughter.[2] *Althénopis*, thus,

Returned mother. Indeed all of this to give priority to some kind
of affiliation. Consanguity. She will not repeat the monstrosities
of paternal fictions her numb lips his humect place of origins, her
hoar tongue his epicurean trope for silence. No, she is returning
to hunger, away from his dead of winter, to take up the questions
of herself, in eastings and southings, whereabouts hereat, to offer
extensions of herself, in writing her experience of contradiction.
Yes, there are

coincides with the loss of a mother and the arrival of motherhood.

In my focus on *Althénopis* itself, I will then consider three forms of the
mother, three 'maternal umbrellas' that will enable me to draw the mother
closer. First, I will examine the case of the missing mother, the mother
dispersed throughout the text, scarcely sighted and sorely missed. The mother
is both part of home and not; she is home and yet conversely, she is not-home.
Second, I will consider the function of surrogate mothers, settling upon the
narrator's larger-than-life grandmother, and the text itself as stand-in mother.
Filtered through my mother-writing-home triad, both grandmother and text
can intercede as surrogate homes. Finally, I will turn to the juncture between
heimlich (homely) and *unheimlich* (unhomely), trespassing upon but moving
away from Freud's notion of the uncanny. I will consider the moments where
the mother is strikingly uncanny, and where the text itself produces similar
moments of discomfort.

The missing mother

What is so often missing from literature, and from daily life, is an expression
of the mother's needs, her desires, her stories, her voice. *Althénopis* does not
represent a mother speaking as a mother, thus providing clear insight into a
mother's point of view, but represents a daughter's shifting relationship with
the maternal, with the mother and with mothering. A number of critics have
privileged a discussion of Ramondino's representation of the mother in their
analysis of her text. Adalgisa Giorgio, in her suggestion that *Althénopis* is a
daughter's recuperation of the maternal, employs Sigmund Freud's model of
the family romance to consider the function of the mother amidst a genealogy
of women (Giorgio 132). Ursula Fanning, in considering the interconnected
ideas of "the mother in the text" and the "mothering of the text" focuses on the
mother-daughter relationship and the narrating daughter's efforts to locate a
voice to represent it (Fanning 211-14). Sharon Wood uses Ramondino's novel
to support her analysis of the myth of Clytemnestra and Electra in relation to
narrating mothers and daughters (Wood 245-53).

In both theory and literature the mother has a history of absence. She is
missing in terms of subjectivity, she is erased or without voice, she serves as
object, she undergoes objectification. Psychoanalytic theory, for example,
continues to produce thought that is

these loves in her, quite harrowing. There are these attachments in her, quite obtuse. She is returning from the one-sided metaphor of confinement to exist in and beyond language. She too will become her own mother. Inamorate with the words that overgo the father's law, I am fidgety already with this longing for a resilient symmetry: the mother a pendulum for the daughter, the daughter a pendulum for the mother.

child rather than mother centred. Psychoanalysis, Sara Ruddick argues, depends upon "the absence or lack of the mother as a condition for subjectivity, language, and culture" (Ruddick 32). For the child to be aligned in relation to the Law of the Father, the mother must be represented as lack, and in terms of the daughter's formation as subject, the mother must be silenced, just as Jocasta remains the silent mother of the Oedipal story. Against such a disturbing mythic inheritance, Hirsch asks "[i]f the notion of the individual *subject* is defined in such a way that its very formation and development, that subjectivity itself needs to take place either against or in relation to the background of an *object* – a silent maternal figure – how can maternity be studied from the perspectives of mothers?" (Hirsch, "Maternity" 93-94) Furthermore, to engage in a maternal quest, the mother remains object, her point of view conjecture, her voice still suffering erasure, her state(s) and circumstance(s) still other.

Critics who attempt to view maternal subjectivity in the light of maternal experience are confounded by a series of discourses – post-structuralist, deconstructivist, feminist – that in deferring meaning and denying the authority of the subject create a dichotomy between 'woman' as theoretical figure, elusive, undefinable, unnameable, and "woman" as a material agent who seeks abortions, childcare, and financial equity in a real world. Elizabeth Bourque Johnson replaces 'woman' with 'mother' in Linda Alcoff's significant question: What can we demand in the name of women if "women" do not exist? (Bourque Johnson 22) *What can we demand in the name of mothers if mothers do not exist?* Against a backdrop of myth, mythification, object, objectification, other, and othering, we are missing the mother, we are trapped in conceptions of subjectivity that refuse maternal subjecthood. (Hirsch, "Maternity" 94)

I am approaching the missing mother in *Althénopis* as part absence and part presence, and as a maternal being who is missed. The structure of the text strengthens a sense of separation alongside a sense of attachment; against the persistent thread of absence we may also locate a variable maternal trace. I will consider this oscillation between presence and absence, separation and attachment in terms of the maternal body and maternal enclosures. Finally, I will use the metaphor of kinesis to consider the movement that on the one hand forms a response to the missing mother, and on the other hand, in the process of writing, filters a form of home through maternal motion.

Pianta di una casa: il Salotto Is the story coming to an end? She said it's time to begin again behind the screen of representation. This inborn sketch of a good-liking name has happened in the lobby. White and black or black and white will welcome you to the other side of the room. We are not thinking of algidity at this measured point. The couch fits in with the right side and the left side and the other side. She has the latitude for likeness in the house and in the garden.

In the first two parts of *Althénopis*, the mother is largely absent. We encounter rare moments of joy and intimacy on the part of the mother when the unaccustomed pleasure infects her children, the narrator and her brother; occasionally the mother would take her children on Sunday picnics in the woods where: "Il vincolo supremo però era quella cesta, da cui ci veniva dispensato il cibo, e quella grande fame infantile, che faceva la gioia della mamma"[3] (Ramondino, *Althénopis* 43). In analysing the mother-daughter relations in Colette's *Break of Day*, Hirsch proposes that "as they tell the story of child development, psychoanalyst theories traditionally cast the mother as the one who desires connection and the child as the one who struggles to separate; however, Colette invents a mother who desires separation, thereby making it easier for her to resolve the conflict between attachment and separation" (Hirsch, *Mother/Daughter Plot* 103-8).[4] Like Colette's example, Ramondino's *Althénopis* represents a mother who seemingly longs for and achieves a state of separation in the first two parts of the text, while the daughter yearns for proximity and attachment. Thus, when the narrator, playing on the rooftop with other childhood friends, observes her mother crossing the piazza, she confesses: "quando usciva nella strada e traversava la piazza, mi pareva un essere piccolo e indifeso, lontanissimo da me, come fosse in un altro mondo, irraggiungibile, come dopo un irreparabile evento si sognano i morti, e volevo correre e volare dal tetto ad accertarmi della consistenza del suo corpo e a richiamarla da un mondo di ombre"[5] (125). Again Ramondino's voice doubles back on itself in this act of mourning and recall, as she attempts to retrieve the diaphanous mother from the shadows of death and the unbearable distance of a childhood memory.

Giorgio situates the narrator's mother as an elusive presence that resists invasion by the daughter; whilst the daughter continues to seek the mother, the mother remains beyond

She has free range of the stretch of her imagination. A clock ticking with desire, or not. A wallpaper distracting us by distinguishing past and future. Or not. She uses couches to trace the rites of order. Where are we to go? We will swing through the garnering of the very roots of the Drawing Room to a sort of cave with upholstered and restitched and carved and scratched armchairs. This will be a refuge and this will be a displacement. Not a frigid zone with little

her, outside the protagonist (Giorgio 133, 143). Nonetheless, in the third part of *Althénopis*, the mother becomes the centre of the daughter's story; the first-person narrator of the first sections shifts to the more impersonal third-person narration, yet the subject matter becomes both intimate and dangerous as the daughter faces the mother on her deathbed. In this final section, where Ramondino employs language differently – no longer simply descriptive but dependent upon metaphor, rhyme, repetition and semantic resonance – the mother and daughter attempt to communicate but do so with difficulty: "Ormai non si parlavano più con parole, la Figlia e la Madre, ma per segni. E i segni erano torbidi, un Logos maligno, escresciuto alla ragione, alla temperanza" (233).[6] Thus, although mother and daughter occupy a shared space, they remain missing, the one from the other.

The text's structure enacts the oscillation of a daughter in her maternal quest; she moves to and fro between presence and absence, from mother sighted at a distance to mother close at hand on a deathbed, from the prosaic absences of the first sections to the poetic, maternal presence of the last. This insistent fluctuation is also evident in the representation of the maternal body, a trope that prefigures attachment and separation, origin and future. Within a few pages the narrator introduces us to the maternal body. Firstly we encounter the mother's hand: "la mano di nostra madre invece era inquietante, pareva sempre cancellare 'sciocchezze', lavare via qualcosa, fresca e odorosa di sapone" (8).[7] The maternal hand so remembered resists the paradigmatic image of a maternal hand as soothing, as nurturing. A few sentences later the mother is now written as lack: "Nostra madre poi, malgrado quel sangue, non aveva un corpo, aveva i gesti, ma sopratutto aveva i

place for herself but by any sketch of the imagination a parlour of amplitude. If he imposed with his nuances what once was, she is impounding her self as if she knows more than the cave as if she needs to draw the free range of where she will stand. How far along is she? Let's say there must be leeway to play with the constant dimness. At best, we are burrowing in to the furrow of a couch.

Il bagno The real mother is dripping wet her sodden towel hereafter a constant

'pensieri,' aveva mal di testa" (8).[8] The mother, disembodied and barbaric fluid, is consistently hard to fathom.

The narrator's mother, lacking maternal gesture yet possessing maternal body, returns us to the allure of the materiality of mothering, to the dilemma of speaking of the mother in physical, psychological or emotional terms, a dilemma that potentially imprisons women in a maternal essence, an essentialising narrative; or that denies women the pleasure to be found in the fundamental relationship to the mother, in a narrative that speaks of breasts, milk, nourishment and care. Ramondino's portrait of the mother clearly gives form to a woman who is complex, and who resists the ideal mothering role that Italian culture has elevated. The mother, we are told, had put herself in parentheses but that "ogni tanto ne usciva" (39).[9] The woman that remains inside this state of enclosure, unknowable, barely reachable for the daughter, is equally so for us as readers. The mother withdraws from the acts of mothering: after watching other children on the beach dried by their mothers, kept warm, safe, and fed, the daughter confesses that "[m]i sentivo come privata di quei riti signorili e materni" (2).[10] Unlike Luce Irigaray's model, where the daughter, in the process of being nurtured, becomes suffocated by food and maternal love, where the daughter devours the mother, and sacrifices the mother in order to live, Ramondino's example exposes a daughter yearning to be fed.[11]

Althénopis represents different journeys; the narrator journeys back through memory in order to give textual presence to the shadowy figure of the mother; the daughter returns home, journeys back to the mother after living elsewhere; the family journeys back after living in France; the mother journeys in the world of fiction away from her children. Cath Stowers, in "Journeying Back to the Mother," moves from the journey and return that is at the very heart of Oedipality, to Melanie Klein's repositioning of the mother, her body, and her departure at the centre of infant development: "For Klein, the infant oscillates

calculation of her fluids. She *withdrew even further into her own entrails, as water into the depths of the earth.* She seeped into solid ground by her own reckoning feasible by virtue of her fluid character. The real mother dreams of soaking in the bath the water a whirl-point a spring-point to her annulled body. The impostume part a projection of his solid logic. She leads you to believe she is divisible in volume and in tenor dropping drop-meal, in some way language.

between 'seeking, finding, obtaining, possessing with satisfaction,' and between 'seeking, lacking, missing, with fear and distress'" (Stowers 62). Stowers, thus, provides a trope of journey that depends upon toing-and-froing. When Ramondino's narrator returns to the mother "[c]on ossa cresciute dalla placenta, dal latte, delle cure, e occhi non strabici" she epitomises Klein's theory of an infantile sway between possession and lack (233).[12] Yet the daughter, grasping "l'amore sordo della Madre," began "a portare la Madre sulle spalle" and yet "[e]ra tornata sconfitta dalla Madre, come a chiederle ragione della sua vita" (236, 234, 235).[13] The seeking daughter, as narrator missing the missing mother, as author missing the dead mother, inscribes a double death, a prefigured death in that the two women survived but their fates separated: "La Figlia trovò il suo destino, ma svaní la Madre" (236).[14]

In a text that builds multiple layers of the missing mother, the employment of any trope must indicate movement that resists linearity, as does Stower's employment of "a fluctuating journey" (Stowers 65). Although I welcome the trope of the journey as cyclical or fluctuating in new critical practice, I want to offer another example, an example that represents movement under stimulus, that implies a change of position, that may be linear, random, circular, haywire, repetitive, rhythmic, comforting, discomforting. I want to introduce the idea of kinesis as a way of approaching mother-daughter movement. In this way the mother functions as stimulus for the daughter's movement; the daughter may move away from the mother as much as she moves towards her and as much as she moves elsewhere. Conversely, and emphatically implicated in this scene of kinesis, is the notion that the daughter functions as the stimulus for the mother's movement; the mother too will move through variable and viable positions and directions. Within this movement, which can allow for both separation and attachment, the two women can acknowledge that origin, future, absence and presence will in different and accountable ways play a role.

And yet you want to say not-denominable the she who *withdrew into her own entrails.* The real mother bears her self (apart from the others) in her baptism: barred from a symbolisation that maintains the walls of a solid. The real mother a casemate fortified against degrees of heat degrees of force degrees of conductivity. This is solid. Or is it? she asks knowing the women of her family disappeared, cancelled themselves out. Soaked up by the men who counted

If the process of writing, in the case of *Althénopis,* filters a form of home through maternal traces, the text itself echoes the maternal kinesis as it shifts from poetry to prose to poetry-prose, from autobiography to fiction to memory to analysis. Above all, the mobile text performs Ramondino's representation of maternal separations alongside maternal attachments in a way that provokes both disengagement and engagement.

In the closing paragraphs of *Althénopis,* the daughter finds a sign, "un gesto, un amuleto, una raccommandazione" that her dying mother leaves: "Ma sembrò a chi lo ricevette – protesa da sempre, ora quasi ansimante, in un vano ascolto, o in un abbraccio mancato – voce chiara, ammonitrice, non contraffatta, seppure grottesca e strana" (263).[15] The mother, still enigma, still faltering, precipitates a flux of daughter movement. Neither completely knowable, nor completely separate, each character is as much daughter as she is mother.

The surrogate mother

Patrice DiQuinzio argues that feminist theory needs to accept accounts of mothering that will "be partial and fragmentary" and that not all accounts of mothering can be reconciled with each other; "feminist theory will have to resist the tendency to totalise such accounts of mothering" (DiQuinzio 28). Moreover, DiQuinzio proposes that whilst critics such as Betty Friedan, Shulamith Firestone and Mary Daley tended to oversimplify and minimise the significance of mothering, women have a great variety of "situations and experiences" in relation to maternal activity (67). Mothering itself can be linked implicitly to the maternal body, but it may also be viewed as separate, as an adjunct from the birthing mother. Such a notion widens the potential of whom and how we will mother, and allows the mothering man, daughter or friend to function as surrogate mothers.

whose deaths counted. A gorget of fluctuating words protects her from his word. Or does it? Along the same shivering lines we will ask why the urine blood milk plasma overflows the subject. The real mother is dripping wet hereafter she is solid and she is fluid. So to speak and denied by another.

La camera da pranzo Swallow the mirror. Suckle the mirror. Then swap glass for ice for summering memory as if we are all hungry for something to heat. *For*

Althénopis produces a surrogate mother in the form of the grandmother. Her powerful presence overshadows a pre-eminent mother-daughter dyad as it also displaces the classic Freudian triangle of father-mother-daughter (Giorgio 135). The grandmother is placed in the text's opening pages, larger than life, a primeval mother who provides continuity and stable ground. The mother, situated on her deathbed in the final pages, remains ambiguous, unknowable, yet an insistent and compelling lure. We have considered the ways in which the mother functions as a missing mother; an interrogation of the figure of a surrogate mother will allow us to question the maternal paradigm. I will consider the figure of the grandmother as a source of nourishment, as mimicking and replacing the gestures of the mother. I will then use the trope of fluids to consider the grandmother as a source of continuity. Finally I will witness a daughter in pieces, surrogate mother herself.

Filtered through the voice of the daughter, the grandmother epitomises the maternal paradigm; she is characterised by plenitude, intuition, excess, irrationality, and a need to feed. Yet she transgresses the role of mother in that each maternal attribute, each act of mothering takes on an extravagant life of its own; by not remaining defined by way of, and thus imprisoned within, a maternal body, the grandmother reinvents a maternal subjectivity. Her maternal body, no longer capable of bearing children, invests plenitude and ripeness in numerous household activities. The Grandmother "amava cucinare, ma ormai da molti anni non era più padrona di una casa, sicché doveva, per seguire il suo estro, violare gli orari dei pasti e i precisi preventivi di spesa" (15).[16] When the children returned home from school they would find "nostra madre a letto col mal di testa e la pezzuola imbevuta di aceto sulla fronte, al buio, e la nonna sfavillante accanto ai fritti e ai mille-foglie colmi di creme, e ci immergevamo in quei pranzi sontuosi, odorosi, gocciolanti, che non avevano né capo né coda, e che irridevano alle preoccupazioni finanziarie, ai mali di pancia e al computo delle vitamine" (17).[17] The surrogate mother, in this example, dependent upon a maternal version of nurturing, reclaims "mother" and "mothering" as expandable terms. The

what she considered burnt out in herself, she considered burnt out in all the world. A culinary tarpaulin is laid upon the table because the mother prepares something to eat as an offering against the ice and the mirror. Or is it instead that the mayonnaise, the *petits pois*, the salted almonds, the béchamel sauces and the cakes are for herself to eat? Here is a memory of dining-rooms because the real mother, the dispenser of milk, put herself less put herself elsewhere

grandmother makes room for fantasy and myth, recklessness and risk. Tasks associated with mothering, such as cooking, sewing, story-telling and even cleaning demonstrate the importance of creativeness, movement, and invention for the grandmother as she practices the art of natural medicine, defies the strict balance of the narrator's mother, writes poetry, scorns wax on the furniture, and revels in water and light in the house. In contrast, the mother withdraws from the world and from her maternal role.

The grandmother's activities function as forms of self-expression that augment the possibility of the maternal. For Giorgio, "Ramondino's writing finds both its origin and its destination in the maternal: it proceeds from women, [and] reproduces subversive female discourse in *mise en abime*" (Giorgio 137). The structure of Ramondino's text repeats the motifs of continuity, conjunction, and connection as the daughter journeys from grandmother (first page) to mother (final page). Yet the overwhelming sense of continuity is located in terms of the grandmother-granddaughter link. This link is heightened in the light of Ramondino's admission that her grandmother provided the impetus to write *Althénopis* when, in a dream, she commanded Fabrizia to write (Ramondino, "In *Althénopis* ci sono" 4).

Eva Cherniavsky prefaces her consideration of motherhood in nineteenth-century America with the following questions: "If postmodernism signifies the end of origin stories is motherhood a residually modern phenomenon? Do we (should we) imagine, with Julia Kristeva, that the mother is the strange fold that changes culture into nature, the speaking into biology? How do we (con)figure a non-original motherhood?" (Cherniavsky viii). I would suggest that to deny origin in maternal narratives reiterates the same loss for women that a denial of the maternal body and maternal activity instigates. My question, then, would be: How do we (re)figure an original motherhood? How do we articulate and perform a motherhood that includes culture *and* nature and that includes speaking *and* biology?

Origin, for many feminist critics, recoups, invigorates and expands our notion of the maternal. For others, it continues to situate the mother as voiceless object despite the good

otherwise. The splendour of the laden table stands in for her disappearance, a sump that is she that is empty of her. And if she leaves if she continues to leave tentacles of blood and milk answer you. How can this be? The real mother the tensile mother reaches from inertia to movement from cave to cellar from oblivion to memory. Sometimes the heavy table is the toll of suffocation: in you I suffocate myself in me you suffocate. Sometimes the heavenly table is the

intentions of the feminist thinker. Many critics argue that in order to reclaim the missing mother, the mother sacrificed at the origins of culture (Irigaray), women need to think back, or write back through their mothers (Virginia Woolf), and to look at the past with fresh eyes, in an act of revision that is an act of survival (Adrienne Rich). The Milan Women's Bookstore Collective coined the phrase "a genealogy of women" to stimulate and maintain a continuum of women's discourse; the multivalent phrase not only makes reference to a reclamation process, to the need to bring to the surface the buried voices of women, the lost novels, the poetry, the autobiographies and the diaries, but to refigure a practice of everyday relations among women in terms of connections and exchange (Milan Women's Bookstore Collective 25). In *Althénopis*, the importance of a female heritage is reflected in the narrator's family, a family that between mother and grandmother contains numerous female figures. The narrator considers the women from her past, the aunts and the cousins, the mother and the grandmother, in order to reconsider her own subjectivity, tentatively speculating the maternal as she tentatively speculates herself.

Testing the potential overlap of nature and culture can lead the critic to an oft-used trope in women's theory and literature; the trope of fluids. Paola Masi proposes "fluids" as an innovative trope through which women represent themselves, but some feminist critics would argue that with the link between fluids and female body so strong the trope serves to reduce rather expand feminine possibilities (Masi 15-17). Dependent upon Irigaray's *This Sex is not One*, Masi explores the metonymical motivation of fluids; fluids enjoy the possibility of conjunction and proximity whereas solids favour the possibility of substitution and association. Irigaray contends that fluids carry connotations of nearness rather than distance, touch rather than regard, softness rather than hardness.[18] She explores the female body and its fluids (blood, milk) and the female body and her words (fluent, fluctuating). She locates a sameness that finds its context or pretext in the preoedipal relationship. Fluids thus signify movement and regeneration, connection and passage, fertility and changeability.

tophus that absorbs a re-conception of the mother over and again. Against ice. Against paralysis. From what we have we will be reborn over and again still remaining alive.

Le cene What is she thinking in her deserted kitchen I ask myself. Eating her simple broccoli with oil and salt and lemon, gone the crust of fat the familiar fry-up of oil and garlic. Transparent skin yes but still I cannot grasp her inner

Fluids can provide access to maternal origins in Irigaray's analysis; milk, blood, and water recall the preoedipal condition of attachment, of lack of separation between self and (m)other. In *Althénopis,* however, fluids are a source of both connection and separation, of attachment and disengagement.[19] When the young daughter discovers "nel gabinetto grandi bacilli pieni di panni e acqua rossa, coperti da una tavoletta," she could not decipher the connection between such findings and her mother's body, "asettico e fragile"; she smelt, too, the blood "come una memoria sbiadita, sulle gonne della nonna" (8).[20] Blood, in this context, alienates the daughter, distances her from the adult female body, allows no connection between the mother's menstrual blood and her own future as a woman. In direct contrast, the daughter finds a direct line of continuity when she herself bleeds in adulthood: standing over the greasy sink, over the grey malodorous water, she discovers that she is on her way "interpretare il mistero della resurrezione dei morti, ché tra i vapori, le acredini e i sudori della cucina vedevo comparire le sembianze della nonna, di cui in quel mestruato inizio di adolescenza con piú forza avvertivo la mancanza" (177).[21] Blood is now a life-line for the daughter, but on this occasion, connection is made with the surrogate mother, the grandmother.

In the final part of *Althénopis*, I find that Ramondino, in her representation of a mother-daughter kinesis, refigures the maternal, the mother, and the act of mothering. The movement that we witness, where the one impels the other, in a dynamic interplay of position, denies a stable function, as daughter or mother, as woman or girl, as complete as incomplete, as knowable as unknowable. The daughter is surrogate mother: "La Madre sino allora aveva portato la Figlia nel suo ventre, da allora la Figlia cominciò a portare la Madre sulle spalle" (234); just as the mother is surrogate daughter: "La bambina scomposta, dai gesti frali e tremanti, dalle incerte risatine, dal latte già oscurato al

Her world kept back and apart and away like the larder that is almost and otherwise empty of food all I will see all I will find are the disconcerting flecks of mould. These bruised smudges of blue and green lead me famelic to the bent figure. What does she do all day I ask myself? The bride and the bride-mother drained of past rituals, not the rituals of feast days or Sunday, for she the non-believer, but the ritual, for example, of a darkened room and a vinegar-

mistero del sangue, nasceva senza trine dal grembo della Madre morente e balbettava sul ventre di vecchia donna in disfacimento." (261).[22] The little girl, ambiguously, cited, may refer to the mother, herself still daughter, still little girl; or the daughter, experiencing a rebirth, a return to herself as newly born; or the baby that the daughter will give birth to, a symbolic daughter prefiguring those who will follow. In *Althénopis*, the figures of the daughter, mother, and grandmother break into pieces as much as they forge connection and continuity; the narrator's representation of each figure is provisional, a personal account that allows the recognition of the maternal, the mother, as relational but separate, as experienced but imagined, as spoken but not-speaking.

The uncanny mother

When Barbara Creed tells us that "the notion common to all aspects of the uncanny is that of origins," we can, in taking Freud's lead, consider "origins" in terms of both the mother and home (Creed 54). This approach to origins, through an uncanny approach to home-doubling-as-the-mother, and the mother-doubling-as-home, ties us to the maternal body, a maternal paradox that is desirable but terrifying, partial, fragmentary, and incomplete. Hélène Cixous asks, "[w]hy is it that the maternal landscape, the *heimisch*, and the familiar become so disquieting?" (Cixous 544-545). First, I want to respond to Cixous' query, and then, as a way of addressing my initial question provide another reading of the mother and of home, a reading that I will filter through the uncanny, a reading that will transform and transgress the unfortunate habit of representing the uncanny mother as monster or monstrous. *How can we represent the mother as a form of writing home, or the home as a form of writing the mother, in a way that will include body and experience but that will resist essentialisation?* In re-writing a version of the uncanny, I will focus upon the final section of *Althénopis*.

Cixous proposes that Freud's text is "a commentary on uncertainty," and that "[n]othing turns out less reassuring for the reader than this niggling, cautious, yet wily and interminable pursuit (of 'something' – be it a domain, an emotional movement, a concept,

soaked rag, entombed in a book as if to save herself from death. Diaphanous arms they once sought to preserve peaches apricots aubergines and tomatoes for the famish winter. Diaphane heart tremulous heart that once ate to her immensurable joy the beauty of dawn and storms and lightning and the manducable spikes of sunlight that recast her youthful body awry. The real mother hidden inside the phantom mother underfed and neglected she is

impossible to determine yet variable in its form, intensity, quality and content)" (525). Thus, to follow the labyrinth-like paths, the entanglements, the hesitations, the ebb and flow of meaning, is to witness the uncanny in Freud's text itself. The uncanny, Freud will tell us, is definitely "related to what is frightening – to what arouses dread and horror" (Freud 339); "the uncanny is that class of the frightening that leads back to what is known of old and long familiar" (340). When he scrutinises the entry on "*heimlich*" in Daniel Sander's *Wörterbuch der deutschen Sprache*, he discovers a capricious word, a word that, in its variance of meaning, exhibits its opposite: *heimlich* in the first signification means "belonging to the house, not strange, familiar, tame, friendly" (342), and in the second signification means "concealed, kept from sight, so that others do not get to know of or about it, withheld from others" (344). Lifting Schelling's definition from the entry, Freud appeals to this coincidence of meaning as the uncanny's point of procedure, extricating the "un" to explicate the disquieting strangeness: "everything that is *unheimlich* ought to have remained secret and hidden but has come to the light" (345).

Freud, in his ebb and flow, moving closer to his uncanny, extending *das Heimliche* (homely) into *das Unheimliche* (unhomely), proposes that "this uncanny is nothing new or alien, but something which is familiar and old-established in the mind and which has become alienated from it only through the process of repression" (363-64). Shortly later, Freud offers a "joking saying," a saying that repeats, in some kind of hidden and uncanny way, the idea that the female body, in particular the female genitals, is the site (or sight) of the uncanny: "[l]ove is home-sickness" (368).

Freud leads us to that class of the frightening which in turn leads us to that which is old and unfamiliar; for a number of feminist critics that journey, which is a journey towards origins, is a journey towards the mother. Nonetheless, Freud's employment of the mother, and in particular her genitalia, is problematic. Maria Aline Seabra Ferreira underlines part of Freud's maternal paradox: "Having expelled the figure of Woman/(M)other from 'The Uncanny,' Freud unwittingly calls all the more attention to it" (Ferreira 474). For Ferreira, Freud's reference to the maternal body performs the version of the uncanny that lies at the heart of his text; thus, the maternal body is something that is both secretly familiar and repressed.

stripped of maternal gestures fed by past uncertainty full of years divided before the promise of death, dead frozen before her broken waters. I would hold her stiff and close.

Gli svaghi The real mother had saved her love of science and numbers for a rainy day or a later day but the day simply filled to the brim with regret and loss. Even the love of French and the books to be read in French slipped through

Having outlined Freud's engagement with the uncanny, an engagement that proceeds at the expense of women, that depends upon an erasure of a woman's point of view, I will now pose some difficult questions: What happens when a woman experiences the uncanny moment, when she herself is led back to that which once was familiar, when she is led to examine and face her origins, when she herself begins to face the mother? Does she face the monster? Does she face a monstrous aspect of herself, a hidden aspect that once repressed, has unexpectedly come to light? We could say that the mother conceals herself and reveals herself, that she is familiar, unfamiliar, home, not-home. We could become caught up in a trap of binary oppositions that limit and disable the object of our study, but I want to retain that sense of kinesis, a movement that will allow the monstrous to vanish. By keeping kinesis at the heart of mother-daughter relations, at the heart of the particular approach I am making, at my approach through the uncanny, I need to consider a cluster of terms that will exist in a state of flux: familiarity, unfamiliarity, recognition, misrecognition, repetition, sameness and difference.

In *Althénopis*, the daughter returns home: "Lei, la Figlia ritornata. Con ossa cresciute dalla placenta, dal latte, dalle cure, e occhi non strabici, né volto tumefatto, né con sei dita, né col morbo blu, né con postumi di febbri meningee, tutta invece una macchina umana buona che si era messa a funzionare per proprio conto" (233).[23] The daughter, in describing herself, signals a shadow image, a phantom body, the dying body of the mother, laced with the memory of milk, laced with trace of placenta. Thus, we recall the old and familiar. Yet, at the doorstep, at the moment the returning daughter encounters her mother, they each remain a secret, as though they are returning us to Freud's uncanny, as though he is trespassing upon Ramondino's narrative: "Ormai non si parlava più con parole, la Figlia e la Madre, ma per segni. E i segni erano torbidi, un Logos maligno, escresciuto alla ragione, alla temperanza. La Madre parlò sulla porta di ingresso con un abbraccio

the debilitating cracks of time. Her thriftiness necessary and calculative went beyond epiphany's gift of exercise books and pencils and sweets to the abrasive amputation of her own pleasures. If French were the only culture for the past-time-mother now her bed, the simulative universe, percolated the cheap and garish thrillers, the infantile Settimana Enigmistica, this her percolated time bitter and riddled with natant echoes. Not just the honeyed youth nor the

fragile, come il penultimo cerchio nell'acqua fatto dalla pietra. Quante volte avevano giocato, e crudele era il gioco, circuiva le radici della vita" (234).[24] The mother withholds herself as the daughter withholds herself; the mother, the destination of the daughter, stands in veiled state, in unfamiliar state, undoing home to the point of not-home.

Shere Lite entitled an essay that considers 874 daughters' responses to questions about their mothers, "I hope I am Not Like My Mother" (Lite 13). Her title, echoing Rich's "matrophobia," leads us to the uncanny moment; now, the daughter casts her eye upon the mother's sameness, terrified to be like, the likeness the hidden secret, the sameness to be obliterated. Nonetheless, the uncanny moment is a moment of discovery, of daughter discovering mother, of mother discovering daughter; and in each other, then, there will be the recognition of a repeated gesture, a repeated trait, a repeated feature, a repeated word. This act of identification carries with it the threat of a loss of individuated identity, as mother and daughter, in some form of symbiotic relation, become subsumed, the one with the other, the one by the other.

The legacy of patriarchy is inscribed in a chain of "repetition"; and repetition itself becomes a key to the uncanny mother as home. Hirsch, in her examination of the mother-daughter plot turns to Tzvetan Todorov, by way of Peter Brooks, to provide an entry point into the term: *repetition* "relates to what Todorov speaks of as the basic constitution of plot out of tension between two formal categories: difference and resemblance or the 'same-but-different'"[25] (Hirsch, *Mother/Daughter Plot* 117). Repetition, in the light of the mother-daughter relationship, produces the uncanny recognition of sameness, a sameness that in being different will exemplify Todorov's "same-but-different" thesis. Nonetheless, Hirsch turns to the examples of Woolf and Colette, two writers who abandon repetition in favour of contradiction and oscillation as alternative (alternate) strategies to think back through their mothers (Hirsch, *Mother/Daughter Plot* 118). In Hirsch's argument, repetition will exist in conjunction with and, in opposition to contradiction and a movement of toing-and-froing.

diluted strength nor her history of sacrifice and tight economies, but a descent into a gabardine dark. The quarantined thoughts sealed after finding her self on her own. The real mother worn by the pages of her children's lives is getting to her children's future in solitude, covered in a shortness of miracles. Now the amusement in day-dreaming, now the diversion from the frangible, echoy rooms. In this mother another mother in this mother another mother in that mother

Ramondino's final pages, the pages where the sorrowing relations gather around the maternal deathbed, where "[l]a bambina che era stata sua madre rinasceva negli ultimi giorni della sua vita" becomes a form of overlap (261).[26] As I have already suggested, the identity of the "she" and "the mother" in the initial paragraph of the final section remains ambiguous. Furthermore, Ramondino extends the range of overlap to include the reader: "Ché ognuno di noi ha un altro se stesso sepolto, che attende, con coperte faville, il suo giorno"[27] (261). We, each of us, participate in a history of overlap: "La bambina scomposta, dai gesti frali e tremanti, dalle incerte risatine, dal latte già oscurato al mistero del sangue, nasceva senza trine dal grembo della Madre morente e balbettava sul ventre di vecchia donna in disfacimento. La bambina che era stata sua madre rinasceva negli ultimi giorni della sua vita. Ché ognuno di noi ha un altro se stesso sepolto, che attende, con coperte faville, il suo giorno" (261).[28]

Ramondino writes the mother and a version of her self as daughter-becoming-mother as she writes a version of home, and in writing her version of home, she resists subjugating or negating the mother figure(s). The mother, sought-after and longed-for, is glimpsed, distanced, fragmented throughout much of the text, but there, in the final pages, the pages where we meet the uncanny, the mother refuses the deathly enclosures of male-biased narratives. Now, at the end of the book, the faltering mother is body, she is female genitalia; we could, taking Freud's cue, apprehend the sight as monstrous, as the lost continent, as the gateway to home (the womb) (the vagina), as the uncanny reappearance of the mother as terrifying origin. Such identifications and apprehensions of the mother still persist in male-bound theory.

I want to return to Ramondino's closing maternal image, move away from a preoccupation with the mother monster, and progress beyond Rich's proposal that "in a

another in that mother whom? Who will account for the fulmineous woman? Thunder and lightning be damned when she sits so still and frozen.

Die mit Tränen säen, werden mit Freude ernten And then in death in the week of dying the other the one in pieces there in the mother dishevelled and trembling la bambina is born again a little girl. Even now close to the end a gesture set free, glimmerous in flight, I am drawn to the frail voice, a tindery

desperate attempt to know where mother ends and daughter begins, we perform radical surgery" (Rich 236). I want to return to the figure of the uncanny mother. The mother, revealing her genitals in public to her sorrowing relations, touches herself, touches her sex: "Senza pudore, con insistenza, nei primi giorni si toccava il pube. Cercavano di distrarla prendendole la mano le cugine piú vecchie, con la voce a lei rivolta nell'infanzia, quando ancora i cinque-dieci anni di differenza contavano, le ripetevano come una nenia: 'Non si fa, non si fa,' e lei con quella voce balbettante, come tagliata con le forbici, rispondeva: 'Sono una bambina, sono una bambina'" (264).[29]

The uncanny mother in this moment is represented, in part, as body, a body that overlaps, that recalls daughter, that overlaps little girl, baby, lover, wife, mother, reader, freedom, binding, baby, desire, desiring self, self-awareness, almost-grandmother. For the daughter facing the sight of the mother touching her genitalia, the gesture signals a moment of recognition, where the horror is not horror; where the reaction is rather astonishment, or dismay, or affiliation, or ambivalence, or difference-in-sameness. The daughter contemplates her mother as her mother contemplates herself. She, too, prefiguring the uncanny, as the buried parts, the repressed parts, resurface to be utterly familiar, slightly strange, to be more than mother but still mother. When she speaks, citing the arrival of the buried part, the woman resembles herself, and in resembling herself, speaks for herself: "Quel gesto, che per tanti anni era rimasto sepolto, venne ad adagiarsi su quel grembo, a reclamare i suoi diritti e a dichiararli, a separarsi dal vecchio corpo morente per entrare nell'anima di chi lo intese, togliere il divieto e fecondarla, affinché vedessero la luce altri nati di donna" (264).[30]

Ramondino's final paragraph, representing the hand of the mother giving birth to herself, is, as Maria Marotti proposes, a liberation of desire and an expression of sexuality, trail that will set alight a flight of fertile signs. If she is now born again as her own mother as mother to herself she the real mother splintered and phantomy, ventriloqous and auxiliary, she becomes both past and future in her present condition of dying. To touch one's sex at the point of death, to measure who one is by the finger of pleasure is to recognise and repeat the human gift of continuity. These are the pages of dying I read again and again never enough

but it is more than that (Marotti 81). The gesture is opening out on the final page in order that we bear to look, so that we may bear to comprehend, so that in repeating ourselves we recognise ourselves. For women to write their mothers is, in some ways, to write a form of home. If we can claim that home is as much people as it is place, if home is as much origin as it is future, if home will be a situation or domain or feeling or idea to comprehend with astonishment, or dismay, or affiliation, or ambivalence, or difference-in-sameness, then home can be the possibility of, a version of, the mother. Writing a form of home and writing a form of mother can at some point, not forever and not always, coincide; and this coincidence can enable us to recognise the liberation of kinesis, a movement that connects, disconnects, contradicts, avows, disavows the maternal. Writing the mother is 'to lift the ban' – to transgress the monstrous, to find a voice with which to speak. Writing the mother is to make her fertile – to write and speak and think the mother in myriad forms, directions, and possibilities. Writing the mother is so that "vedessero la luce altri nati di donna" (262).[31] Writing is to become human.

still not finished with these melliloquent words sweet at the moment of grief her grief my grief the thought of the skeletal mother bereft of honeyed embrace, inducible love indurate love, withstanding the inexpressible heat and chill that tied this hand to that hand, this heart to that heart, this mouth to that mouth, this word to that to word. In the guts of this simmering lamentation the sentences breathe familiar air down my nerve-struck spine the thickening sentences deliver a resilient hymn or ode or lyric to maternal symmetry.

Notes

1. The principle source for this poetic banner is the final part of *Althénopis*, "Bestelle dein Haus" (Set Thy House in Order). I borrowed each section heading to produce a text that reflects (upon) Ramondino's novel, my theoretical considerations, and in a longer version (that will appear in my doctoral thesis) autobiographical traces. My volume of poetry, *chrome*, also owes a great debt to Ramondino's novel.

2. Adalgisa Giorgio, proceeding from Nancy Chodorow's notion that mothering is a reproduction of oneself as daughter and woman, proposes that Ramondino's text works as an example of a daughter reconstructing herself in relation to her mother. (137)

3. "The supreme bond, though, was the basket from which the food was dispensed, and our great childish hunger, which was our mother's delight." (49) Note all translations of *Althénopis* are taken from 1988 version by Michael Sullivan.

4. See Giorgio's analysis of Ramondino's representation of separations and attachments. (142-46)

5. "when she came out on the street to cross the piazza, she seemed small again and defenceless as if in a world far removed from me, unreachable, as after some irreparable happening one dreams of the dead, and I wanted to run, to fly from the terrace to make sure of her solidity and bring her back from a world of shadow." (128)

6. "By now the Daughter and the Mother no longer spoke in words but in signs. And the signs were clouded, a malign Logos, uncontainable by reason, by moderation." (231-32)

7. "while my mother's hand disquieted instead. Cool and smelling of soap, it seemed always to wipe out 'nonsense,' to wash something away." (14)

8. "And then my mother, despite that blood, didn't have a body, she had gestures and above all she had 'things on her mind,' she had headaches." (14)

9. "on occasion she would come out." (45)

10. "I felt as if I had been deprived of those well-bred maternal rituals." (78)

11. see Giorgio, 142.

12. "[w]ith bones grown on placenta, on milk, on cures, and eyes without a squint." (231)

13. "the Mother's dumb love," (234); "to bear the Mother on her shoulders," (232); "[d]efeated she had come back to the Mother, almost as if to ask her the reason for living." (233)

14. "The Daughter discovered her destiny, but the Mother vanished." (234)

15. "a gesture, an amulet, a word of counsel;" "But to her who received it – straining forward from the start, now almost panting, in futile listening, or in failed embrace – it seemed a clear voice, admonitory, not faked, though grotesque and strange. Nor did the gesture seem like the flight of the dove which alights on the shoulder of the predestined, but rather the blind flight of the bat, zigzag but responsive to its promptings." (260-61)

16. "loved to cook but it was years since she had been mistress in her own house, and thus her urge led her to violate meal-times and the shopping budget." (21)

17. "Mother lying down in the dark with headache and a vinegar-soaked rag on her forehead, and Granny in sparkling form over the fritters and creamy pastries. And we dived into those gorgeous offerings, which dripped and smelled so good, which had neither beginning nor end, and which mocked at questions of expense and vitamin count." (23)

18. See "The 'Mechanics' of Fluids" and "When Our Lips Speak Together" in *This Sex Which is Not One* 106-18 and 205-18.

19. Sharon Wood considers the ubiquitous fluids in *Althénopis* in terms of "the female physical and sexual body." (245)

20. "large board-covered basins in the toilet full of cloths and red water;" "ascetic fragile;" "like a bleached-out memory, even on Grandmother's skirts." (14)

21. "interpreting the mystery of the resurrection of the dead, for in the vapours, the acrid smells, the sweat of the kitchen, I saw the semblance of Grandmother appear, whose absence I was then feeling more, for I was at the onset of adolescence and menstruation was coming on." (178)

22. "Up till then the Mother had carried the Daughter in her womb, from then on the Daughter began to bear the Mother on her shoulders" (232); "The restless little girl of the frail and tremulous movements, of the faltering giggles, of the milk darkened already by the mystery of the blood, was born without frills from the womb of the dying Mother and prattled in the lap of an old woman falling apart." (258)

23. "She, the returned Daughter. With bones grown on placenta, on milk, on cures, and eyes without a squint, nor swollen heart, nor the hangover of meningitis, but altogether a human machine in good condition, which had begun to operate on its own account." (231)

24. "By now the Daughter and the Mother no longer spoke in words but in signs. And the signs were clouded, a malign Logos, uncontainable by reason, by moderation. The Mother spoke at the front door with a hug fragile as the last ring made in the water by a stone. How often they had played, and the game was cruel, squeezing the roots of life." (231-32)

25. See Todorov 233.

26. "The little girl who had been her mother was born again in the last days of her life." (258)

27. "For each of us has another buried self which awaits its day with blanketed spark." (258)

28. "The restless little girl of the frail and tremulous movements, of the faltering giggles, of the milk darkened already by the mystery of blood, was born without frills from the womb of the dying Mother and prattled in the lap of the old woman falling apart. The little girl who had been her mother was born again in the last days of her life. For each of us has another buried self which awaits its day with blanketed spark." (258)

29. "Without shame, insistently, in the first days she touched her sex. The older female cousins tried to distract her by taking hold of her hand and chanting over and over in the tone they had used in childhood, when the five or ten years difference counts: 'You don't do that, you don't do that,' and in that voice, faltering as if snipped by scissors, she replied; 'I'm a baby girl, I'm a baby girl.'" (261)

30. "That gesture which had remained buried for so many years alighted in her lap, to reclaim her rights and assert them, to peel away from the old dying body and enter the soul of her who grasped it, to lift the ban and make her fertile, that others born of woman might see the light." (261)

31. "others born of woman might see the light." (261)

Across Borders

Writing Outside the Borders: Personal Experience and History in the Works of Helga Schneider and Helena Janeczek

Maria Cristina Mauceri

An interesting phenomenon, which has already occurred in several other Western European countries, is taking place in Italy. There are a number of significant and successful authors, who are not native Italians but come from other European countries, and who write in Italian and publish with prestigious Italian publishers. These authors include Giorgio Pressburger and his late brother Nicola, Edith Bruck and Fleur Jaeggy. Recently this group of writers has expanded, with the arrival of more authors from central and eastern Europe who have chosen Italy as their literary motherland. These authors are different from traditional migrant writers in several ways: their works are not inspired by the experience of migration and they do not deal with themes linked to this phenomenon, such as the departure, the journey, the difficulty of being accepted in or of adapting to a new country, or nostalgia for the abandoned homeland. But they all call into question the traditional definition of Italian literature.

In this chapter, I will discuss the autobiographical works of Helga Schneider[1] and Helena Janeczek,[2] two writers who are interesting for two reasons: first, they left their native lands to move to Italy, and second, there are striking thematic affinities between some of their works, although their backgrounds, ages and experiences are very different. Both these writers emigrated because of the negative effects of Nazism and the Holocaust on their families, but these effects and their experiences were very different. In their autobiographical texts, Schneider in *Lasciami andare, madre* (2001) and Janeczek in *Lezioni di tenebra* (1997) contemplate very different consequences of the persecution of the Jewish people.[3]

I propose to examine the relationship between writing and expatriation from a formal and from a thematic point of view. I will deal with the choice of the language and genre. The language, which is not their mother tongue, allows the two writers to detach themselves from painful memories, while autobiography allows them to reflect upon their relationships with their mothers and their maternal heritages together with their decisions to abandon their mother countries. I will further investigate how the conflictual relationships of Schneider and Janeczek with their mothers is linked with their attitudes towards their mother countries, and also how this relationship is a key to understanding the authors' connections to the Holocaust. *Lasciami andare, madre* and *Lezioni di tenebra* are transnational texts, having been written in Italy and in Italian about events and people of other countries. I will therefore suggest ways in which they are related to other literatures, but as they were written for Italian readers, I will also relate them to contemporary Italian reality.

The lives of both authors were indirectly scarred by the Holocaust. Schneider is the daughter of a Nazi. As she describes first in *Il rogo di Berlino* (1995), the story of her "stolen" childhood in a Germany devastated by the war, and then in *Lasciami andare, madre*, her mother abandoned her and her brother, who was nineteen months older, in Berlin in 1941, in order to become first a political activist and later a guard at Sachsenhausen, Ravensbrück and Auschwitz. Schneider met her mother for the first time since the war in 1971, and discovered her involvement in the Holocaust.[4] As she revealed in an interview with Catherine Simon of *Le Monde*, she saw her again in 1998 because, after the success of the publication of her childhood memories, the Italian television corporation *RAI* decided to make a film about her life and insisted that she meet her mother. This encounter lasted only five minutes and left the writer very upset. When she received a letter from a friend of her mother informing her of the precarious health of the ninety-year old woman, she decided to meet her once again. *Lasciami andare, madre* was written in two weeks to try to deal with the shock of this tragic encounter.

Janeczek comes from a family of Polish Jews: her mother was deported to Auschwitz but survived the Holocaust. After the war, her parents settled in Germany, more by necessity than by choice. They would have preferred to migrate to the United States but they were denied visas because of the father's health. They never assimilated there; on the contrary, they maintained a suspicious and critical attitude towards the Germans and never allowed their daughter to develop any feelings of belonging in Germany or friendship with the people.

Both Schneider and Janeczek felt alienated from their countries of birth. Schneider's childhood and adolescence were sad and lonely. After her mother left, her father remarried, but the stepmother rejected Helga who, unable to cope with the loss of her real mother, became a difficult child. Schneider's sense of alienation increased when she discovered her mother's past. Janeczek's situation was different, because she never regarded Germany as her motherland; nor does Poland, her parents' country of origin, have any sentimental significance for her. She moved to Italy in order to escape the constant parental pressure to be different from the Germans. For these authors, writing is a symbolic return to their countries of origin and to the persons who gave birth to them. The need for this internal journey does not arise from any nostalgic desire to return to these countries, but from their personal need to come to terms with their pasts, their reasons for expatriation and their feelings of estrangement from their home-countries.

In both works the journey has real and metaphorical meanings. Luce Irigaray's suggestion that the mother-daughter relationship is "le continent noir par excellence" (14) is very pertinent to these two works, in which the daughters revisit their mothers and try to explore their mysterious pasts. In *Lasciami andare, madre*, Helga, the daughter, returns to Austria to meet her old mother and to find out whether she regrets her past. The narration in *Lezioni di tenebra* starts with a trip to Poland by Helena and her mother, whose main destination is Auschwitz. The title, *Lezioni di tenebra*, not only refers to *Leçons de Ténèbres*, a work by François Couperin, quoted in the epigraph of the book, but also hints at Joseph Conrad's *Heart of Darkness*, as the author revealed to me (Janeczek, personal interview). According to Janeczek, there is an analogy between the journey in her book and the journey into the African jungle described in Conrad's novel. *Lezioni di tenebra* is a journey into the heart of darkness, because she starts to explore her daily life and history and then makes a physical trip to Auschwitz, the centre of darkness and fear. By reliving her mother's journey into the abyss, Helena understands how Auschwitz branded her for life, and she also understands how her mother's experience affected her own upbringing.

The personal relationships of the writers with their mothers and their countries motivated them to write autobiographical texts. The mothers are the "pre-text for the daughter's autobiographical project" (Brodzki 245). Apropos of ethnic autobiographies, it has been remarked that these can be considered "a microcosm of larger political and sociocultural issues. They are no longer regarded as records of individual lives, but as a story of a life embedded in a particular history" (Seyhan 67). This remark applies to Schneider's and Janeczek's texts as well. *Lasciami andare, madre* chronicles the brief encounter of the writer with her mother in 1998 and includes memories of the past. Dialogues prevail over the narration, giving this text a strong theatrical character; it is not surprising that Lina Wertmuller described it as a family psychodrama. Indeed she is so enthusiastic about *Lasciami andare, madre* that she stages a theatrical adaptation in Rome in February 2004 (Manin 24). This psychodrama often turns into an inquisition, as Helga questions her mother about her involvement in the Holocaust.

As suggested by the word *lezioni* in the title, Janeczek's book is a *Bildungsroman*, in which the story of the development of the daughter interweaves with that of her mother. The *lezioni* refer not only to the teachings of the mother but also to the things that the mother learnt as a victim of the Nazi persecution. The structure of the book mirrors this intertwining, because the narration moves between the past of the two women. To the young Helena, her mother's teachings seem to come from a dark and hidden past that the woman is prepared to disclose to her daughter only during their trip to Poland. At the end, reflecting upon her relationship with her mother and on her own past, the protagonist comes to understand herself better.

In both texts the daughters are the narrators, but the mothers are the co-protagonists and perhaps even the antagonists. However as narrators, the daughters manage to retain a degree of autonomy, and the overwhelming power of the mothers is reduced because they appear in the texts in the third person. To understand what might have induced these two authors to write autobiographical texts, it is useful to recall Bloom's remarks on mother–daughter relationships in women's autobiographies. She argues that, in recreating and interpreting her childhood and maturing self, a daughter assumes functions that her own mother fulfilled. In her role of autobiographer, the daughter becomes her own mother and recreates her maternal parent as well. In this new literary relationship the daughter is the controlling adult. Bloom concludes with the statement that "the autobiographical act has added another major dimension to the ways in which mothers and their daughters get along in addition to those that constituted their actual lives together [...] it is certainly a reversal of power and dominance" (292).

The two works are mostly set in Germany, but they are written in Italian. When she moved to Italy, Schneider forgot German quickly, as if leaving her motherland coincided with forgetting her mother tongue. Janeczek has a more complicated relationship with language, because her real mother tongue ought to be Polish or Yiddish, but these languages were rarely spoken at home, and being born and brought up in Germany, the closest she has to a mother tongue is German. Nevertheless German is for her a language associated with sad memories of loneliness and pain. Speaking and writing in Italian is a kind of liberation, and a way to come to terms with the burden of descending from a Holocaust survivor, as she told me (Janeczek, personal interview). Both writers admitted to me that for them, Italian is a language with which they communicate and detach themselves from painful themes. As Zaccaria maintains, the use of a new language by expatriate writers is a form of defence, because by living in a culture far from the problems of the motherland and communicating in a language which does not remind one of one's past, one protects oneself and creates new ways of living which lead to a reorganisation of identity and writing, though they may also cause division and internal exile (58).

Abandoning one's language can be interpreted as abandoning one's identity, or at least a part of it, according to Christiana de Caldas Brito, a Brazilian expatriate writer and psychologist who lives in Italy and writes in Italian. She believes that language is not only a means of communication, but above all it defines one's identity (136). If we consider that the words motherland and mother tongue associate the mother with the native land and its culture (and even in German, where the native land is the *Vaterland*, the mother tongue is the *Muttersprache*), Schneider's decision to abandon both clearly manifests her wish to detach herself from a mother who was never present in her life, but whose memory haunts her.

Schneider and Janeczek write in Italy about events that took place in Austria and in Germany, and in Janeczek's case, in Poland too. Their situation as diasporic writers is mirrored in their texts. As they review their childhood, they also reflect on the history of their countries. Their decision to live outside their countries of origin, to detach themselves from their past identities, and to use a different language, can be interpreted as a criticism of the idea of deriving one's identity by being part of a place with strong and well-defined borders, as Sinopoli remarks (*Diaspora e migrazione intraeuropee* 176). For both writers, Italy has become a new literary and linguistic homeland; in Apter's words, "'narration' becomes a substitute of 'nation'" (90). In *Reflections on Exile*, Said remarked, apropos of the German philosopher Adorno, who was forced to flee during Nazism and wrote his autobiography, *Minima Moralia. Reflexionen aus dem beschädigten Leben*, in exile, "The only home truly available, though fragile and vulnerable, is in writing" (184). This applies to Schneider and Janeczek equally well.

As well as expatriating to Italy and choosing to write in Italian, Schneider and Janeczek share another common aspect: the mother-daughter conflict is the central feature of their works and their difficult relationships with the history of their countries of origin is mirrored in their difficult relationships with their mothers. The mother-daughter conflict is the starting point of the narration in *Lasciami andare, madre* and in *Lezioni di tenebra*, but private relationships and tragic historical events are tightly intertwined.

The reasons for the conflicts of the writers are different. Schneider has not yet come to terms with the fact that her mother abandoned her and became an accomplice of the Nazis, and she is even more upset when she reflects that her mother does not regret her past, even though she is old and close to death. The daughter perceives herself as her mother's first victim, and identifies with all her other victims: the children and women she helped to eliminate:

> "Non avevi pietà nemmeno per i bambini?" chiedo. … "E perché avrei dovuto averne?" ribatte prontamente. "Un bambino ebreo sarebbe diventato un adulto ebreo, e la Germania doveva liberarsi di quella razza odiosa, quante volte te lo devo ripetere?" Inspiro profondamente. "Ma tu eri madre," obietto "avevi due figli. Mentre i bambini venivano spinti nelle camere a gas, non pensavi mai a noi?" "E questo che c'entra?" "Voglio dire … non ti veniva mai in mente che se fossimo stati bambini ebrei ci sarebbe toccata la stessa sorte?"[5] (71)

Schneider deals with a personal issue, but at the same time she demystifies the mother as a symbol of love and self-sacrifice. The agitated dialogue between mother and daughter reveals that it was the mother's will for power that induced her to become a fanatic supporter of Nazism. It was this lust for power that made her prefer a public role in the party to a private role in her family. And even now she still wants power over her daughter, and continues to demand from her an undeserved love and respect.

In *Lezioni di tenebra*, the mother-daughter conflict seems to arise from the fairly normal tension between family members of different generations and with different personalities. However, the Holocaust affects this conflict. Janeczek reveals how this experience led to the authoritarian and sometimes violent upbringing that she underwent as her mother attempted to prepare her to face the perils of life. It is evident that Janeczek's mother's educational methods were a reaction to the terror she experienced at Auschwitz. Helena describes her upbringing as an *addestramento*, a "training," a term usually applied to military life rather than to the family:

> I genitori sanno che i figli sbagliano, e che bisogna educarli a non sbagliare. Ma certi, credo, sanno che dagli errori si impara [...] Mia madre invece sa che se commetti un errore, puoi essere spacciata. Per questo non deve solo educare sua figlia a non sbagliare deve impedire che sbagli [...] Per questo mia madre non educa, ma addestra. L'addestramento si differenzia dall'educazione perché cerca di trasformare ciò che insegna in riflesso ... Nell'addestrare è contemplato l'uso della violenza come metodo e come sanzione, e mia madre infatti urlava.
> [6] (52–53)

Helena's mother tries to suppress her daughter's will and normal desire to be different, in order to improve Helena's chances of surviving in extreme and extraordinary situations. The daughter sees herself in the role of a victim of her violent mother, although she understands that this verbal violence is a consequence of misdirected love.

Schneider's work reveals the falsehood underlying the Nazi myth of motherhood, while Janeczek shows how the Holocaust can impinge on the mother-daughter relationship. Both works point out how private life and historical events cannot be separated. However, there is a difference between the two writers: Nazism separated Schneider from her mother forever, whereas the understanding of her mother's tragic experiences draws Janeczek closer to her.

The interpersonal conflicts also arise because the daughters are frightened of being mirror images of their mothers, physically and psychologically. In *The Mother/Daughter Plot*, Marianne Hirsch suggests that the image of the mirror emphasises the mutual dependency between mothers and daughters (21). In *Lasciami andare, madre*, Helga is regretful when her mother remarks on their physical resemblance, but she is even more concerned that the resemblance might be psychological as well:

> "Non hai niente di tuo padre, somigli tutta a me." Ha ragione penso con rammarico. Avrei tanto voluto somigliare a mio padre, e invece è stato mio fratello a ereditarne le fattezze, mentre io sono il ritratto di mia madre.[7] (90)

> Mi folgora un pensiero. Che in me, nei miei geni, ci sia qualcosa di questa donna. Provo repulsione, disgusto, ma già lei reclama la mia attenzione.[8] (115)

Schneider's feelings of not having an autonomous identity, but of being a *Doppelgänger* of her mother, have been clearly described by Dan Bar-On, author of the first socio-psychological study of the children of the Nazis, who noticed that some of them are frightened that they may have inherited their parents' "bad seed" (330).

In *Lezioni di tenebra*, Helena reflects how her own character shows the effects of the Nazi persecution of her mother. For example, she sometimes has violent desires for a piece of bread, and as a child she was afraid of being chased and murdered. But Helena admits that as she grows up she comes to understand that the person whom she really fears is the one who transmitted all these anxieties to her: her mother, who sometimes (perhaps unintentionally) adopts the tones and attitudes of her past persecutors:

> "Più tardi ... ho avuto tanta paura solo di lei ... Paura dei suoi interrogatori, delle domande, del suo controllo su di me. E poi degli urli, delle parole che mi gettava in faccia, del suo verdetto di condanna."[9] (110)

The words *interrogatori, controllo, urla* and *verdetto di condanna* all remind us more of a Jew being persecuted in a concentration camp than of a daughter being reproached by her authoritarian mother. It is as if Helena's mother had introjected a certain model of behaviour and made it her own, even though her intention is not to persecute her daughter, but to protect her from future perils.

In *Lezioni di tenebra* and *Lasciami andare, madre*, the two authors attempt to come to terms with their past experiences: they both feel that they are their mothers' victims, and that they are still at the mercy of the power exercised by their mothers. Nevertheless, there are moments when the roles of mothers and daughters are reversed, but with differences that depend on the pasts of the mothers. This reversal of roles reminds us of Adrienne Rich's comment that "We are, none of us, 'either' mothers or daughters; to our amazement, confusion and greater complexity, we are both" (253).

The daughter in *Lasciami andare, madre* meets her mother with the intention of closing a chapter of her life. When she does not reach an understanding with her mother, she feels the urgent and wicked wish to interrogate her, and sets up her own personal Nuremberg trial. She hopes that by listening to her mother talking about the monstrosities perpetrated by her, she will find the courage to sever the family ties forever. But in the end she is not able to sever these ties because she is torn between the natural tenderness of a daughter towards her old mother and her moral duty to detach herself from a criminal who was involved in the Holocaust:

> Ti guardo, madre, e provo un dissidio terribile, lacerante: l'istintiva attrazione per il mio stesso sangue e l'irrevocabile rifiuto per ciò che sei stata – per ciò che ancora sei.[10] (70)

> Il mio pensiero corre ancora una volta alle vittime, alle tante storie che conosco, che ho letto o che mi sono state raccontate. Penso, anche, madre, che solo odiandoti sarei finalmente capace di strapparmi dalle tue radici. Ma non posso. Non ci riesco.[11] (73)

> Provo angoscia e una irrazionale tenerezza. È mia madre, nonostante tutto è mia madre. Devo vergognarmi se qualche volta l'istinto, il mio istinto di figlia, prevale sulle ragioni della morale, della storia, della giustizia e dell'umanità?[12] (126)

It seems difficult for the daughter to hate the frail old woman, even though she still tries to appear strong and powerful, because the biological impulse of procreation is stronger than the crimes the mother committed (Golino 135).

In *Lezione di tenebra*, in Warsaw and Auschwitz, Helena adopts a protective role towards her mother, who cries because she feels guilty of having once abandoned her own mother in the ghetto, who was then deported and murdered in Auschwitz. It is as if the daughter had to play a mother's role:

> ... accarezzandola come una bambina cui è successa una tragedia, come aver perso una bambola o aver trovato morto qualche piccolo animale ... Poi si è messa a urlare "mamma, mamma" e io ho di nuovo cercato di calmare mia madre come una bambina che piange strillando "mamma, mamma," ma non è servito ...[13] (15)

The themes of abandonment and roots are connected. After considering the case of the daughter in *Lasciami andare, madre*, the reader comes to the conclusion that it is not enough to leave one's country and forget one's mother tongue to sever one's roots. An invisible umbilical cord seems to bind Helga to her mother, whom she still misses, in spite of all her crimes. The trauma of having been abandoned by her mother still oppresses Schneider, and remains a source of inspiration for her writing. While not all her are autobiographical, all are set during the Nazi period.

Helena too chooses to leave Germany and to detach herself from her excessively threatening and intrusive mother. In the end she finds a solution to her uprooting by accepting that she belongs to more than one country, an experience she shares with many other people in this period of mass migration. In *Lezioni di tenebra* she remarks that her multiple belonging is mirrored in the mobile identity of her family: "Nella nostra famiglia i nomi [of the people] hanno una natura mobile" (70) ("In our family, names change"). In fact Janeczek is not the real surname of her father, but the one he adopted to escape persecution. The multiple belonging of the author's family is also mirrored in their choice of language, which varies according to circumstances and the moods of the speakers:

> "Litighiamo in tedesco quando siamo in Italia e al telefono, io a Milano, lei a Monaco, ragion per cui io tendo a cadere nell'italiano che ora viene più spontaneo a me ..."[14] (72)

And discussing the language used for the names she calls her mother, Helena declares:

> Più le voglio bene, più aumentano i suoi nomi e le lingue dei suoi nomi. Così diventa mamma e mammina, mame e mamele, e ai confini fra lo yiddish e il polacco maminka e mameshi, mameshi kroin "mamma corona," ma è la prima volta che ne traduco il senso, e poi matka, matusia, matuska, mamusia, mamuniu.

Se c'è pace, non dico più né Mamma, né Mammi con due emme, mentre l'altro modo dei bambini di dire mamma in tedesco, "Mutti," non l'ho mai usato ... Lei invece, se è proprio arrabbiatissima o deve impartire un ordine, talvolta parla di sé come "deine Mutter," "tua madre," alla stessa stregua in cui io per lei divento "meine Tochter." Se mi vengono i nomi italiani o più ancora quelli in yiddisch e in polacco, vuole dire che è un momento veramente buono, non capita cosí spesso.[15] (73)

Janeczek recognises that her knowledge of her supposed mother tongue, Polish, is mostly passive and that for people who did not go through her experiences it is difficult to understand her situation, which is quite similar to that of many children of migrants:

"Io non lo so, il polacco, ma se è facile riesco a capirlo e se è ancora più semplice, ridotto a singole parole o frasi fatte, lo parlo anche, lo parlo quasi tutti i giorni. Sono convinta di avere una lingua madre che non conosco, ma vallo a spiegare a qualcuno."[16] (76)

But reading the following, one arrives readily at the conclusion that Janeczek has come to terms with the existential situation of her displacement:

Non trovo che sia importante (e buono) conservare le radici e il passato, penso anzi che sia impossibile, quello che è importante è l'essere consapevoli di avere un groviglio di appartenenza e non appartenenza, perché fa parte della costituzione di qualsiasi individuo.[17] (Bregola 132)

Lezioni di tenebra and *Lasciami andare, madre* are transnational texts that call into question the traditional Italian literary canon. From a thematic point of view, they belong to the intergenerational Holocaust literature, which started in the United States in 1979 with Helen Epstein's book *Children of the Holocaust*. In the 1980s, the first memoirs of the children of the perpetrators of the Holocaust were published. In 2001, the American psychologists Alan and Naomi Berger edited the first anthology that brought together the memories of the children of the victims and of the persecutors. The Bergers indicate interesting similarities and differences between the two groups (8–11). Both feel the need to define their relationship with their parents and to understand the impact of their parents' involvement in the Holocaust. The two works discussed in this article reflect their authors' wish to face this problem in their relationship with their mothers. It is significant that Schneider feels guilty about her mother's behaviour and takes on the task of bearing witness against the Nazi crimes in her writing. On the contrary, *Lezioni di tenebra* illustrates how many children of survivors want to connect with their parents' pasts, in order to understand them and themselves better, because they are often born and brought up far away from their parents' countries. Because of the pivotal role of the mother-daughter conflict, these texts also belong to a specific thematic stream of German feminist literature, exemplified in the studies of Katharina Aull and Renate Dernedde, which began in the late 1970s as a consequence of the interest of scholars in the function of the mother-daughter relationship in shaping the daughters' identity.

What is the relationship between these works, which were written for an Italian audience, and contemporary Italian reality? Before the official institution of *il giorno della memoria* in 1997, a number of books on the Holocaust were published in Italy. It is hardly a coincidence that Roberto Benigni's film *La vita è bella* was released in the same year that Janeczek's book was published.

The comparatively recent Italian interest in the Holocaust certainly influenced the reception of these two texts. Schneider hopes that both her books document the horrors of the past so effectively that they can be avoided in the future. She wants her readers, particularly the young ones, to become aware of Nazism and of the means that the Nazis employed to obtain popular consensus. This is particularly important nowadays, because neo-Nazi web sites are becoming more common and neo-fascist attitudes are being revived in Europe. Schneider's questioning of her mother reveals what induced her to follow the National Socialist ideology and where blind hatred of the other can lead.

Janeczek's book about multiple belongings and identities touches on an existential situation that is typical of our times. The Jewish diaspora is very old and the Jewish people are used to multiple belonging. However Helena, who lives in limbo because she is not allowed to take root in Germany, also seems to reflect the situation of many children of migrants who are not allowed to identify with the country where they are brought up. But there is an important difference, as Wajnryb remarks in *The Silence. How Tragedy Shapes Talk*: the children of migrants live between two countries, while those of Holocaust survivors have been deprived of their roots (130).

Lezioni di tenebra and *Lasciami andare, madre* are interesting examples of a new transnational literature. From a literary point of view, they open the borders of Italian literature, by linking it to intergenerational Holocaust literature and German literature. At the moment, works like these written in Italian by non-native authors do not belong to the mainstream of Italian literature, but they challenge the way in which this literature is considered. As Sinopoli remarks (*Poetiche della migrazione* 206), we should broaden the concept of Italian literature and consider it not a closed and monocultural system, but an open and transnational one, which includes the works of migrant writers who write in their adopted language, as has already happened elsewhere in Europe. Beside this, these texts face the relationship between autobiography and emigration from a historical and private perspective and link it with the figure of the mother. They confirm Melanie Klein's theory of artistic creation that the mother remains an important psychic presence throughout life, even motivating the production of art and culture (334). The autobiographical act becomes a way to exorcise this presence, by gaining control over their mothers, at least in their literary relationships. Furthermore, recalling the past gives the narratives of Schneider's and Janeczek's lives the continuity that expatriation had broken.

Finally, expatriation allowed Schneider and Janeczek to look at the histories of their countries of origin with the critical detachment that comes from being at a distance. Their autobiographical texts are important witnesses of the negative effects of Nazism on public and private lives. They describe the past, but they can be read as a warning for the present, because by denouncing anti-Semitism, they denounce the hatred for everyone who is 'different' as well.

Notes

1. Helga Schneider was born in Silesia into an Austrian family. Her early childhood was spent in Berlin and she returned to Austria after the war. Having married an Italian, she moved to Bologna in 1963, where she wrote for *Il resto del Carlino* and published her first book, *La bambola decapitata*, in 1993. In 1995, she wrote *Il rogo di Berlino*, at the suggestion of a journalist of *La Stampa*. The book, published by Adelphi, was a great success and in 1996 an edition for schools appeared. As a result, she is often invited to talk to students about her experiences and Nazism. She then wrote two works of fiction set during this period: *Porta di Brandeburgo. Storie berlinesi 1945–47* (1997) and *Il piccolo Adolfo non aveva le ciglia* (1998). *Lasciami andare, madre* was published in 2001 and has been translated into seven languages. The German edition (2003) sold out in a few days. Her latest book is a story for teenagers, *Stelle di cannella* (2002).

2. Helena Janeczek was born in Munich in 1964 to Polish Jewish parents who settled there after the war. She used to spend her summer holidays in Italy and learnt Italian as a child. In 1983 she moved to Milan to attend the University. In 1989 she published a volume of German poetry, *Ins freie*, with Suhrkamp. *Lezione di tenebra* (1997), her first book in Italian, was awarded the *Premio Giuseppe Berto* and the *Premio Bagutta*. Janeczek lives in Gallarate and is a contract reader of German books for Mondadori. In 2002 she published her second book, *Cibo*. The opening chapter of *Lezioni di tenebra* has been translated into English and published in Bukiet.

3. The following books are also accounts of the Holocaust written in Italian: *Chi ti ama di più* (1959) by the Hungarian Edith Bruck, and *Il silenzio dei vivi* (1997) by the Austrian Elisa Springer. These authors are from an older generation, and are not considered here.

4. This traumatic encounter is described at the beginning of *Il rogo di Berlino* and reappears in *Lasciami andare, madre*.

5. "'You didn't even feel sorry for the children?' I ask [...] "And why should I have felt sorry for them?" she answers promptly. "A Jewish child would have become a Jewish adult, and Germany had to get rid of that loathsome race; how many times do I have to tell you?" I inhale deeply. "But you were a mother," I protest, "You had two children. While those children were being pushed into the gas chambers, didn't you ever think of us?" "And what does that has to do with it?" "I mean [...] didn't you ever think that if we had been Jewish, the same would have happened us?"'

6. "Parents know that children make mistakes, and that they should be educated to avoid them. But some parents, I believe, know that one learns from mistakes [...] On the other hand, my mother knows that if you make a mistake, you can be ruined. So she must not only educate her daughter not to make mistakes, she must prevent her from making mistakes [...] For this reason my mother does not educate, but she trains. Training is different from education, because it tries to turn what it teaches into a reflex [...] In training, violence can be used as a method and as a punishment, and in fact my mother shouted"

7. "'You do not look like your father, you look very much like me." She is right, I think with regret. I would have preferred to resemble my father, but my brother inherited his features, while I am my mother's portrait."

8. "I am overwhelmed by the thought that something of this woman is in me, in my genes. I feel aversion and disgust, but she is already clamouring for my attention."

9. "Later [...] I was so afraid only of her [...] of her interrogations, of her questions, of her control over me. And then of her shouts, of the words she threw in my face, of her judgment."

10. "I look at you, mother, and I feel myself terribly and painfully divided: between my natural attraction to my family and my irrevocable refusal of what you were and you still are."

11. "Once again, I remember the victims, the many stories I know, that I have read or that were told to me. I think then, mother, that only by hating you can I finally manage to break away from you. But I can't. I am not able to."

12. "I feel anguish and an irrational tenderness. She is my mother, in spite of everything she is my mother. Should I feel ashamed if sometimes my instinct, my instinct as a daughter, prevails over the reason of morality, history, justice and humanity?"

13. "stroking her like a child who has just been involved in a tragedy, such as losing a doll or finding a small dead animal [...] Than she started shouting "Mummy, Mummy" and I again tried to calm her, as if she were a crying child, screaming "Mummy, Mummy." But I could not."

14. "We argue in German when we are in Italy or on the telephone, when she is in Munich and I am in Milan, so I tend to slip into Italian, which comes to me more spontaneously now"

15. "The more I love her, the more names I give her, and in more languages. So she becomes mamma and mammina, mame and mamele and, blending Yiddish and Polish, maminka and mameshi kroin "mother crown" (but it is the first time that I translate this), and then matka, matusia, matuska, mamusia, mumuniu.

When we are at peace, I do not call her Mamma, nor Mammi with two ems, and I never used the other word German children call their mothers, "Mutti" [...] On the other hand, when she is very upset with me or she must give me an order, she sometimes speaks of herself as "deine Mutter," "your mother," just as I become "meine Tochter" for her. When I call her an Italian name, or, even more so, a Yiddish or Polish name, it means that it is a good moment, it does not happen very often."

16. "I can't speak Polish, but if it is easy I can understand it, and when it is very simple, just single words or standard expressions, I speak it too, I speak it almost every day. I feel that I have a mother-tongue but I don't know what it is – try to explain that to someone."

17. "I don't think that it is important or useful to maintain one's roots in the past; I think that that is impossible. What matters is to be aware that one has a tangle of belongings and not belongings, because every individual is made that way."

Weaving Textual Tapestries: Weaving the 'Italian Woman-Writer' into the Social Fabric[1]

Maria Pallotta-Chiarolli

The pattern of the carpet is a surface. When we look closely, or when we become weavers, we learn of the tiny multiple threads unseen in the overall pattern, the knots on the underside of the carpet. (Adrienne Rich)

I lived many lives as a child in Australia

Whatever I saw was fractured into many pictures, multi-faceted and yet crystal clear

I grew up as part of a tapestry, rich with the colours of many realities, woven with the threads of many places, spaces and times, that existed alongside each other. (Pallotta-Chiarolli, *Tapestry* Preface)

A tapestry is a fabric in which multicoloured threads are interwoven to produce a pictorial design. The design of a tapestry often seems three-dimensional with layers of interwoven images of people and events from various times past and present. I use the tapestry as a motif or metaphor to describe the bordering and interweaving of my "multiple lifeworlds" (Cope & Kalantzis 8) as an Italian-Australian woman, academic, writer and social activist. Within and between each of these worlds are points of tension and confluence, questions and emotions that motivate my own research and writing, and motivate my work with young people to articulate their own 'multiple lifeworlds' through writing and art.

In this chapter, I will draw from my published books to explore my *mestizaje* or border-dwelling self (Anzaldua; Lugones; Molina) in relation to my autobiographical writing and the issues with which I engage. I will illustrate how who I am, my Italian-Australian woman self, frames and informs my work with culturally diverse young people in the articulation of their border existences. In other words, arising out of this academic/researcher/writer/ activist positioned as outside/inside/no-side both Italian and Australian identities, this chapter will explore the tensions and points of confluence between constructs of "social diversity" and "multiculturalism." It will discuss the interweaving between cultural diversity and other social justice issues such as gender diversity and sexual diversity that often remain silenced or denied beneath the surface of "official multiculturalism." This chapter will also explore the diversity and hierarchies within Italian-Australian identity and community; how my work grapples with the tangles and knots, and celebrates the design of multicoloured threads.

You will see that this chapter itself is a tapestry, taking you into my different worlds through the interweaving of theory, research and narrative.

The warp and the weft: the writer as weaver

Identities and community allegiances are not fixed and dichotomous, but rather fluid, transitory, fragmented, episodic. Because my life has been lived within, beyond, and underneath the simplistic surface of the carpets of 'Italian' and 'woman,' I want to explore other lives lived within, beyond and underneath the surfaces of many carpets. I want to pick at the multiple layers, threads, knots and tangles. I want to suture together supposedly conflicting and oppositional colours and textures.

In order to effectively convey this interweaving of lived experiences, I construct textual tapestries. My tools as a textual weaver include theory, research and narrative, each informing and augmenting the other. I am the theorist and the researched, as well as the narrator of my own autobiography and the biographies of family, friends and young people who have participated in my research-weaving. I stand both inside and outside my life and my work. The reader views the complexity of the pattern from multiple perspectives, including the multiple perspectives of the Italian-woman-researcher-author-narrator-research participant (see Brew).

As a mestiza-researcher-writer, or textual tapestry weaver, my own background is a pertinent factor that positions me alongside my research participants when voicing their experiences and perspectives. When I was five in 1965, I was thrown into a monocultural Australian working class urban school and drowned/cleansed in English. Much later, I was told in order to have some measure of credibility in academia, (my so-called "wog-chick look" was already problematic) I would have to learn academic language. I now bridge and border the three-dialect Italian, working class wog-English, academic-speak- sometimes comfortably, but they each only convey a part of the multiple. As a weaver-researcher-writer, my challenge is to interweave the words, the ways of communicating, and their worlds. I want to show that one is not only Italian, but a particular type of Italian, and one is also a particular version of a gender, and a particular version of a sexuality, and a resident of a particular geographical place, and of a specific age and level of education, and with a certain economic framework. This awareness of context and specificity is drawn from my own experiences and becomes a tool to explore and challenge the hierarchies and presumptions of the wider world.

She's always been what no-one quite expects. Wherever she's worked, Maria has never really known how to wear the uniform, how to speak, what cult behavior to adopt, what fundamentalist phrases to spout, who to insult. And it's either been attributed to her or excused in her for this thing they all seem to be able to define, confine, undermine called "Italianness."

First job teaching at a boys' high school and for a few weeks she hears things like, "You don't have to worry about attending that meeting tonight/ the staff do at the pub/ helping run the parent info nights because we know you won't be allowed to/you need a chaperone/ your Italian father/brother/boyfriend won't let you."

Or

"The headmaster doesn't really think women should wear short skirts/ no sleeves/ that much make-up/ long hair so wild but he's not really going to say anything much about it because you're Italian and that's what Italian women are like."

Or lecturing in Women's Studies at a uni, a colleague says, " I think some of the students don't quite feel comfortable with you because you wear skirts/ makeup/ long hair so wild but they're not really saying anything about it because you're Italian and that's what Italian women are like."

Should she swap uniforms, should she pull that hair back, wipe the make-up off, cover up in long black skirts and baggy pants[...]and then they'd only say she looks so much like a traditional Italian peasant woman.

The use of narrative descriptions and storytelling research methods to 'unsilence' and destabilise homogenizing labels and social hierarchies also have their beginnings in my Italian childhood. I come from a Southern Italian peasant family oral storytelling tradition as a way of teaching and discussing political and sensitive issues. In this tradition, the anecdote **is** the explanation. Indeed, this position is supported by ethnographic research methodology. Many ethnographers argue that there is no such thing as simple description or simple storying. Both the storyteller and the ethnographer must make decisions about what is important, guided by an analytical process based on implicit and explicit concepts, assumptions and theories (see Fitzgerald; Lincoln).

My Italian childhood has also made the issue of accessibility central to my work. I try to move beyond the dry and impoverished language of traditional academic writing as that writing is alien to the Italian migrant working class worlds I come from (see Hooks). As Altork states,

> We need to ask, first of all, whether we want to study a culture in a calculating, solely intellectual way, and then – when we turn to the task of bringing the culture to others – whether those whom we study would want to be represented in that way[...] Do we really have to avoid lyrical description, subjectivity, and the personal voice in order to hold our place in the line-up of respected social scientists? (Altork 129)

The mestizaje border-dwelling researcher-writer-weaver inhabits the factory and the academy, writes theory and engages in action. I want to work with my research participants to reconstruct their lives and knowledge into a text within which they are still able to see themselves. How do I reconstruct people's intimate details in ways that do not exploit nor appropriate? How do I write so that the 'written-about' can access the work, identify themselves, and collaborate with me in the portrayals of their realities? If I write about my mother migrating to Australia, or a Lebanese friend's bisexual Muslim realities, will they be able to see the journeys they make through my words even if they haven't stepped into a university, apart from cleaning its toilets and cooking in its cafeterias?

The outcome of a wide range of narrative research instrumentation is what Lionnet describes as "text as metissage." This is the weaving of "different strands of raw material and threads of various colours into one piece of fabric" which "free" the mestizaje researcher-writer "to enlarge, redefine, or explode the canons of our discursive practices" (Lionnet 213). The texts I produce are an interweaving of diverse textual threads: autobiography, fiction, narrative, participant observation, interview transcript. It is a deliberate patterning to textually represent the major themes of hybridity and metissage, the dynamic and powerful interplay of confluence and difference, a polyphony of voices as well as the polyphonic in one voice.

> In looking at this book [...] I see a mosaic pattern [...] Too, I see the barely contained color threatening to spill over the boundaries of the object it represents and into other 'objects' and over the borders of the frame. I see a hybridization of metaphor, different species of ideas popping up here, popping up there, full of variations and seeming contradictions. (Anzaldua 66-67)

Collage-like strategies of research and writing that endeavour to engage with collage-like lives many of us live as Italian-Australian women writers, allow for "contradiction, [...] difference, doubt, inconclusiveness and ambivalence," therefore articulating in text the experiences of mestizaje or border-dwelling (Brewster 90). As I have tried to do in *Tapestry,* and in the design of *Girls' Talk* and *Boys' Stuff,* Ely and others encourage experimentation with "different fonts, boldness or type size" to draw readers' attention to complex and multiple perspectives (Ely et al. 94). They also call for experimentation with layout techniques that disrupt linear representation such as the use of columns, juxtaposed text, textual layers and pastiche "to emphasize ambiguity and uncertainty" (Ely et al. 97). Significant suturing and scissoring strategies in *Tapestry* include the fragment form or use of vignettes, anecdotes and layered stories which may or may not be linked chronologically or systematically. The book has no neatly sliced chapters but rather demonstrates a thematic or symbolic coherence and pattern of plural connections, surfaces and directions. It "leaves the seams there, it makes a virtue of showing the gaps" (King, Miller & Muecke 9). It is a method well-suited to the evocation of mestizaje as "narrative, human inquiry and lived experience go hand in hand" (Goodfellow 184).

Thus, in summary, my role as mestiza-interweaver-researcher-writer is to search for different ways of describing the complexity, the multidimensionality, the organization and disorder, the uncertainty and incongruities of the social worlds that we and others inhabit. (Evans 245)

Walking the multiple-within: the writer as tour guide

I was born into a life of many worlds and communities in Australia, each with their own codes and expectations, that I had to learn to weave and mesh, untangle and knot, and I am still doing so with both joy and pain. *Tapestry* documents the processes of suturing and scissoring that have gone into the weaving of my multiple-within self. The whole journey back into my past – physically going to Italy, emotionally travelling back into the lives of the past generations in my family, and interweaving all this with the way I was raised in Australia – was important for me to make sense of why I think, live, love and act in the multiple and sometimes seemingly contradictory ways I do as a woman, as a feminist, as a straight queer activist, as a mother, as a daughter, as a lover, as a professional well-educated middle-class Italian-Australian. I needed to know who and where and how and why in my family history in order to answer those questions about myself and the legacy and questions, indeed, the tapestry, my daughter has inherited and into which she will undoubtedly interweave her own threads and colours. I needed to make sense of those tangles, those times of confusion and clarity, insecurity and exhilaration I have experienced, and still do experience, in Australia and experienced in Italy.

> I bind
> the threads
> create
> a coat
> of colours
> know
> at last
> who I am
> (Saunders 317)

As the writer-weaver of *Tapestry*, I become a tour guide, taking the reader on a 'walk' or journey into the world of metissage where many worlds and boundaries, assumptions and stereotypes, are problematised, negotiated and traversed (see Robb). The family history I grew up with and my own life's experiences often don't match the stereotypes and assumptions of an "Italian family" or an "Italian woman." Indeed, a publisher rejected the manuscript because, as the publisher's report stated, my family did not sound like a "real" or "true" Italian family. The report expressed doubts that an Italian family could NOT be homophobic. And why wasn't there more intergenerational conflict between my parents and myself? Also, the fathers in my manuscript didn't sound "convincing;" why didn't I write more about an Italian father's violence? So basically I was being told that in order to publish a biography about a 'real' Italian family, I had to rewrite or fictionalise the story of my real

Italian family to conform to an Anglocentric definition of a "real" Italian family. Needless to say, if I had agreed to these criteria in my desire to be published, I would've evoked the wrath of my real Italian family (and thereby actually met the criteria of conflict in an Italian family the publisher expected!) Finally, after several further rejections from publishers, most of them to do with the fact that they had "published their ethnic minority/migration book for the year," the manuscript was accepted by Mark McLeod from Random House for the very reasons it had previously been rejected- it challenged gendernormative and heteronormative assumptions and stereotypes about Italian families. This publisher wanted me to take the reader on a tour of the multiple realities under the stereotyped surface.

For example, Italians as devout Catholics is a dominant Anglocentric construction, especially in relation to Italian women. However, I have grown up with stories of women's resistances to the patriarchal injustices and power of the church. How can I submissively accept the dogmatic and destructive statements made by some Australian church leaders and the Vatican about young people, homosexuality, women's rights, contraception, and the 'real family' as married and heterosexual, when I come from a long line of men and women who faced and resisted socioeconomic and gendered oppression coming from the joint forces of church and state? Thus, my role as tour guide is to 'walk' readers through the realities of religious oppression and how it impacted upon my family.

Dora vows that when she gets to Australia she'll never step foot into another church apart from days like weddings and baptisms when the Church celebrates life rather than represses it. She vows she'll never be at the mercy of priests and nuns again; she'll never allow the Church to direct the way she and Stefano conduct their family.

"Why?"her more devout friends ask.

"How can you forget? " she retorts sharply. Everything she's suffered as a girl and young woman seems to have a direct line to the pulpit. Being hit by her brother for not removing all the stains from his shirt because "God said" women were meant to serve men. Sewing herself a dress and admiring the low neckline, which accentuates her ample bosom, until her father storms into the room and tears the dress. It's fit for a whore, he yells, because "God said" women were meant to be modest, not arouse men's lusts, or else whatever happened would be their fault. Sitting in the village Church and listening to the priest preaching about the sin that some young women commit if they ride bicycles as "God said" it's immoral for young women to have their legs apart on a bike. Learning to ride a bicycle with girlfriends in the field where they hope no-one's watching, and going home to find relatives have seen her riding the bike, and she must now be beaten and go to church to confess "to God." Having her name proclaimed from the pulpit as one of the evil girls who had been "tempted by the devil" to ride a bike rather than staying inside or working in the fields with her family where "God said" she belonged. Being beaten by her father for having attended a dance because "God

said" girls who danced were puttane and temptresses. Her brother had followed her and dutifully reported to their father because "God said" brothers should protect the virtue of their sisters as this would maintain honour in the family.

"I never actually heard God," Dora says. "God couldn't get a word in what with all the nonsense being said on his behalf."

Stefano agrees. "Maybe that's why they don't shut up. Because if we heard God, we wouldn't meekly accept the way things are for us. We'd stop putting up with oppression, ignorance and obedience all in the name of something called "sacrifice in order to reap a heavenly reward". We would've demanded the Church lead us in seeking some justice for our village." (Pallotta-Chiarolli, Tapestry *79-80)*

In his sister's cafe, Stefano notices how the men stop talking to watch the priest go by in his immaculately clean black gown, shiny crucifix and stiff white collar... They feel helpless for the priest serves both the Pope and Mussolini and if they want to keep their livelihoods and not have their village reduced to rubble, they have to keep their priest and keep him well.

Stefano's family live next to the church grounds and his mother often watches the women heading there in the evening as she sits outside, inhaling a couple of breaths of the evening air before the next round of household chores. "Aren't you coming, Maria Giovanna?" they ask.

"I've worked all day and I have a family to care for so I don't have time to sin. I'm sure God will excuse me if I don't waste my time in his house with his family, who seem to have plenty of everything, when my own house is falling down around me and we can't work out how we're going to survive tomorrow. But his sons, the priests, are very welcome here if they make themselves useful," she retorts. (Pallotta-Chiarolli, Tapestry *167-168)*

With *Someone You Know,* my first book (Pallotta-Chiarolli 1991; new edition 2002), my Italian-Australian self is there alongside my feminist self, and my Italian-Australian family and community are there woven into the biography of Jon, a very dear friend of mine, a gay HIV-positive teacher in a Catholic boys' school. As a tour guide, I take the reader on a journey into our friendship, explore the themes of birth and death, the Christianity that is love and acceptance, and the Christianity that is bigoted and destructive in both my Catholic and his Seventh Day Adventist frameworks. I invite the reader to walk the border where two worlds meet and mesh, the Italian subculture and the gay subculture, worlds that are supposedly opposed or unaware of each other due to the prolification of divisive myths and ignorant stereotypes:

As our neighbour, Jon was now able to investigate what he called "the ethnic scene."

"I never realised what diversity existed in an ethnic minority culture," Jon said one evening after a party at my place. "You for instance," and he pointed his finger. "You're so typically Italian, your talking hands, your flocks of family. But you're so different. You speak with an educated Aussie accent. You hang around with all sorts. You hate some Italian traditions, but you hate some Australian ways too. You refuse to be categorised. You're a feminist, and you won't be caught dead without make up. You're married and haven't a clue about so-called wifely

duties and resposibilities. You're suburban, rustic and a fringe dweller all at once. We're a couple of chameleons, changing colours to survive and living on to full existences."

We'd been talking about Jon and Kevin renting the place across the road. My parents thought they were "bravi"

... I would often stand back and watch my parents talking to Jon and Kevin over the front fence, their cheerful voices carrying across the road. I was so proud of them. My father discussed his vineyard and winemaking with Jon, an interested listener, unlike his own children, who wouldn't drink his wine but bought sweet wines full of chemicals. My father's tall dark frame shadowed Jon's and his hands cupped a bunch of grapes from which Jon selected one. My mother would invite them to come over any time and take eggs from the chickens because her daughter rarely cooked decent meals and they'd rot

My brother enjoyed a good family debate. "What if I was gay?."

"Well, if that's the way God made you, what could we do?" Dad said. "I'd feel sorry for you. It would hurt me to think you have to face so much trouble but[...]" and he shrugged, holding the palms of his hands to the sky. "There's an old saying, 'Il mondo e bello perche e vario.' The world is beautiful because it is varied." (Pallotta-Chiarolli, Someone You Know *21-24)*

Weaving a tapestry of social diversity: multiculturalism as surface

Multiculturalism, as officially espoused by the Australian government and as taken up by many Italian community leaders/gatekeepers in Australia, is not enough. Multiculturalism as policy has become a way of controlling the diversity of the others by the centre, and thus still maintaining either/or divisions (see Gunew). First, the focus on cultural heritage and the maintenance of cultural tradition has been used to hide, ignore and perpetuate the injustices, hierarchies and prejudices inherent within those traditions (Vasta). Second, the focus on establishing and developing one's own "Italian" culture, producing 'Italian' cultural narratives and texts for ourselves, may be perpetuating insularity and apathy in regard to the responsibility the Italian community has to engage politically and socially in the issues facing Australia and the world. The descent into 'ethnic chauvinism' often parallels Anglo-chauvinism (Patterson 42). Within the binary framework of Anglocentrism and ethnic fundamentalism, official multiculturalism cannot address the silences and gaps within and between other forms of mestizaje differences such as those formulated around sexuality and gender:

> the whole notion of authenticity, of the authentic migrant experience, is one that comes to us constructed by hegemonic voices; and so, what one has to tease out is what is not there. (Gunew in Spivak 61)

Multiculturalism as surface constructs Australian society as composed of basically internally homogenoeus units, an hegemonic majority, and small unmeltable minorities with their own essentially different communities and cultures which have to be understood, accepted and basically left alone (since their differences are compatible with the hegemonic culture) [...] Multi-culturalist policies construct cultures as static, ahistoric and in their 'essence' mutually exclusive from other cultures, especially that of the 'host society.' (Yuval-Davis 185)

My writing is about the social diversity within, beyond and underneath the surface multiculturalism. As Trinh T. Minh-Ha writes:

Multiculturalism does not lead us very far if it remains a question of difference only between one culture and another [...] To cut across boundaries and borderlines is to live aloud the malaise of categories and labels; it is to resist simplistic attempts at classifying; to resist the comfort of belonging to a classification. (107-108)

However, questions of risk pervade the work of mestiza-researcher-writers. They are usually positioned precariously on the borders of their various communities and families if they dare to weave tapestries of social diversity that engage with issues of *onore e vergogna* such as gender and sexuality. Social isolation and harassment may be the result of having disclosed facets of one's life or represented the community in ways that are considered by the community gatekeepers to be damaging and 'unrepresentative.' My work is often a researcher's confrontation with herself, her communities and her location in relation to the wider society. For example, not only do I receive hate mail and have had my car vandalised by members of the wider Australian society due to my work with same-sex attracted youth, telephone calls have been made to my parents' home by members of the Italian community stating how "shameful" and "disgusting" my books are as they reveal "things about the community that shouldn't be talked about" and "promote homosexuality and sexual freedom for women that are not Italian values." Chicana lesbian mestiza researcher-writer Cherie Moraga questions the implications of writing about herself in terms of ethnic community ostracism because of her sexuality:

I felt I could not write because I have a movement on my shoulder, a lover on my shoulder, a family over my shoulder. On some level you have to be willing to lose it all to write- to risk telling the truth that no one may want to hear, even you. [...] Sometimes I feel my back will break from the pressure I feel ... like I am being asked by all sides to be a 'representative' of the race, the sex, the sexuality – or at all costs to avoid that. [...] The only way to write for la comunidad is to write so completely from your heart what is your own personal truth. (Moraga v-vi)

The following anecdote about one of my experiences within an Italian 'community event' illustrates how within surface multiculturalism, women are subsumed into the category of 'migrant,' or subordinated in relation to the Italian male whose experience becomes the generic experience of 'Italian migrant.'

It's a conference on Italian migration. The audience is mostly migrant women. The guest of honour is a well-known doctor. He's a prominent citizen within Australian politics and society, because he's a prominent Italian community leader.

He begins to talk about his own migration experience with a nonchalance and arrogance that troubles Maria. "It was very easy for Italians to settle into this beautiful country. We were able to achieve whatever we wanted. We found freedom and success.

And as he gives his particular details, Maria realises what he is inclusively referring to as "we" is really exclusively "he." He was Northern Italian, blonde wisps of hair still peeping through the styled grey; and his blue eyes scan over the group of mostly dark-haired, dark-eyed, olive-skinned women.

His parents had lived middle-class lives in a prosperous Northern Italian city. He had come to Australia knowing English, and having completed high school. While he went on to earn his doctor's degree, his wife raised his four children.

After his presentation, there's an unspoken restraint in the clapping. Maria's hands have had trouble coming together.

It's question time. Maria waits to see if someone else will do it. But the two questions before hers are both from men, one positioning himself next to the doctor in terms of his own experience and importance; another seeking clarification of some petty detail about historical dates.

Maria's hand is up, alone, and just as she's wondering whether it'll be worth it, the speaker turns to her and nods. She stands and his eyes scan her. He smiles benevolently, paternally, at her. She introduces herself, her work as a lecturer, writer and researcher, and asks, "Do you think that the fact that you already knew English, had a good education, and were able to pursue tertiary studies, and that you are a man, were the reasons for why your migration was easier? Do you think your situation was typical of Italian migrants, particularly women?"

Audience members have turned around to see who this upstart is. But some of the women are beaming at her. The doctor's face composes itself into a look of condescending patience, one reserved for naughty or silly children who don't know any better. His hands come together in front of him in a praying motion and he begins, "Ma figlia mia" which literally translated means: "But, daughter of mine."

Maria can barely focus on what he says after this verbal cementing of a hierarchical wall. He has established the binary zones: positioned himself as a father figure, powerful, all-knowing, all-encompassing, and she is the rebellious young daughter who doesn't understand and must be reprimanded, brought back into line, the Italian (male) community line.

Thus, ethnic communities can be "divided, segmented, hierarchical, patriarchal and potentially narrow in outlook just as much as the institutions and 'communities' within the wider society" (Skrbis 14). My border-positioning within the Italian 'community' as a woman-weaver-writer is strategically useful in exploring and highlighting those divisions, hierarchies and oppressions. Likewise, I can make strategic use of my border-positioning within the larger world of national and international concerns and social groupings. In other words, as an Italian-Australian woman and writer, my gender identity and cultural location should be instrumental in and inform my engagement with the broader socio-cultural, political and economic issues of Australia and the world. As well as actively supporting and celebrating positive socio-political achievements in our country, these are some of the issues that concern us all in Australia and that our Italian-Australian communities should be actively involved in challenging: sexism, racism against indigenous people, heterosexism and homophobia, racism and political expediency displayed to recently arrived asylum seekers and refugees, the oppressive dogma of religious institutions, inequalities in educational opportunity, poverty, intergenerational concerns and youth issues such as suicide and drug abuse, inequitable workplace practices, a health system that disadvantages the poor, the aged and the marginal.

In *Tapestry,* I explore the racism inherent within segments of the Italian community towards more recently arrived migrants and refugees:

Maria's sitting with some older rellies at a wedding reception held in the Adelaide Town Hall. They all seem so joyous, basking in their traditions in this display of middle-class migrant success. The bomboniere are crystal vases, each of the five bridesmaids wafts around in a thousand dollar dress, and the couple, he Protestant English-Australian and she Catholic Italian-Australian, grin brightly as if their future's secured. Well, financially it is in good Italian style, Maria thinks with a smile. They'll be moving into a double-storey house bought by her family and it'll be fully furnished with engagement and wedding gifts, ranging from fridges to freezers, carpets to curtains. The groom's parents and the sprinkling of their relatives and friends throughout the vast hall look rather overwhelmed tonight. The parents are probably just beginning to calculate how much their share of all this Cecil B. De Mille wedding extravaganza is going to be. They've already gone way overboard in buying a TV set for the new couple but what could they do when their daughter-in-law's parents asked them what piece of furniture their children would remember them by, and waited expectantly for an answer. Could they say a toaster? But apparently they already had three of those.

The conversation at Maria's table now gets political over the lasagna as Italian folksongs are sung in the background by a second-generation band. The older rellies speak Italian of course, or more accurately, their Napolitan and Calabrian dialects.

"It's the bloody Asians. They're ruining this country."

"They should be sent home. They're taking the jobs, they work for nothing."

"They're destroying our culture. Notice all the stinking restaurants, all the Japanese language and Chinese language going up everywhere. Being taught in our schools. What do my kids need to learn an Asian language for?"

"I'd kill my daughter if she ever married one of them."

"They're dirty. They stink of curries."

"Their skin is like rotting rice."

"Australia is going downhill letting all those foreigners in."

"Like the bloody Arabs. We fought them in wars and now we have to live with them."

"They're terrorists. They're bringing crime into this country."

"I'm voting Liberal so we can get rid of those bloody bastards."

The groom and the bride are about to begin their first dance, and the politics is wolfed down with the last of the lasagna and a strong swig of red wine.

But Maria's left staring into her lasagna, her fork raised at the beginning of the admonition she didn't get to make. She wonders when the "Them" became "We," when the fence was jumped. (Pallotta-Chiarolli, Tapestry 125-127).

When, why and how did the oppressed become the oppressor? (Freire) What happens when migrants become economically successful and climb the ladder? Did we learn so well from being on the receiving end of such racism that we are excellent at doing it to others? And how is all this allowed to sit mostly unchallenged within the official policy and rhetoric of Australian multiculturalism? What would it mean to shift the focus from multiculturalism to the development of social cohesion through social diversity?

Tomorrow's tapestries: the writer as travel agent

When approached by a publisher to do *Girls' Talk: Young Women Speak Their Hearts and Minds*, who I was and the absence of girls like me from the books I had read as an Italian girl and young(er) woman, directly influenced the metissage content and tapestry style of the book.

sometimes, when she's reading about Dick and Dora, Nip and Fluff in her reader, she can't help thinking that the Dora in the book has a mother who is not a bit like the Dora who is her own mother. The mother in the book has a tiny waist, a triangle dress, and wears a clean white apron and high heels and even make-up as she's cooking or doing the dishes. And she's always smiling. And the Dad in the book always wears a suit and hat, and carries a black bag and umbrella when he's coming home from work, driving a car of course, unlike her own Dad in greasy overalls arriving home on a bike, sometimes drenched. Maria studies many of the pictures in her books like the plates of green peas and mashed potatoes next to a piece of meat that all book-families seem to eat all the time. No-one has spaghetti or minestra. And they have things like a telephone and gramophone. She never finds a book that has pictures like her family. (Pallotta-Chiarolli, Tapestry 124)

I wanted this book to be a tapestry: culturally diverse girls interwoven into a fabric of debate/writing/drawing around shared themes such as gender, identity, school, family, friendships, sexuality, sex and love. This would not be a book for and by Anglo-Australian girls with the obligatory, token 'ethnic girls' chapter at the end of the book. *Girls' Talk* had to be inclusive, multiple, diverse, with a polyphony of voices. From 1996 to 1998, I became a travel agent for over 150 girls and young women from around Australia in the planning of their own journeys, the production and publication of their own tapestries of writing, photography, cartoons and art that explored the multiple lifeworlds they belonged to and the impact of these 'worlds' on issues such as bodies and health, school and friendship, love and sex. Australian schools, youth organisations, young women's organisations, ethnic, lesbian and health organisations were informed of the project and girls and young women were invited to participate in the compilation of a book 'by girls for girls.' My own writings – introductions, commentaries and questions – were then positioned in marginal spaces on the pages. These often included anecdotes or opinions based on my Italian-Australian background and experiences of growing up as a girl.

My next two books, *Boys' Stuff* and *So What's A Boy?*, co-researched and co-written with Dr Wayne Martino from Murdoch University, himself from an Italian father/Croatian mother family background, again wove tapestries, this time from the diversity of masculinities in Australia. While acting as travel agents with over 300 boys and young men for these two books, facilitating their own journeys in exploring their lives and worlds, it was disturbing to see the racism, sexism and homophobia in many young men, some of them from Italian-Australian backgrounds. This often reflected the prejudices and injustices they had inherited from their parents and grandparents, particularly fathers and grandfathers. Is this the legacy we want to be remembered for in Australian history? That, as discussed earlier in this chapter, multiculturalism was only a surface veneer that concealed or actually condoned the continuation of other discriminations? And what is the role of an Italian-Australian border-dwelling woman-writer in exposing, challenging and engaging with these hierarchies and discriminations?

The textual tapestries from girls and boys for these books illustrated the way culturally and sexually diverse Australian young people are negotiating potentially homogenising and conflicting categories such as gender, sexuality, ethnicity, indigeneity and other factors such as class and disability. In other words, they are assertively interweaving 'lifeworlds,' positioning themselves and others as home-sites of confluence and intermixture, rather than as having to assimilate to one 'world' or the social rules of one category at the expense of others. Three processes were particularly evident in our multicultural and multisexual tapestry-weaving young people:

- the critiquing and interweaving of socially ascribed categories and labels within themselves;

- the crossing, bridging and bordering of "worlds" and the regulations and codes of those 'worlds;' and

- the employment of strategies of adaptation, negotiation and selection in order to live their lives as satisfactorily and successfully as possible.

As Ayse Unguytemur writes in *Girls Talk* about the interrogation of her Turkish, Muslim, Australian, feminist self:

> I believe in rights for women [...] I am a feminist [...] I am not a victim, and certainly not a second class citizen as you may think Islam classifies me ... I was born in Australia, have lived in Australia, in fact have never left the east coast of Australia but I'm too dark to be an "Aussie" I guess. And, well, I do wear the hijaab, so I am considered a "radical Muslim" by my family and Turkish community. Therefore, they don't consider me "one of them." (Pallotta-Chiarolli, *Girls' Talk* 205-6)

Christian was one of many young men from a mixed cultural family background who used the skills he'd gained in living and understanding social diversity within his own family and community to interrogate the hierarchies he saw around him at school, as well as wanting to participate in the many worlds outside school:

> My father's side is Italian and my mother's side is English. At school, the Italian boys had a lot of respect for each other [...] but they didn't show the same respect towards people of different descent like the Asian boys. I'm willing to participate in or have a look at different cultures and different people and the way they operate. Whether it be gays or lesbians or whether it be Moroccan, I'm really interested in the way that other people live their lives and the culture that they live amongst. (Martino & Pallotta-Chiarolli, *Boys' Stuff* 167)

Many young people are publicly resisting the combination of Anglocentrism and ethnic chauvinsim in their schools and social spaces. In "Wandering," Jewish-Australian Naomi Ullmann presents the contradictions and paradoxes inherent within her inheritance of the Palestinian/Israeli chasm, "a Jewish state Palestinian land/ Arab killing Jew Jew killing Arab" and the added intricacies and insights of living in a socially and religiously diverse Australia where she is forming friendships with Palestinian and other Arabic girls such as Julieanne, Australian-born with Arabic grandparents, who tells her

> it's important to me that the Jewish people have a safe place to live [...] have somewhere for their children ... but it's just as important for everybody else too. No one deserves it more than anyone else. (Pallotta-Chiarolli, *Girls' Talk* 212)

Ullmann also presents the complexity of "Jew killing Jew" by interrogating her ancestors' complicity in the condemnation and destruction of homosexual Jews.

> "HOW CAN YOU, OF ALL PEOPLE, WHO HAS BEEN PERSECUTED YOURSELF, PERSECUTE OTHERS?"
>
> I think to myself, and, out aloud,
>
> **"The Nazis also persecuted homosexuals."**
>
> (Pallottta-Chiarolli, *Girls' Talk* 211)

Luc is a young gay man who was born in Italy and migrated to Australia as a child. He recalls 'coming out' to his father:

The first time I'd ever seen my dad cry was when we went for a long drive around the block for five hours, just kept encircling the block, while I talked to him about being gay and he wanted me to change […] he was going to send me to Italy because he thought that somehow that would change me. He said, 'I'll send you to Italy, maybe you'll meet a nice girl.' (Martino & Pallotta-Chiarolli, *Boys' Stuff* 144)

As well as these initial ethno-hetero-normative assumptions from his home world, Luc also experiences sets of assumptions and hierarchies, inclusions and exclusions, from his world of school as fellow students try to fragment and categorise him:

There's a kind of notion that if you're a wog you're cool. But the people from Asian backgrounds get very much picked on [… but] I got harassed by some of the Asian boys for being gay. I said to them, "I'm in a minority group but so are you, so what are you talking about?"[…] I was also abused by one group of very woggy boys, Greek and Italian students. I was harassed by them, and yet I kind of belong to their community as well in that I'm Italian. They said I wasn't Italian even though I was the only one that lived in Italy. But I wasn't Italian because no Italian male was supposed to be gay. I remember one Italian student saying to me, "You're either not Italian or you're not a faggot," with that really serious look that I was making it up that I was gay. (Martino & Pallotta-Chiarolli, *Boys' Stuff* 171)

As travel agent-writers, we can encourage young people to be social weavers, to undertake journeys of self-reflexivity and socio-political exploration, in order to construct tomorrow's textual tapestries.

"More threads weave their way in"

In this chapter, I have argued that Italian-Australian women writer-weavers need to unpick the tangles and suture discordant threads in our Italian-Australian community which is both a site of support and interrogation, celebration and devastation. As I present in *Tapestry*, I remember all too well the ridicule, gossiping and ostracism my parents faced from members of their Italian community for daring to raise my brother and me with equal expectations and opportunities, regardless of gender. I remember my mother being shunned by other Italian women for being strong and independent and expecting her husband to treat her with respect and do his equal share of parenting and domestic work. I remember my father being ridiculed and homophobically harassed by other Italian men for preferring women's company and conversation in the kitchen over coffee rather than their company over beer, wine and cards; for knowing how to cook and clean, change our nappies and lavish my mother with affection.

My parents taught me that 'community' is not always 'home,' and that it may sometimes be better to dwell on the borders of a community than be enmeshed in its conformist net. This lifelong learning and experience of exclusion/inclusion boundary demarcation processes can strengthen Italian women-writers-weavers to claim our space in social and political debates in wider national and international sites, as well as inform the work and legacy we are passing on to future generations. We cannot hold hypocritical and bigoted views, using the rhetoric of multiculturalism to bolster the ambitions of our community gatekeepers, and protect them from external criticism, while others in our community are stifled and marginalised. We are not meant to use multiculturalism as a shield to deflect internal criticism and interrogation. We are not meant to use constructions of cultural heritage, tradition and insularity inherent in a fixed and fossilising concept of multiculturalism to ignore our responsibilities and accountability to social injustices happening in the wider Australian and international setting, as well as those within our community.

I wish to conclude by addressing one more aspect of my tapestry-weaving, tour guide and travel-agent roles. At some point in the future, what I am saying today will no longer be important or necessary. At best, the completed tapestry of my life work will decorate a museum wall as a relic from the past. Indeed, it will appear flawed and simplistic, and if the critic is generous, it will at least be set aside with comforting labels such as "pioneering," "significant in its day," "paving the way for the better work that followed." For isn't that the measure of our success? As social activists, we are working towards a point where we will not be needed anymore, where our stories will have been told and retold and have become part of the fabric of history. Where the issues we consider contentious and struggle for social justice with today will have been resolved or will require a new generation to take up the challenges in ways that are far more applicable to their context. At that point, I hope to be able to bow out gracefully or to keep supporting those who come after me.

Thus, one of my greatest joys in the research, teaching and writing that I do is the opportunity to empower, to open rusty gates, act as a mentor to those who will come after me. More spaces need to be provided for the multicultural, multisexual generations that will come after us to weave their own tapestries into the social fabric, to cross borderlines and expand boundaries, to explore the contradictions and confluences inherent in the construction of their multiple social positionings as both endproducts of larger sociopolitical and cultural forces, and beginnings of new inscriptions into society, politics and culture. As Trinh T. Minh-Ha writes:

> as long as the complexity and difficulty of engaging with the diversely hybrid experiences of heterogenous contemporary societies are denied and not dealt with, ... the creative interval is dangerously reduced to non-existence. (229)

> *I cannot unthread the tapestry. It is vast and more threads weave their way in even as I speak*

> *I can show you only what I see and what my fingertips touch. What will you see and touch?*

> (Pallotta-Chiarolli, *Tapestry* Preface)

Notes

1 The first version of this paper arose out of a panel session given at the Inaugural *In Search of the Italian Australian into the New Millennium* Conference in Melbourne in May 2000. The panel included fellow Italian-Australian sorelle weaving their specific tapestries as Italian-Australian women and using their learnings and insights into gendered, cultural, sexual and other social processes and hierarchies to weave themselves into the fabric of Australian society as social thinkers and social activists. These women were: Josephine Cafagna, Teresa Crea, Anna Maria Dell'Oso, Melina Marchetta and Virginia Trioli. I also wish to acknowledge the initiatives of Dr Ilma Martinuzzi O'Brien and Ms Diana Ruzzene Grollo, themselves inspirational writers and activists, in the planning of that panel and in encouraging women's voices at the Conference.

Imagining Homeland in Anna Maria Dell'Oso's Autofictions

Susanna Scarparo and Rita Wilson

For a man [or a woman] who no longer has a homeland writing becomes a place to live. (T. Adorno)[1]

Italians in Australia often construct what Stuart Hall has called a "narrative of the self" (277). When presented with the task of describing their path of life up to the present time, often in biographical interviews, this narrative of the self provides them with a coherent identity. Yet this coherent picture is made up of various experiences, constructed from different elements that change all the time and therefore also change the outcome of what is seen as a continuous narrative. In this chapter, we discuss the early works of the Italo-Australian writer, Anna Maria Dell'Oso, whose writing crosses the boundaries of both culture and genre. Standing between two cultures, she writes stories that are on the cusp of autobiography and fiction, and that allow her simultaneously to stage and to question her own desire to construct a narrative of the self.

Dell'Oso was born in Melbourne in 1956 of Italian parents who migrated from Abruzzo and for many years worked double shifts in inner city factories. She started to play the violin at the age of 12. After completing secondary school, she studied briefly at the Tasmanian Conservatorium before winning a cadetship on the *Christchurch Star* in New Zealand where she trained as a journalist. She returned to Australia in 1978 and worked for the *Sydney Morning Herald*. Her weekly essays for that newspaper's weekend magazine, *Good Weekend*, attracted a large number of faithful readers and were republished in 1989 as a book entitled *Cats, Cradles and Chamomile Tea*. Since working for the *Sydney Morning Herald*, she has written poetry, short stories, two opera libretti, plays and film scripts, has contributed regular columns for *New Woman Magazine* and other newspapers and magazines, and has worked as a film critic for ABC television. In 1984 she was awarded a general writing grant by the Literature Board of the Australia Council and in 1987 she won a three-month grant (also from the Australian Council) to attend the Australian Film and Television School to study screenwriting. In 1991 she won the Noosa Arts Theatre Playwriting Competition for the Play *Tinsel and Ashes*, and in 1999, she was awarded the Steele Rudd Australian Short Story Award for *Songs of the Suitcase*, published the previous year.

Writers like Dell'Oso are difficult to categorise. In the preface to *Cats, Cradles and Chamomile Tea*, Australian journalist Phillip Adams, with conscious irony, describes her as a "female foreigner." Generally, literary critics use the label "migrant" for writers whose names signal their descent from non

Anglo-Celtic parents or grandparents. Sneja Gunew points out that the term "'migrant writing' is used not simply to designate those writers born overseas, but rather misleadingly to describe the writings of all those Australians perceived as not belonging to the literary and cultural traditions deriving from England and Ireland" (xi). According to Gunew, related expressions such as "'ethnic' or 'multicultural' writer are coded terms for continuing to maintain these divisions" (xii). Perhaps a more appropriate definition for non Anglo-Australian writers would be that of the 'hyphenate' writer. In the context of North American literature, Daniel Aaron is one of the first scholars to introduce the notion of the 'hyphenate' writer. According to Aaron, the hyphen initially represented older North Americans' hesitation to accept the newcomer; it was their way to "hold him [or her] at 'hyphen's length,' so to speak, from the established community" (11). It further "signifies a tentative but unmistakable withdrawal" on the user's part, so that "mere geographical proximity" denies the newly arrived "full and unqualified national membership despite [...] legal qualifications and [...] official disclaimers to the contrary" (11).

Aaron distinguishes between three possible stages which may differentiate non Anglo-American writers. The first-stage writer is "the pioneer" spokesperson for "the unspoken-for" ethnic, racial or cultural group. This writer writes about his or her "co-others," with the aim of debunking negative stereotypes ensconced in the dominant culture's mindset. The second-stage writer abandons the use of preconceived ideas in an attempt to demystify negative stereotypes. Different from the first-stage writer, this writer presents characters who have already sunk "roots into the native soil." This person readily indicates the disparity between dominant and marginalised groups, and, in some cases, may even engage in militant criticism of the perceived restrictions and oppression set up by the dominant group. In so doing, this writer runs the risk of a "double criticism:" from the dominant culture offended by the "unflattering or even un-American image of American life" but also from other members of his or her marginalised group, who might feel misrepresented and might have preferred a more "genteel and uncantankerous" spokesperson (Aaron 12). By contrast, the third-stage writer travels from the margin (ethnic culture) to the mainstream (dominant culture), viewing the latter no less critically but more knowingly than the first- or second-stage writer (the "local colorist" and the "militant protester" respectively). Having appropriated the tools necessary to succeed in the dominant culture – for example, the skill to manipulate its language – this third-stage writer feels entitled to participate in the intellectual and cultural heritage of the dominant group without renouncing the cultural heritage of his or her ethnic group. Indeed this writer, as Aaron reminds us, transcends a "mere parochial allegiance" in order to "transport [personal experiences] into the province of the [general] imagination" (13).

We find Aaron's distinction more useful than the distinction of "ethnic" writers into first-, second- and third-generation. Of Aaron's different stages of the hyphenate writer, Dell'Oso represents the third-stage writer. She inhabits this cultural position self-consciously and makes it a part of her writing, using her hyphen to reflect on the ontology of writing from a position of displacement. Dell'Oso is not, technically speaking, a migrant; after all, as she states, she is "inescapably Australian, whatever that means (aside from the undeniable fact that [she] was born at Queen Victoria Hospital in Melbourne)" (*Cats* 94-95). Claiming her non-migrant status allows her to complicate the meanings associated with the term migrant when used as a category for theorising notions of social identity and belonging.

Through a reading of the essays and stories published in *Cats, Cradles and Chamomile Tea*, we will examine the ways in which Dell'Oso turns theory into praxis. All the pieces in the collection are short takes of personal experience, mostly written in the first person, playing with the fact that the name on the cover of the book marks her as a foreigner of a sort. We interpret these writings as autobiographical acts in which Dell'Oso questions her cultural identity and its relationship to individual autonomy. This is clearly set out in both the content and organisation of *Cats, Cradles and Chamomile Tea*. The collection is divided into stories dealing with childhood recollections of working-class life with migrant parents, reflections on the role of writing and story-telling, the struggles of feminist young women living in inner city shared terraces, and the experience of giving birth and of motherhood. In all of these stories and essays, Dell'Oso deliberately positions herself as a working-class Italian woman while at the same time writing as an educated, feminist and multicultural social critic who can define herself outside the origins and categories of working-class and migrant. Taking on these various positions, she focuses on the relationship between writing and self-fashioning.

Reflecting on the dismantling process involved in recreating the self, Dell'Oso explains why she did not grow up with an understanding of herself as constituted in one place:

> [W]e come from the Abruzzi region of Italy. It's central Italy but it's psychologically and economically part of the Mezzogiorno. Part of the soul of southern Italy, even though technically (geographically) some of it is north (of Rome), but it's actually south […] So, […] we were on all these borders (Cafagna et al. 816)

In a recent interview, she defines writing as a continuum, "ranging from the most obviously factual and reporterly to the most fictional and novelistic" ("Interview" 2). Reflecting on her writing in the ironic piece "Sometimes Reality can Drive you into the Light Fantastic," Dell'Oso recalls feeling completely unprepared for the transition from childhood to adulthood marked by the sharp distinction her high-school teacher made between writing "compositions" and writing "essays:" the former allowing the imagination to run free, the latter being located in the dominion of reality. She describes how she felt as if a "crack [had] split our minds into left and right brains:"

> Fantasy, my companion, was leaving me south of the border as I crossed into
> adult life. From now on, I was to face nothing but Reality - a jungle leading to
> the desert plains of Logic. [...] (*Cats* 25-26)

Dell'Oso goes on to probe the ways in which adults attempt to bring fantasy
back into their lives, from dreaming to writing the past. Her own choice is
neither simply to write an autobiographical past nor simply to write fiction,
but rather to write a form of autofiction.[2] Thus, in her works numerous textual
markers signal a deliberate interplay between the autobiographical mode and
the fictional story (Smith and Watson, *Reading Autobiography* 186). Dell'Oso
uses the mode of autofiction to construct and deconstruct notions of home and
identity. The choice of this form of life narrative is not accidental. As Nancy
Miller points out, "autobiography in *its performance as text* complicates the
meaning and reading of social identity, and hence of the writing subject" (468).
For Dell'Oso, like other writers of autofiction, the performance-as-a-text of
this type of writing lies in the ways in which it plays around the borders of what
is fact and what is fiction:

> The frankness of the narrators encourages the belief that the 'I' of the stories is
> always the writer. But as you read you realise this cannot be. Or at least, not all
> the time. It plays around the borders of what is fact and what is fiction. I hope
> the effect is that the reader feels that there is an untold story behind the stories,
> one that links them all. ("Interview," 1)

The effect of such writing, generally, is to unhouse or estrange oppositions
such as inside/outside, public/private, self/other and past/present in the
representation of identity, and thus to signify the inorganic links between
writing and subjectivity in relation to the experience of displacement.

Between a here, a there, *and* an elsewhere

Conscious of her interstitial position, Dell'Oso uses class, gender and ethnicity
to assume the paradoxical position of outsider and insider in both Australia and
Italy. This reversible duality transforms her into a "double-agent" (as she calls
it[3]), offering her the possibility to create a self akin to the travelling self theorised
by Trinh T. Minh-ha; that is, as a "self that embarks on an undetermined
journeying practice, having constantly to negotiate between home and abroad,
native culture and adopted culture, or more creatively speaking, between a
here, a there, *and* an elsewhere" ("Other Than Myself/My Other Self" 9). *Cats,
Cradles and Chamomile Tea* can be interpreted as a staging of this journeying
practice through which the imaginative elsewhere that was once a place of
exile becomes the place of self-creation.

In the essay "Scaling the Linguistic Wall of Indifference," the journeying
practice towards the elsewhere begins with the ability to translate between
words and meanings, developing what Dell'Oso calls "the ESP technique,"
"second guessing between parents and bureaucrats, working out people's

intentions" not from words, but from the "ability to imagine being somebody else" (*Cats* 77). This, however, can be dangerous because it can lead to exile:

> Translating comes easily to me after a lifetime of crossing both sides of the language barrier, Australia's Great Wall of Indifference which is protected by the barbed wire of custom and the watchdogs of a savage schoolyard education.
>
> Since babyhood I have been crossing this Wall. Sometimes, however, I don't duck quickly enough across the firing lines of English and Ethnic. Sometimes I get stuck on one side of the Wall, usually English [...]. At other times I am caught in the middle watching the bullets whistle past. The no-man's land where migrants' kids retreat continually changes its geography: one day it is extraordinarily lush, thick, fertile; the next treacherous, empty, raped. To be split between two cultures gives you a passport to both sides of the Wall. But during a war you're either on one side or the other or in exile. (*Cats* 77)

There are two aspects to this exile. On the one hand, there is the state of exile, which, according to Edward Said, is that of "unhealable rift, a discontinuous state of being [...] with very little to possess, you hold on to what you have with aggressive defensiveness. What you achieve in exile is precisely what you have no wish to share, and it is in the drawing of lines around you [...] that the least attractive elements of being an exile emerge" ("The Mind of Winter" 51). This is how Dell'Oso describes her family's state of exile:

> I grew up without kin. Apart from my mother and father, brother and sister, I had no blood relations. Emigration had made us a 1950s urban nuclear family. In Italy my mother had been the fourth of a family of five children, my father the third of a family of nine. In Australia they found themselves alone together, two shy newlyweds who barely knew each other. In the early years we lived on the main street of Collingwood, an industrial inner suburb of Melbourne. Papa and Mamma went out to work each day and my brother, sister and I walked to the local school, the house-key pinned firmly to my innermost pocket. We were the Five Bears living alone in a house in the woods of a foreign land. (*Cats* 78)

On the other hand, to be in exile also means that you have been expelled, sent away from your homeland. The consequence is often homelessness. But what home did Dell'Oso have, previous to her expulsion, and who exactly sent her into exile? Her own particular exile – which is to be distinguished from her parents' exile and the state of exile they shared as a family – commences when she starts school and begins to label her native language as useless, and English as useful. As Dell'Oso explains in the story "English as a Sekon Langwidge," "the assimilation of the 1950s and 1960s was a savage process which forced us to choose between the brutalities of Useful and Useless and no matter which cassette tape we identified with we were losers, either culturally or academically or both" (*Cats* 72). Faced with the brutality of the "two tapes jamming inside" her head, she retreats in what she calls "the no-man's land." This turns out to be analogous to what Trinh T. Minh-ha calls "that undetermined threshold place" which enables the writer-in-exile to look in from the outside while also looking out from the inside. Like the outsider, she steps back and records what never occurs to her the insider as being worth or in need of recording. But unlike the outsider, she also resorts to nonexplicative, nontotalizing strategies that suspend meaning and resist closure. [...] She refuses to reduce herself to an Other and her reflections to a mere outsider's objective reasoning or an insider's subjective feeling [...] she stands in that undetermined threshold place where she constantly drifts in and out. (*Woman, Native, Other* 218)

This place is by no means a home. For Dell'Oso, this liminal space at best gives her two sides of a wall which could both be, but are not, her homes. The wall makes it impossible for her to reconcile the two sides because she is a stranger on both sides. Born in Australia, she cannot claim a belonging to that side of the wall on account of her parents' birth somewhere else. However, she cannot claim her parents' homeland as her home either, on account of having been born in Australia (the other side of the wall, so to speak). The question is, how does the migrant child turn this so-called "no-man's land" into a home?

It is almost a commonplace to link the concept of home to the notion of identity. But identities are not free-floating. They may be in flux, and continuously transforming, as Stuart Hall contends, but as Dell'Oso's metaphor of the wall suggests, they are also limited by borders and boundaries (Sarup 94). However, as Stuart Hall reminds us, for diaspora artists "[t]here's no place to speak from except from somewhere. But at the same time as somebody has to speak from somewhere, they will not be confined to that person or that place" (quoted in Ferguson 1).

For other exilic writers such as, for instance, Edward Said in *Out of Place* or Andrè Aciman in *Out of Egypt*, their first-hand memory of home plays a crucial role in their exploitation of homelessness as a condition inspiring creativity. In both cases, the remembering self describes his homesickness out of remembered places constituted of and constituting defined borders and boundaries attached to an original homeland. For Aciman, in particular, writing means "the overcoming of despair at not having his home again" (Porter 308). In other words, he was born with a homeland he later lost. Dell'Oso, by contrast, was born without a homeland. The borders and boundaries of her identity pre-dating her 'exile' were defined and imagined within the borders and boundaries of a blue trunk her mother had brought with her from Italy. From this trunk came the images of her homeland brought to her by the ghosts of her parents' homeland, turning their *Italia* into "a web of memory and dream, a truthful fiction" for the young Anna Maria (*Cats* 81). This is how she describes them in the story "Ghosts:"

Weaving out of dreams and stories, ghosts were a part of life; if they were not always welcomed, at least they were noticed. I grew to like them as they walked everywhere around us, the spirits of the past: the unknown aunts, uncles and cousins, the war-torn villages, the small precious farms with poor soil or bad harvests and the rituals of crops and animals. Out of the old blue trunk papered with passenger labels from the *Oceania*, lived the family ghosts transported from the Mediterranean and those that had sneaked in after the trunk was dragged to Collingwood from Port Melbourne: photographs, a small statue of the Virgin, rosary beads belonging to my grandmother, a posy of white paper wedding flowers, two ornamental baskets of roses made entirely from plaster. (*Cats* 15-16)

However, in this story the narrator also recounts how as a child still in primary school, she used to spend a lot of time at the local hospital as one of the unofficial child translators for the women who grew pale, gave up work, and continued to see doctors in the hope of a cure. The young child, however, could see that "the doctors didn't know how to cure them because they didn't understand how losing a homeland can become a sickness. They couldn't see the ghosts that came begging at the women's back doors" (*Cats* 18). Able to comprehend but unable to explain, Dell'Oso's words were useless: "I was blowing dirt from a crack between one language and another. In the chasm there was a third language, the language of the women's ghosts and stories, the dialects of the past but that was something else, something [...] I couldn't translate" (*Cats* 18).

The realisation that there is a "third language" which may be found in the crack between the language of the 'old country' and that of the 'new country,' is a partial answer to the constant search for one's 'own' language. Writers like Dell'Oso question how one can speak of 'my language(s);' in other words, in what sense are the languages they currently speak and write theirs or not theirs? It is not only a question of knowledge, or usage or ability, but a question of belonging, of familiarity and nearness. Language itself becomes a country, a homeland.

Coupled with the jamming tapes labelled Useful and Useless, the inability to translate the crack between one language and another confirms Dell'Oso's exile from the home and identity provided by the contents of the blue trunk. In fact, without the possibility of translation, ghosts, story-telling, dream and nostalgic memories become untenable:

> Italy had gone, no one there thought of the ones in Australia anymore. The truth was that the migrants themselves had become ghosts, staring from 1940s photographs stuffed into an envelope somewhere in a drawer in Naples or Palermo: the brother or sister who had gone to 'America' clutching a suitcase and streamers from the deck of a ship. From the other side of the world we kids began to feel the effects of this ghost-making process; as the airmail letters dwindled, something from our parents was being drained away, pulled back to a distant shore. (*Cats* 19)

And so the daughter in exile begins to hate Italy and everything that came out of the blue trunk: "just the smell of it, the smell of the past" made her hostile (*Cats* 19).

Yet the ability to recognise one's ghosts is fundamental. To deny them is to forfeit the possibility to find one's home. The ghosts, however, are intrinsically bound to the process of story-telling to the point that for the migrants and their children, "ghosts and stories became indistinguishable, their boundaries blurred." For as Dell'Oso clearly states: "a world without ghosts is a world without a story. A world without story is a world without the possibility of beginning, middle and end, and then the miracle of end-as-beginning again. If you can't tell your own story, your soul is lost: if you can't imagine the story of your life, you can't conceive of how to live it" (*Cats* 20). The women who grew pale and continued their futile search for a cure by seeing doctors and taking Valium, lacked the ability to give their stories legitimacy and consequently lost the ability to conceive of how to live.

For Dell'Oso, legitimacy comes with writing her own stories as well as those of others. In doing so she becomes a third-stage 'hyphenate' writer: able to travel from the margin to the mainstream, and feeling entitled to take part in and comment on the intellectual and cultural heritage of both dominant and ethnic groups. Writing becomes a way to construct a form of public self-fashioning that would facilitate a process of self-authorisation.

The permission to write is closely connected with self-fashioning which for women has often been problematic. But, again, how may a woman come to writing when she is without any legitimate place, or land, or native country, or history of her own? An answer may be found in the story of two members of the feminist collective Libreria delle donne di Milano, Emilia and Amalia.[4] Theirs is an example of a relational life narrative, albeit an asymmetrical one. On one side of the narrational exchange we find Emilia, with her vital need to tell her story again and again, on the other side Amalia, who, having listened to Emilia for a long time, one day decides to write this story for her friend, and to give it to her. Probably without the patient presence of Amalia, Emilia wouldn't have found the way to tell her story. If we define identity as the stories we tell of ourselves and also the stories others tell of us, then we can see that by writing Emilia's story, Amalia completes the cycle of self-fashioning: Emilia's self-knowing is routed through another (Amalia). Thus the process of writing this life story involves a double feminine narrator as well as all the different moments of narration: the oral narration of Emilia, the writing on paper of Amalia and, further, the reading of it by Emilia. Narrative coherence is created by the friendship, confidence and trust between two women. Dell'Oso develops a similar "narrative friendship"[5] in recounting the story of Hana and Marina in "Without Clichés, Migrant Children are Lost Souls" (*Cats* 73-75). Hana, a sixteen year-old of Yugoslav origins, calls Dell'Oso in order to tell her the "real story" of her younger friend Marina, "a Greek girl." Marina had left home, and her story had been reported in the Sunday papers by an Australian reporter who had "missed the point:"

> Hana insisted. He hadn't seen, he hadn't probed and he would probably never understand even if they rang him and told him. I had a foreign surname. I was a woman. I should visit them to let them tell their side of the story.

> [...] I met Hana and Marina in a suburban bungalow [...] We sat on the floor around the heater drinking coffee. Marina was shy and quiet. Hana was the talker. (*Cats* 73-74)

What emerges is a "tale of exile from their communities," one that is singular, unique, but at the same time is the meeting point of several lives and stories. By showing how Marina's story is bound up with Hana's, and how both stories resonate with her own (after all, she, too, is a migrant child), Dell'Oso composes a "relational narrative:"[6] one that reveals some of "the different kinds of textual others through which an 'I' narrates the formation or modification of self-consciousness" (Smith and Watson, *Reading Autobiography* 64-65). Dell'Oso infuses her ambivalent sense of her own cultural identity into her characters (in this case, Hana and Marina), linking her quest for authorial self-definition to their multicultural identities. Interweaving ethnicity with issues of gender and class, she borrows from other ethnicities the elements necessary to authorise her own autobiographical narrative, thus populating her stories with a variety of 'significant others.'[7]

Relationality: writing (m)others and homes

A natural extension of this concept of relationality, the other side to self-creation as it were, is telling the story of the other, the mother and my/other country without appropriating either her or her story, being close to her and yet different. Dell'Oso lets the strangeness or otherness of language pass across/through her writing. She describes the effect of playing as a child with the letters in the blue trunk:

> The Italian language seemed like gossamer veils over blue ink that called to me – and has for 40 or more years. It has been this anima (soul) that I have never been able to really get near, to fathom or to grieve over, for historical reasons (reasons of migration and geography and social custom). (Cafagna et al. 815)

Should we consider this as a refusal to appropriate her "mother('s) language?" Hélène Cixous remarked in one of her seminars that in the word "mother" there are me and other, so if we write it like this "m'other" that suggests another form of hyphenation, that space which separates "me" from "mother" (other in relation with/to mother). This borderline becomes a living fact of individual life, a symbolic link with maternal and mother, that is, gratitude, if it is not repressed or converted into hate.[8]

The titles of Cixous's two most recent books are revealing: *Osnabrück* (1999) is the name of her mother's birthplace in Germany, and *Les rêveries de la femme sauvage, Scènes primitives* (2000) is about her complex relationship to Algeria, her native country. In the first book, the writer (the daughter) cannot recall if she really visited Osnabrück with her German grandmother; perhaps she only dreamt it. So Osnabrück continues to be her mother's town, coming out from the stories she tells her daughter / biographer. *Les rêveries* begins with "Tout le temps où je vivais en Algérie je rêvais d'arriver un jour en Algérie"

(9). ("All the time I lived in Algeria I dreamt that one day I would arrive in Algeria"). Was Algeria a dream or a reality out of dream, nothing that you can hold, that you can keep? Where is the border between the dream of Algeria, the promised land, and the 'real' Algeria? Are these (symbolic) starting points / points of arrival of a personal story which concerns the destiny of the author and her family, or does this singular, unique history reveal the way in which a woman refers to her own origins and relationships constituting her identity as different? As it becomes clear in her stories about home, Dell'Oso continues to be a traveller (like the travelling self theorised by Minh'ha and mentioned previously) who does not really reach a point of arrival, so that any notion of homeland remains a dream, like Algeria for Cixous.

As we have seen, Dell'Oso did not grow up with a sense of belonging to her native city, Melbourne, or, for that matter, to her native country, Australia. In several stories, she recounts how her family's Australian home constituted a kind of backdrop to the 'home' where her mother and father had lived a substantial part of their lives: the Abbruzzi region of Italy. This is the home of the relatives who sent gifts of gold jewellery so precious it was never worn, and the country for which they became nostalgic when airmail letters arrived. However, to Dell'Oso, the photographs, mementos and keepsakes, the suitcases filled with memories were never real, existing only in fantasy, glimpsed as the wistful longing she read in her mother's eyes when the subject of *l'Italia* came up:

> Our extended family was a Kodak film-roll family, reduced to nostalgic memory, a shared name and the sending of blessed money to La Madonna di Villa Marino. Tears, pleas and prayers wouldn't flesh them out, wouldn't make them real. (*Cats* 70)

Like Osnabrück for Cixous, Italy was completely fictional to Dell'Oso because it grew out of dreams, and her parents' nostalgia and glorification of their homeland. Her mother, in particular, "was the principal creator and story-teller of the world of the photograph album" (*Cats* 81).

In his memoir, *Out of Place*, Said describes his relation with his mother as that of "colony to metropole" (60), thereby revealing that his ambivalence towards his own past is represented by his mother and his "mother city," Cairo, both now beyond his reach. For Cixous, Said and Dell'Oso, the mother and the homeland are the crucial elements in their past and in their memoirs. For all of them, the mother defines and complicates their identity and their relationship to the 'homeland.'

Dell'Oso's sense of identity was shaped by ever-changing stories of the past, of family and of Italy, that unknown land of peasants, priests, donkeys and treasure troves of gold. The memories of the first generation and the way in which they idealise and sanctify the image of *l'Italia* within the family is a source of conflict for Dell'Oso and for many second-generation writers. From Dell'Oso's point of view, time had stood still for her parents in the Italy they had left. "Nostalgia was becoming the older generation's strongest defence against having to live and deal with some troublesome, disrespectful and culturally alienated young people," who previously had been fairly compliant with their families' wishes and "delighted to get bomboniere at weddings" ("The Sewing Machine" 59). The adolescent problems of Dell'Oso as a subject were worsened by the knowledge that her position as both an insider and outsider in her interactions with peers was precarious and that any "transgression" (such as being forbidden to join in what were considered normal activities for teenagers) was likely to tip the balance against her. Looking back, she realises that her friendships with "disenchanted, long-haired middle-class kids with permissive educations" were part of her reaction to her "traditional, still very rural-minded" family ("The Sewing Machine" 58-59). As she grows older, Dell'Oso begins to perceive displacement and her own 'state of exile' as ways of gaining a perspective on her life, and that of her family, and thereby achieving a more complex identity.

"Il bel paese" or "the lucky country"?[9]

In Dell'Oso autofictions we find representations of a 'homeland' which are linked to but never contained by geographical boundaries, and which effectively shape "a place in-between, a 'space/spazio' that cuts across the hyphen, a space the elusive borders of which fluctuate between the real and the imaginary: a space that is continuously re-invented" (Giunta iii). Dell'Oso's ambivalent attitude towards her two 'homelands' is incisively summarised in a comment she made during a panel discussion on exploring identity and community through culture:

> A crucial part of my life in Australia is the experience of having spent over 40 years of *not* living in Italy […] I have not been to Italy so many times that I am a permanent resident of this inverted place of borders and shadows where I search for somewhere to belong while still calling Australia home. (Cafagna et al. 814)

In "Once Upon a Country," Dell'Oso describes how, pregnant with her first child, she and her husband decide to travel overseas. Driven by a longing to know more about herself, her family and her people, she decides to go to Italy:

> not to the tourist, gourmet or art-lover's Italy, but to the isolated rural Italy of my family, the Italy of the emigrants where for centuries the land was both a tyrant and a mother. It was this Italy that had flung its children all over the New World […] I wanted to see the people who had stayed behind in the villages, I wanted to trace their fates against mine. I wanted to meet my relatives. (81)

But amongst her relatives in the rural villages where her parents were born and grew up, she feels self-conscious and a stranger from half-way around the world (82). She is afraid to speak the local dialect that was once her native language, which in these villages is "the language of belonging and community, not the language of difference and isolation that it was in Australia" (82). Choosing to remain a stranger, she speaks standard Italian, however badly. This choice is motivated by her desire to remain outside the identity that the dialect would have given her.

She finds herself once more in the position of insider-outsider. She compares her feelings of ambivalence to the attitude of a third generation Italian-American, Anthony, who is also visiting relatives in the village, and for whom the need "to work out his place in the past" (92) has become an obsession. And she concludes that "all people need to know from where they come in order to be able to give something to the present. The past needs to be respected, the stories need to be told" (100-1).

The stories written in the shadow of a place named "Italy" explore domestic and private alienation. Here the routine and the predictable are in constant danger of being shattered. In the villages of her parents' homeland, a place that both confirms and contradicts her childhood image of Italy, Dell'Oso realises that to feel and understand a place she needs to be somewhere else, so that paradoxically she is "home" only when she is not home. Thus, while she's in Italy she dreams of "scrubland and a high endless sky," of "gum trees," and of "a wide tangled brown horizon," and misses "the bigness and wildness of Australia" (94).

At this stage in Dell'Oso's journeying practice, with the recognition that, for her, "home" is not located in a physical reality, comes the realisation that "home" is the site of creativity and imagination, precisely because of its intangibility, its shifting ground. In other words, Dell'Oso defines herself as a writer exactly at the point when writing becomes the means for her to overcome the sense of loss at not having a 'home(land).' In examining the construct of 'Australia' from 'elsewhere' (Italy), Dell'Oso implicitly poses the question: what might 'Australia' look like when these other homelands (the villages in the Abbruzzi, or the "different world" of the Milanese relatives), and mother languages (Abbruzzese dialect, standard Italian) are acknowledged as constitutive repositories for these mediated views of "the lucky country," Australia? Dell'Oso's work consistently depicts narrators who question and disrupt unexamined assumptions about ordinary 'Australian' life. In her writings there is always the threat of a nameless element that will reposition and rename both the traditional narrative conventions and the subject positions which go with them. Yet, when viewing Australia from the 'elsewhere' that is Italy, she realises that

> Australia is seen as a kind of mythical place and a proof that one has undergone a rite of passage into fortune. Australia is a dream, a fairy story. The women ask me if there are oranges in Australia, are there olives, are there apples? ... I am lulled into telling fairytales about my own country [...] I tell them that in the north there are pineapples and palm trees and that the rain is hot, I tell them there are black swans and red deserts. ("Once upon a country," *Cats* 90)

By acknowledging Australia as a place of belonging, she constructs a mythical country, an elsewhere in relation to the inner city and suburbia of her life in Australia. This 'elsewhere' is the place from where she articulates "the untold story behind the stories, one that links them all." Here, to use once again Minh-ha's words, the

> complex experience of self and other (the all-other within [oneself]and without [oneself]) is bound to forms that belong but are subject neither to 'home,' nor to 'abroad': and it is through them and through the cultural configurations they gather that the universe over there and over here can be named, accounted for, and become narrative. ("Other than Myself/My Other Self," 21-22)

The ability to name and account for this metaphorical elsewhere (which is also the only home possible for the daughter of migrants) gives her the power to speak the "third language, the language of the women's ghosts and stories, the dialects of the past" that as a child in the story "Ghosts" she had been unable to translate. However, the ability to translate and, therefore, to turn her third language into narrative is fully realised only once she travels to the elsewhere of her childhood:

> When I stepped inside the picture and talked to the characters of the photograph album, they told me other stories, the tales to the edge of the frame with characters and motivations unknown to me. I saw our family photographs stuck in other people's albums: we were characters in their stories. [...] I came to see [my parents] not just as two great forces from where my tale began but as people in the larger mosaic of other people's lives. I saw that there was always another perspective, another story. [...] [U]nwittingly we carry the family stories, the light and the dark, deep within ourselves. How we will pass them on to the next generation depends on how much we struggle to know about them. (*Cats* 101)

The architecture of a collective memory is always bound to a particular place. But in the case of 'writers on the borders,' the fictions, or meanings, of the allegories attached to the 'old' landscape and the 'old' language, as figured in a tradition of writing, have been transposed or transported to a 'new' place. Dell'Oso's cultural hybridity enlarges the task of recollection. And so the vignettes that describe the different layers of experience (of the I-narrator as a non English-speaking child in an Anglo-Celtic school, as an adolescent rebelling against her parents' values, as the narrator of the stories of related others) suggest the halting quality of a personal search. Dell'Oso seeks an identity that is at once Australian, Italian and Abbruzzese, but foremost her own.

This quest for her identity is also a search for possible connections between a here, a there and an elsewhere which ultimately becomes the untold story behind the stories, one that links them all into a search for an imagined homeland. This search results in the discovery of home as a site able to contain and accommodate an ever changing and evolving sense of identity shaped by the stories we tell of ourselves, and also the stories others tell of us.

Notes

1. Quoted in Kaplan 119.

2. According to Smith and Watson, "Autofiction […] is the French term for autobiographical fiction, or fictional narrative in the first-person mode. […] Despite the difficulty of fixing the boundary between fiction and autobiography, the reader comes to an autobiographical text with the expectation that the protagonist is a person living in the experiential world, not a fictional character, and that the narrative will be a transparent, truthful view of that world." But, as autofictions like *Roland Barthes par Roland Barthes* (1975) suggest, "no definitive truth about the past self may be available. The referential 'real' assumed to be 'outside' the text cannot be written; the subject is inescapably an unstable fiction; and the autobiography-fiction boundary remains illusory." (Smith and Watson, *Reading Autobiography* 186)

3. "Sometimes I get stuck on one side of the Wall, usually the English, unable to reveal my double-agent status for fear of copping flak or ruining my cover along with all other agents quietly posing as natives" (Dell'Oso, *Cats* 77).

4. Initially recounted in the collective publication Libreria delle donne di Milano, *Non credere di avere dei diritti* (Don't believe you have rights) 123-24.

5. See Adriana Cavarero, chapter 2, "Alla periferia di Milano" 74-88.

6. "Relational narratives incorporate extensive stories of related others that are embedded within the context of an autobiographical narrative" (Smith and Watson 65).

7. We use the term in the same way that Smith and Watson do to describe "those whose stories are deeply implicated in the narrator's and through whom the narrator understands her […] own self-formation" (65).

8. See gratitude and "affidamento" (entrustment) in Cavarero, chapter 4, and particularly, "Nell' orizzonte della differenza sessuale" 158-60.

9. Although meant ironically by its author, the words from the title of Donald Horne's famous book, *The Lucky Country: Australia in the Sixties* (first published in 1966) have been interpreted as an affirmation of the Australian way of life, and have been used in numerous ways to describe everything that is great about Australia. *Oh Lucky Country* (1984) is the English title of Rosa Cappiello's novel, *Paese Fortunato* (1981). The novel reinforces the original irony of Horne's title, and gives it a parodic account of life in Australia from the point of view of an Italian migrant.

My Other, My Self[1]

Suzanne Branciforte

I celebrate myself,
And what I assume you shall assume,
For every atom belonging to me as good belongs to you. (Whitman, *Song of Myself*)

In tenth grade, our English teacher asked us to write a 'Song of Myself' modelled on Walt Whitman's great poem. Growing up on Long Island, we could all aspire to that self-expressive lyricism of our fellow Long Islander. I wonder what happened to my verse; I'd like to know now what aspects of myself I chose to celebrate. Some twenty years later, I was reminded of that creative writing exercise while preparing a talk for a women's studies conference called *(Re)Searching Ourselves* at the New England college where I was teaching. I had intended to talk about how my research had shifted from Italian Renaissance literature to cultural identity and the Italian American experience, that is, how I had come to research my *self*. Only while writing that paper, in a catalytic moment of life writing, I realised that what I was researching was really my *other*.[2]

For years, I had been an American Italianist, that is, an American woman who studied and taught Italian language and literature. Suddenly, for a series of reasons I will briefly explain, I discovered I was an *Italian American* American Italianist (in a subsequent, complex turn of events which I explain elsewhere, I eventually became an Italian American Italian Americanist).[3] The revelation had a profound impact on my teaching, on my writing, on my perception of self. For years, the slippage between my American and my Italian identities had given me a perpetual feeling of alienation: more Italian when in America, more American when in Italy. I shifted languages and personalities like I changed planes, and sometimes, quite honestly, I missed my connection.

Years of travelling back and forth between Italy and the US 'to do research,' to better understand 'the Italians' (the *others*?), had set me off on a path of discovery: an introspective journey aimed at better understanding myself. The quest for self-knowledge (and what greater intellectual motivation than to know thyself?) led to a complex unravelling of my hybrid cultural identity, forcing me to address a split personality. The role life writing assumed in this painstaking, archeological sifting for the artifacts of my development became pivotal. A different form of discourse led me away from academic writing and into 'creative writing,' a world I had wanted to inhabit but never felt completely at home in. Like Dorothy, carried away by a baffling twister to a land of mystery and magic, I found myself in Italy/Oz on an intensely personal journey, accompanied by the haunting and elusive refrain: 'There's no place like home, there's no place like home.' But where *was* home?

In years of training to become an (American) Italianist, in the tradition of the poet Henry Wadsworth Longfellow who founded the Italian department at Harvard, my alma mater, I had carefully avoided researching my *self* and had focused on the *other*, my cousins in the homeland, Italy. To research my *self* would have meant looking at the Italian American experience, something which not only had held little interest for me, but which quite frankly I found distasteful, un-sexy, maybe even dangerous, risking associations with ugly, spaghetti-and-meatballs clichés and the mafia. I didn't want to spend my time convincing people that my Sicilian origins had nothing to do with Cosa Nostra, I didn't want to dedicate my energies to analyses of *The Godfather* or Francis Ford Coppola or the Sopranos. It wasn't my intention to distance myself from other Italian Americans, but I didn't want to risk association with them either. Quite neatly and conveniently, I had avoided the whole kit and caboodle by being an American-American who studied Italy. In Sandra Gilbert's "hyphen-nation," hyphenated Americans are on a perpetual quest for a cultural identity, clutching some genetic claim like a passport to a past not ours (Gilbert 52). Not I! Like Longfellow, I positioned myself in the Anglo-Saxon tradition of Italophiles, denying my roots. But the involvement with Italy impassions and transforms, and like E.M. Forster's Lucy Honeychurch, "Italy was offering (me) the most priceless of all possessions – (my) own soul" (108).

So I clothed myself in Armani and filled my head with Dante, Petrarch and Boccaccio. I learned to speak the 'real,' mellifluous Italian, not the down-home, chunky dialect my grandparents spoke when they landed at Ellis Island. I learned about Barolo and Simone Martini and Renzo Piano and Pantelleria. I was determined to be more Italian than the Italians. And although I retained a slight, betraying and temptingly sexy American accent in Italian, I was not American. I was not Italian, either. But most of all, I was not Italian American. As I vested myself with traditions and histories I felt a birthright connection to, I danced a dance of seven veils in reverse: I covered myself in thinly transparent layers, beautiful and effervescent, distracting and colourful, just enough to hide the form beneath.

I donned the first veil by becoming an Italianist. An Italianist is someone who studies things Italian, but the word reveals nothing of one's ethnic identity. For an Italian American Italianist, it's a good cover. You're not saying you're *Italian* – you are an Italian*ist*. But my entrance to Italian Studies was through the back door. People often automatically assume that my interest in Italian language and culture is due to some genetic predisposition. Once upon a time, I would have said 'nothing could be further from the truth,' but I'm now a believer in DNA *über alles*, and less convinced that I made a choice exercising free will. When I was growing up, French culture was the defining *haute culture* (cuisine, fashion, language, literature) and in fact, my first foreign language was French. I went so far as to try to invent French roots for my chameleonic surname: pronounced with the right accent, it could pass for French or even British (just drop the final vowel, an innocuous, silent -e). I was subconsciously denying my roots every chance I got.

Then, the defining moment: that first trip to Europe, a Modified American Plan version of the Grand Tour. High school graduation, destination: Paris. Then, in the once-you-cross-the-pond,-make-the-most-of-it mode, Rome, Florence, Venice, Vienna. The overnight couchette from Paris to Rome passed through the Italian Riviera (later to become my home) in the early morning hours. My first vision of Italy. The alternating blues and blacks: the sparkling blue of the Mediterranean and the sudden black of dark tunnels as the train sped through rocky cliffs. Blue, black, blue, black. It was a real awakening; something stirred in me when I saw for the first time the land my grandparents had left. What was this sudden sense of identification? Discovering the artistic treasures of the Renaissance, I took pride in what my ancestors had produced. *My* ancestors? Where was this unfounded, unjustified pride coming from? There was a birthright that I was just beginning to claim. Like that first liberating swim in the Mediterranean, I wanted to steep myself in a Western tradition that in large part my forebears had shaped. I was staking a claim on my heritage. And I needed to know more. Hence the directional shift: Renaissance studies, one part France, two parts Italy. And the real journey began.

It's a professional hazard, identifying with the culture that is the object of study. But the subtle and complex transformation had started: I conveniently traded my American identity for an Italian one, and skipped the very important, essential link – my Italian American heritage. To the Italians, I was *"l'Americana,"* my nationality was currency abroad. And it could be bartered for a better, closer look at the object of my desire. I was focused on the *other*. It took years for me to understand that I had overlooked my *self*, and that in effect, I was dealing not with two but with three distinct and separate if interrelated cultures: the American, the Italian and the Italian American.

How does one overlook one's own ethnicity? In the America I grew up in, it was easy: the process of assimilation was just being completed. Our parents were born on American soil of people who had made the crossing, who spoke other languages and ate other food. Our parents spoke English only, even if they understood their parents' strange dialects. They ate strange-smelling food in their parents' homes and American food in their own homes. We were born into an English-speaking, American food-eating environment. Some of us were curious enough or comfortable enough to go delving into that disappearing culture of our grandparents. Sometimes it took another generation before that 'return crossing' could be made.

Raised with a healthy, 'normal' tolerance and appreciation of other cultures and traditions, I never really questioned if my upbringing was Italian American or not, or how that might have influenced the formation of my own identity, values, lifestyle. I freely participated in my Jewish friends' family celebrations, from Bar Mitzvahs to Purim, and in my Chinese friends' New

Year celebrations. I revelled in the differences and marvelled at the similarities. An anthropologist manqué, I always had an acute interest in cultures, rites, rituals, societies and behaviours. But it's easier and safer to study the *other*. Beneficiary of a privileged upbringing, I had never felt like the *other*. I was mainstream: an upper-middle class white woman, growing up in suburban New York, the product of a fine education. As a trailing member of the baby-boomer generation, I shared an upbringing with millions of other Americans that made me one of the crowd. Or did it? As a woman student at Harvard in the early 1980s (closer to the innovation of coeducation than I care to admit), I first became aware that perhaps I was not 'entitled' – not because of my gender, but because I was Catholic and Italian. Not 'ethnic' enough to be hip, not WASP enough to be in. On the cusp of acceptability, I played to the E.M. Forster crowd and passed from Italian American to American Italianist. One went to a place like Harvard because one wanted to meet, to be exposed to, to become friends with people who were different. In a quest for exposure and education, I started to distance myself from my very non-exotic New York nerdy roots. I sought the *other* and began the journey that took me back to me.

As an American student of Italian language and literature, I am unusually comfortable about my split personality and living in two cultures, one foot firmly planted in each. ('*There's no place like home, there's no place like home*') Like a snail, I carry my home on my back. It's a trick I learned early on in my vagabond existence: make yourself feel at home in the humblest *pensione* or the most grandiose villa: it goes a long way towards getting a good night's sleep. But my immediate adaptability in Italy may be attributed to an underlying connection to my Italian American identity – something I only started to uncover in Italy – that particular understanding of my cousins 'in the old country,' the familiar ring of the language I had struggled to learn, gestures and behaviours that vaguely reminded me of my father's cousins or great aunts. I was never really a foreigner in Italy, and the more time I spent there, the more I became a 'stranger' (*straniero*) in the land of my birth.

When did I become Italian American? Perhaps it was some kind of '*Nel mezzo del cammin di nostra vita*' realisation, a Dantesque midlife crisis. If so, then the '*selva oscura*' was the academic environment in which I found myself: a small liberal arts college in New England. The seven years I spent in a small New England town in a tenure-track position in Italian were an awakening for me, a gradual process of consciousness-raising that led me to the margins. Hired to be a teacher of Italian language, literature, and culture, I could not have anticipated that I would become a magnet and a resource for Italian American students. I realised for the first time (naively?) that we do not define ourselves, others do: you are what/who you are perceived to be. And I was the *Italian American* professor. In an amazing and appalling revelation, students confessed how isolated and alienated they felt as Italian Americans at a college that was predominantly Irish American. It was news to me; I had always worn the security blanket of belonging like some kind of mantle. My head-in-the-sand unwillingness to acknowledge discrimination against Italian Americans had impaired my vision considerably. The epiphany: in my professional life I was constantly bridging two worlds, but as I did so, I represented (to others) a 'third world' – that of Italian Americans and in particular of Italian American women. The state of Italian American women is like an under-developed country: rich in natural resources, in some ways untamed, politically disorganised, and exploited by the dominant culture.

At the same time, one of my best students, an Italian American woman from New Jersey, was researching the hagiography of medieval Italian women saints for her senior thesis. Conversation inevitably turned to our common roots, and the discussions were stimulating. She was trying to understand the source of the strength of Italian American women, and decided to do a thesis on that instead. This was not a simple switch from art history to immigration studies; this was a major intellectual inquiry guided by careful consideration of many sources. This was researching yourself! My own research took another direction, too, confirming what I thought I already knew: that the quest for self-knowledge is perhaps the greatest intellectual motivation we can have. As I examined my own intellectual development and choice of profession, I realised that knowing where we come from in a multicultural, pluralistic society, is the anchor of our identity. A profound understanding of the struggles faced by our own people leads us to a fuller awareness of our own situation. And so I began to question why I had ignored where I fit into this rich heritage for so long.

Despite an earlier letter to the editor of a major New York newspaper to protest appalling clichés and inaccuracies about Italian Americans and their culture – prejudices which I thought had long been laid to rest – proving that I was not oblivious to the existence of bias, I was still far from taking up the cause. Instead of acknowledging difference, accepting it, embracing it, celebrating it, we sometimes seek, chameleon-like, to pass unobserved, to blend in, to be one of the crowd, to assimilate. Thus we negate the essence of our difference, the qualities that distinguish us, and become a part of the hegemonic enterprise that keeps those qualities from emerging.

Part of my reluctance to approach my Italian American ethnicity through a formal inquiry stems, obviously, from the negative connotations of Italian American culture. For a long time, American society 'didn't like' Italian Americans; the most common associations were with the mafia or Al Capone, over-eating, or loud, foul-mouthed, vulgar, gold-chain wearing, garlic-eating mobsters. Successful Italian Americans were assimilated Italian Americans; they no longer spoke the language of their ancestors, often mispronounced their own last names, and rarely knew where their grandparents actually came from. How many of us forfeited a heritage that then took years and an enormous effort to recover?

The distancing is done by degrees and over generations, although it is remarkable how much is lost in only one generation. First there's the linguistic break, then some of the culinary traditions slowly disappear: the tomatoes in the garden, the feast days, the big Sunday midday meal with the extended family. I divested myself of an Italian American identity early on. It was easy: in the 1970s and 1980s, as Americans started to travel more, 'Northern Italian' things became chic. Restaurants touted 'Northern Italian' cuisine, even though tomato-based sauces still dominated the menus. In effect, the red and white checked table cloths started to disappear along with the straw-covered flasks of Chianti, and people marvelled at the fact that cream sauces (traditionally French in Americans' minds) could be used on pasta. One Northern Italian pasta sauce was even green: *pesto*. Of course, this was just another import: the famous 'Southern question', *il problema del Mezzogiorno*. Now even Americans looked down their noses at the lower end of the peninsula: Southern Italy after all was the birthplace of organised crime. The agricultural south, home to peasants and mafiosi, vs. the industrial north, home to fashion and fast cars. And so Italian Americans of Neapolitan and Sicilian origins got busy inventing northern connections for their families. We denied our connection to Southern Italy and heard the cock crow three times. How many times did people say to me, "With your height (I'm five-foot-ten) you must be Northern Italian." It took me years to reply with pride, "My height is 100per cent pure Sicilian; my Sicilian father was six-foot-four."

Little protest is ever made about the Hollywood representation of Italian Americans, mostly because it is an image in large part created and promoted by Italian American artists. From Scorsese to Coppola, De Palma to Tarantino, from De Niro to the Sopranos, the image of Italian Americans and Italians as gangsters is benignly accepted by the American media. Nick Pileggi, Don De Lillo or Gay Talese write stories about the 'hood' and pass them off as a representation of the Italian American experience. The publishing houses and movie studios love it: because it sells. That the glamorised vision of corruption and organised crime presented has no bearing on or resemblance to the Italian American experience as experienced by the majority of Italian Americans means very little.

This is not my story, these voices are not my voice. Where is the voice of the Italian American experience? Of the Italian American family? Of Italian American women? Where is our Amy Tan? Our Alice Walker? No narrative of the Italian American experience *not* focusing on the mafia has reached the broad audience of *The Joy Luck Club* or *The Color Purple*. The problems with Italian American ethnic identity have to do with image and voice: a bad image and a lack of voice. As a group, Italian Americans don't have the reputation of Jewish or Asian-Americans, who, even if from poor and humble beginnings, as a culture endorse the value of education, ensuring that their sons and daughters are educated. Italian Americans don't buy books, they don't read, they are not seen as intellectuals.

That is why those students made me realise that by helping them discover their ancestry, by reconnecting them with their roots, I was helping them to understand where they came from and where they could go. Nurturing pride in Italian American ethnicity is a significant part of what I do, and I hadn't articulated that when I started out. It is one of the most rewarding aspects of my job. When I teach students about Dante or Rossellini, about Lorenzo de' Medici or Rita Levi-Montalcini, about Galileo or La Guardia, I am teaching them to take pride in their heritage, in the accomplishments of Italians and Italian Americans.

The inquiry into my Italian American identity and what it means to be Italian American changed my way of seeing. So the invitation to the *(Re)-Searching Ourselves* conference came as a challenge, not to explore just gender but ethnicity or what I now call cultural identity. Feminists have long pointed out that the personal is political, so I took that and applied it to my Italian American identity. Prodded to find the academic parameters of my personal discourse, in an attempt to anchor what I had to say in a language I already knew and that I knew was acceptable, I forayed into a multidisciplinary field where 'people like me' had already been dissecting, deconstructing and reconstructing for decades. Interdisciplinary discourse had always been my bag, but turning the lens on oneself requires particular discipline, rigour, and courage. It also helps if someone holds your hand. By entering the field of Italian American Studies, I found not only a group of talented and congenial scholars, I had located a support group. It takes courage to apply a methodology of which we are presumably already convinced on ourselves. Deconstructing your own identity is a bit like psychoanalysis: are you ready to accept the results of the inquiry? The first question: why had I not been willing to look at my Italian American self? Denial? Fear?

The more familiar I became with the literature, the more comfortable I became with who I was. Oddly, the same cannot be said of those who knew me 'before:' the more comfortable I became with who I was, the more uncomfortable the people around me became with the direction of my research. The consternation was apparent: what *was* I talking about? Italian American ethnicity wasn't *ethnicity*; ethnicity meant Hispanic, Latino, AfricanAmerican, Asian American. Sociologist and anthropologist friends so used to studying 'other' cultures and being outsiders looking in, could not understand the impetus to study my own culture, my overlooked culture. Why couldn't they appreciate my interest in learning about things Italian American? Because they couldn't see 'Italian American.'

Like the Adam and Eve of Masaccio's Expulsion, for years shame had me cover up those private parts I didn't want the world to see. And like Masaccio's Adam, one hand was also over my own eyes, blinding me; shame impaired my vision. But realising you are naked can also be an eye-opening experience. After the epiphany, I was standing naked and proud – the Italian American American Italianist – and it was the others who averted their gaze.

My presentation was scheduled for the session 'Other Cultures, Other Selves' and I liked this rubric because I had researched and discovered *my* other self. My Italian American self. The one who'd been in the closet these many years.

Because I was the American who had become an Italianist and who only of late had discovered she was an Italian American American Italianist and now wanted to proclaim this discovery. As scholars, we don't often sing of ourselves; we sing of others. I thought I was researching my *self*, but discovered I was researching my *other*.

If it wasn't the mafia, it was the peasant image that plagued us. At the conference presentation of my paper, one woman academic stood to make a question, framing it by saying "Since Italy is principally an agricultural society" No one seemed to know that Italy has been ranked in the top six industrial nations in the world for the past twenty years, that it is a member of the G8, that Italian women have all the same rights as American women, and then some. Despite my Armani suit, the image of the Contadina tomato paste lady, with a white babushka and a basket of tomatoes on her head, came dancing into the room and was now sitting beside me. I felt the audience's stares, and their suspicion when I spoke of Italian feminism, as if I were making up stories, perhaps to make myself feel better. After all, it was perceived, I was talking about my *own people*, not a group of *others* that can be analysed and discussed rationally, objectively, professionally and with scientific rigour and detachment that permits an impartial evaluation of that group's customs, habits, behavior. For my academic colleagues, I wasn't talking about the *other*, I was talking about my *self*. What they could not realise was that I was not my *self* that day, I was my *other*.

When I started the voyage I didn't yet know her, my *other*. As I have come along the road, I got to better understand my *self*. I'm glad I found my way in time.

Notes

1. With apologies to Nancy Chodorow.

2. An earlier version of this essay was presented as a paper at the conference *(Re)Searching Ourselves: A women's studies conference at Holy Cross* in Worcester, MA in March 1996.

3. See my article "Politica radicale/pedagogia radicale: l'esperienza di un'italianista italo-americana."

Across the Nation

Lost in Transition[1]

Ida Dominijanni

In 2003, three films which were screened in Italian cinemas signalled the need to revise the nation's political memories which had, up until then, been crushed into the collective unconscious or segregated in the consciousness of certain minority groups. In their order of screening, these films are *La Meglio Gioventù (The Best of Youth)* directed by Marco Tullio Giordana, *The Dreamers*, directed by Bernardo Bertolucci and *Buongiorno, notte (Good morning, Night)* directed by Marco Bellocchio. They differ from each other both in the message they contain and the language they use, but they are linked, in my opinion, by the same intellectual practice and by the same intention of rewriting the last 35 years of Italian political history: they all attempt to alter its accepted periodisation and to move the narrating subjectivity from the seat of power to the individuals and the avant-garde who were its true protagonists. These films have another common theme which can be found in their singling out of the relationship between public and private spheres as the fundamental motive behind the 'attack on above' on the traditional idea of politics attempted by the protest movement of the 1960s and 1970s. Another factor which links them is that the directors are all male and that all belong to the same political generation: Giordana, born in Piacenza in 1939; Bertolucci, born in Parma in 1940; and Bellocchio, born in Rome in 1950, were deeply affected both by events prior to 1968 and by its aftermath. I do not intend to present a critical or canonical review of these three films but rather to use them as sources for the reconstruction of an Italian political autobiography different from the official biography written by the mass media and political scientists over the last fifteen years.

First, however, I would like to establish a premise. In these times of globalisation, the controversy over the symbolic nature of identity has become increasingly bitter regarding the material and immaterial processes which tend to homogenise and disintegrate the kernel of identity. The world over, this tension between the real and the symbolic avails itself of a rewriting of history – both recent and remote – which is useful to the current political struggle and may resort to different languages. As we know from the bloody accounts of recent years, in many parts of the world the preferred language is religion. In Italy the language of choice is political. For reasons which can probably be tracked back to remote beginnings, the land of Machiavelli, Gucciardini and Gramsci is incapable of conceiving of politics as a simple technicality. People speak of it – and is spoken by it – as a language, even if this language is limited to television small talk or to a self-referencing or captious jargon. The 'identity controversies' regarding the nation's biography and autobiography are played out in the politicial arena: the collective and individual 'I' depends on the political narratives of 'the way we were.' Politics, although apparently in its death throes is still our *Heimat,* the conscious or unconscious seat of our 'Italianness.' This makes the study of how the language of cinema has intervened in such centrality of political language all the more interesting – either by restoring its sense and meaning or by decreeing its absolute senselessness.

Written for television, *The Best of Youth*[2] adheres all too rigorously to the requirements of small screen productions, managing to compress the story of 30 years of conflict which originated within the family nucleus into a form that a prime time audience made up of that very same family unit can absorbe. In Giordana's film, which narrates the story of the 'abnormal' generation of '68, set within a lower middle class family, these conflicts never reach breaking point, remaining unacknowledged within a context of bitter-sweet compatibility. Although political and family sagas intertwine, it is the family and its values which triumph over the drama and tragedy of events. History penetrates the domestic walls leaving them cracked but otherwise still standing, rather as if it always comes back to an inviting maternal womb. Even the clash between state and revolution, public order and subversion, is simultaneously expressed and contained within the family. Nicola and Matteo, the main characters, are two brothers who go their opposite ways when one joins the protest movement and the other the police force. However, they come face to face in crucial scenes right up until Matteo's death which signifies – in a Pasolini-like context – that in the conflict between protesters and policemen, these latter were the weakest and the most exposed.[3] In the two brothers' *Bildungsroman* we find – bordering between public and private – the official and unofficial history of Italy between the 1960s and the 1990s. It covers the demise of authoritarian universities and the Basaglian struggle against mental institutions,[4] the myth of Swedish modernity and the commitment displayed by young people during the 1966 floods in Florence, the uprisings at the University of Turin in 1968, terrorism, the abduction of Aldo Moro, *tangentopoli* and *mani pulite*.[5] Time passes: the best of youth reach maturity, children grow up, and mothers remain or return if they had embarked on a journey into the world to find themselves. For those who lived through these times, something rings untrue in this account – at times, painful and moving – which, in the end, is resolved in a 'happy families' solution. Whatever our perceptions, on the surface at least, things seem to have gone exactly as Giordana depicts them. In the laboratory which is Italy, everything has been tried out, all 'attacks on above' have been carried out, and everything, from the political parties to the universities, has been ruined or is unravelling: everything except the family – unassailable institutional bastion of an otherwise 'lost' nation.

The Dreamers[6] however, presents another version of the facts. In the middle class apartment in the centre of Paris, history does not enter on tip-toe nor does it come with the – albeit tragic – stealth of mental illness; it appears with all the unpredictable strenght of a cobblestone hurled from the street. And the family is not strengthened but, like the university, it is overrun, defiled and distorted. It is not the children who leave home only to return at some later stage but rather, the parents who are forced to abandon their role, traumatised by their children's sexual games which completely invert Freud's main tenet. And if, within the apartment's four walls, the youthful protagonists' illicit behaviour runs the risk of becoming a deadly nightmare, that stone intervenes to awaken the three dreamers to reality. Was '68 made of dreams and dreamers? 'Yes!' claims Bertolucci with an anachronistic doggedness, raising a clenched fist.[7] We must restore to the word 'dream' both its meaning of an unreal utopia as well as its significance as an expression of the unconscious, the imaginary which *generates* reality. Contrasting the pernicious realism of 'tiny steps' politics, the film suggests that only dreams have the power to recreate reality, to rewrite it from the minutiae of the everyday. Without dreams there is no reality; without desire there is no politics; without a revolution from within, there can be no collective revolution. Moreover, if there is no intellectual extremism, if we are not willing to risk ourselves radically, there can be no shift – neither big nor tiny steps. Bertolucci's message to the anti-globalisation youth of today is that change comes about only through enormous presumption. Failing this, conformism, a colourless adaptation to the social norms always at the beck and call of the powers that be will prevail over realism. Heralded by the 'magnificent obsession' of the cinema of the 1960s which had already replicated and subverted images of reality, the movement which drags youth from their homes into the streets did not overthrow power, but challenged something much broader and more radical, the very notion of politics. It questioned politics not just as a rational doctrine of government and not even as a representation of the governed but rather, as a marshalling of forces, both collective and individual, of all individuals and the entire collectivity: body and mind, reason and passion, knowledge and sexuality, noble sentiments and wicked perversions, plans and dreams. The personal and political spheres united in a common revolution, twins, like the characters in the film, out to discover happiness on this earth.

However, even the unconscious – especially the unconscious – reveals its ambivalence: it is a dream and it is a delirium, it is liberating imprint and paralysing removal. The season of '68 not only lasted longer in Italy than in other countries but it also ended more tragically, abducted and murdered by terrorism together with Aldo Moro. So if Bertolucci's The Dreamers calls to mind the dawn of the movement, its outburst of energy, its dream-like potential, Marco Bellocchio's Buongiorno, notte evokes its tragic waning, its deadly implosion and its paranoid demise.[8] This time, there is no rock hurled from the street to intrude on Aldo Moro's nightmare in that outer suburban apartment, elevated by his five jailers to the status of 'People's Tribunal.' The sounds of desire have been replaced as violence subdued the creative pretexts of the movement of 1977, the road has instead been plunged into the silent tunnel of widespread and internalised fear similar, in that season of Italian terrorism, to that which we are all reliving in these times of international terrorism. Even politics has renounced its aspirations: it is no longer interested in society's demands or its transgressions but has withdrawn into the narrow confines of power. Under such conditions, the delirium of the five members of the Red Brigades can continue regardless in its paranoid attack on the 'heart of the state.' Then again, covert operations are merely the manifestation of a displacement of the mind from the outside, where it may be surprised and questioned, to the inside, where it is possible to build an artificial world which lends substance to its obsessions. It is a fine line that distinguishes a house from a 'people's prison.' Bellocchio's message is that the terrorists were not monsters, but rather ordinary left-wing militants who had crossed that fine line which marks the boundary between being in touch with reality and the delirium which reconstructs reality for its own purposes. It was a mistake to follow them into that delirium; to listen to the insanities of the kidnappers and to disregard the abducted victim's human plea for help. The political establishment should have negotiated with the Red Brigades but it did not, remaining like them locked inside its own self-referencing apartments. By negotiating it might have brought them back to reality, but it merely followed them into their escape out of reality. Once again, just a dream could have interrupted the cold, deadly drift of political reasoning. The only female member of the Red Brigades dreamt that she let the prisoner escape but, unlike the story of the three *Dreamers*, she did not act upon her dream. Moro was murdered, not symbolically as a beloved and internalised father, but in actual fact, and that is why his ghost seemingly wanders without burial and an unresolved trauma of republican political history remains. Bringing that dream to the screen is the step which redeems the past, rehabilitating a foregone chance; and simultaneously burying the ghost, releasing the memories, liberating the past.

2. Three things come to our attention when we compare these three films: an intellectual practice, a re-elaboration of the notion of politics, and a radical challenge to the accredited story of the so-called 'Italian transition.'[9] In my opinion, each supports the other, creating space in the collective imaginary for a new type of biographical and autobiographical narrative of Italian society between the 'First Republic' and its aftermath.

Here we should mention a preliminary problem. For the last few decades, the narrative function of historical texts has been the subject of much debate among historians, philosophers and literary critics both in the United States and Europe; so much so that any attempt to summarise here would be impossible.[10] It should suffice to recall that this debate has made a significant contribution to a re-evaluation of the interconnecting notions of history, politics and subjectivity and the relationship between the discursive order prevailing in a given society, the practices which give rise to it and which sustain it and those which, wittingly or unwittingly, avail themselves of the linguistic-symbolic conflict in order to undermine it and challenge its injunctions. It is obviously not a question of denying the validity of authoritative discourse by inverting the elemental order and arrogating truth and authenticity to the narrative discourses put forward 'from the base' (there is no such thing as a 'pure' narrative, one which is completely independent of the requirements of the discursive order and of the context in which they appear). We must restore to history that conflictual plurality of facts, subjects, ends and drives which are an integral part of it and which the official political narrative tends to diminish, hierarchise, remove, mutilate and censor according to the orientation which it wishes to bestow upon the present. Neither is it merely a matter of restoring the voice of the lost and the forgotten so that they might bear witness to the victors. We must restore to the past those circumstances of which it was stripped so that the present and the future may avail themselves of those and future new circumstances. Narrative as a discursive practice and narratives in the form of plural (and often alternative) accounts of events do not confine themselves, on the whole, to finalising history; rather, they reveal its violent side and alter its concept. They do not confine themselves to making the past more complex or problematic but they do open up new possibilities for the present day and the future. Narrative practice is therefore laden with political overtones (when, as I will discuss in the case of feminism, it is not openly and manifestly political).

Wittingly or unwittingly, the position assumed by these three directors is typical of this practice and is laden with political consequences. The effect of these three films – achieved through their distinctive and separate languages, incisiveness and strengths – is that they not only evoke memories of past seasons of Italian (and international) political history, but they force us to ask why and how these times have been progressively banished, disowned and diminished in the collective memory, erased and disgraced in the official political and media versions of the transition. As a result, they show the violence and the bias of this account of events and substitute the belief in it which begets consensus with the disbelief that threatens conflict. They throw open the possibility not only of another version of past events but also of another way to imagine future events.

Before taking a more detailed look at how and why this process evolves, it will be helpful to discuss at some length the intellectual practices which sustain it as well as the implications for the role of the intellectual in contemporary Italy.

3. The transformation undergone by the figure of the intellectual in Italy is a crucial but little recognised chapter of the more complex re-construction of Italian public life over the last decades. Briefly, this transformation depended on two separate processes, a strictly Italian political one and a socio-economic one, common to all post-Fordist and postmodern societies. On the one hand, the restructuring of the Italian political system into a bipolar form as a consequence of the upheavals in the early 1990s has brought about an unprecedented bipolarisation of intellectuals.[11] Quintessential to the New Right that is grouped around Berlusconi, is a new class of intellectuals fostering historical revisionism (targeting the antifascist roots of the Italian Republic, the Constitution of 1948, the history of the left with particular reference to the Italian Communist Party – the PCI – and the decade of the protest movement between the 1960s and 1970s). It also attacks the hegemony of the left over Italian culture, targeting the whole of the 'First Republic' as 'old' and forcing left-wing intellectuals into the 'conservative' position of preserving a number of basic principles of democratic society and the Constitutional Pact. At the same time, left-wing intellectuals had been left in turmoil by the demise of the PCI. This came about officially as a result of programmatic changes (the so-called 'svolta della Bolognina') in 1989,[12] but it had been materialising during the protracted crisis of the form of the party for more than a decade. It brought to an end that distinctive form of mediation among intellectuals, society and politics performed by this party. Such mediation ensured the synthesis – or at least the exchange – between different roles and specialisations and gave intellectuals a space in which to practice, not just enunciate, their discourses. Briefly: in the early 1990s, the organic intellectual proposed by Gramsci has moved from the left-wing to the right-wing arena.

In the afore mentioned socioeconomic context, the figure of the end-of-century Italian intellectual is characterised, on the one hand, by a tendency towards a higher degree of specialisation and scholarship in his/her work and, on the other hand, by increased mass media attention. It is a fact that this simultaneous two-fold tendency has placed him/her in crisis everywhere.[13] Once a channel between the elite and the masses, the intellectual of today finds him/herself divided between an elite specialised academic career and a lesser role in the mass media. In other words, the intellectual is either an academic, an expert, a 'qualified' someone to whom politicians turn to as an occasional consultant, or s/he is a columnist for the mass media. In the first case, s/he has a public voice only sporadically, if at all; in the second case, s/he has a vast audience which guarantees his/her popularity but is not necessarily receptive to his/her message. In both cases, what is missing is the context of practice and the political feed-back that were intrinsic to the Gramscian organic intellectual.

The final element and, in my opinion, the most important in the transformation of the intellectual figure, lies in the fact that what Marx referred to as a "general intellect" has become a reality in late capitalist societies.[14] Although typical of all modern democracies, this transformation has had particularly important consequences in Italy. As the more sophisticated analyses of modern capitalism have revealed, in post-Fordist societies – in which production is primarily dependent on knowledge and on interactive and communicative relationships – the intellectual figure has been shattered, disseminated and generalised. In the knowledge economy, where material and immaterial production – ranging from culture to microchips – as well as capital flows and share market speculation originate, there are no longer merely *'hands at work'* but *'minds at work'* as well. The opinion of the traditional public intellectual regarding this or that policy is less crucial than the acceptance or challenge of values by this mass of intellectual workers who constitute the mind-body core of production. In my opinion, it is precisely this mind-body alignment that has provided the basis for the transition of the Italian cultural hegemony from the left to the right. We should not forget that Silvio Berlusconi is, first and foremost, a television magnate not a politician. During the 1980s, his television companies were the first to identify this trend and to offer intellectuals working in the mass media and in the 'industry of the imaginary' a space in which to find employment and a voice. Berlusconi understood in good time that which the left failed to grasp, i. e. that the cultural, communications and information industries would play host to a decisive game in post-Ford, postmodern Italy. He played the game, utilising his own capital, his own tactics and his own content and he won, while the left refused to play at all or played a defensive game, merely 'imitating' the form and content of Berlusconi's television.

In a context like the one I have briefly described, the act of the three directors whom I am discussing becomes even more interesting because it is not inspired by traditional intellectual figures. Furthermore, it does not merely respond to the rewriting of the country's history in terms of content, reasoning and pedagogy but launches a counter-offensive in the same sphere of the imaginary in which Berlusconi's attack took place. It is easy to recognise here a very simple trend – the umpteenth example of in the Americanisation of the Italian public sphere. Hollywood has long accustomed us to search the big screen for the elaboration of American history and collective memory that we will never find in official political language. Even if this were the case, it is still a significant example of a loss of meaningfulness of that traditional, rational language used in the public sphere and especially of a weakening of political language's ability to decipher and give voice to the political crisis.

It is not a coincidence that we are indebted to another director, Nanni Moretti, for his 'j'accuse' against the self-referencing typical of 'professional' politics which he made on 3 February 2002. It helped to re-open a channel of communication (and confrontation) between the centre-left leadership and its disillusioned electorate as well as breathing new life into a discussion on the relationship between politicians and intellectuals which had been totally discarded.[15] However, while Moretti's attack on the political language gave way when directly confronted, the choices made by Giordana, Bertolucci and Bellocchio are anchored in cinematographic language. By avoiding a direct confrontation with political language they demonstrate more effectively its loss of meaningfulness and sense; by avoiding direct confrontation with the political bureaucracy they show, at a distance, its loss of charisma and position. The three directors do not question the relationship between politicians and intellectuals, but rather resort to a given function of the intellectual. They do not protest over the outdated procedures of modern politics, but rather raise awareness of different practices which have been ignored or have been twisted by the ascendant version of events.

4. We can now take a closer look at the messages of these three films, dividing them into two main categories. One covers the underlying notions of politics and history, the other covers the relationship between present and past as well as the function of memory in Italy's autobiography:

It should be noted that in all three films, History with a capital 'H' is never given any conclusive or factual role. Rather, it appears in the guise of a quotation or a context and always filtered through the characters' subjectivity. It is their stories which determine History and not vice versa, not only regarding the plot but particularly regarding its symbolisation or, in other words, the way in which it is imprinted on the individual and collective memory. More important than the facts themselves is the manner in which they are selected and perceived by the subject – which means that the narrative is more important than history. However, the priority given to the subjective eye is never allowed to overstep the mark (not even in Giordana's film which tends to restrict history's wide horizons to the narrow perimeter of the family) of that decadent and narcissistic intimacy which has not been absent from other Italian films in the most recent generations. Far from diminishing it, the subjective point of view is useful in emphasising the importance of history and the impact it has on individual lives: history and life are bound together by a virtual loop. Thus, in all three films, 'politics' represents that process of putting into the loop personal with public, subjectivity with the real, the intimate with the external, emotions with intentions, the transformation of self with the transformation of the world.

Once again, 'politics' is not the realm of reason, nor of order, nor of purposeful actions. Reason and the unconscious, intention and desire, the will to impose order and the energy that creates disorder all traverse both the personal and the public spheres. It is this mixture that makes politics impredictable, and it is its varying dosages which often, in just as impredictable a manner, give rise to 'good' or 'bad' outcomes. The trajectory of the cobblestone which lands in the Paris apartment in *The Dreamers* is also unpredictable: it thrusts the lives of the three young people towards the public good in the very same moment that they could have been burdened with a sense of sin and death. Here politics plays on dreams and on vital energies; it wins and a period of a seminal conflict begins. But just as unpredictable is the fate which awaits Aldo Moro: here the alliance with the female terrorist's dream in which she frees him does not bring about the desired results and politics intervenes in the guise of reasons of state and the revolution: it loses and a gray period of order is restored. The First Republic died at Aldo Moro's funeral and Italian politics began its decline.

Here there is an arc where the two categories which we established, and which link the three films, come together, in other words, a junction between the function of memory and the periodisation of the Italian transition, which completes the deconstruction and reconstruction of the Italian autobiography of the late 1990s. Indeed, if the first category demolishes the restrictive and stifling idea of politics which characterised the 1990s, the second category dismantles the framework of chronological falsehoods which sustained that idea. I would now like to consider the main points of contact.

5. As I have already mentioned, in the early 1990s the Italian political system was hit by a wave of judicial inquiries that highlighted the corruption of the parties that had governed, amid ups and downs and by excluding the PCI from its alliances, for more than 40 years. We know that corruption is a constant in contemporary political systems and that this leads to an increasing number of conflicts between executive power and the legal controls exercised by the judiciary. Nonetheless, the revelations of *Tangentopoli* – as the corruption scandal became known – and the operations of *mani pulite'* – as the investigations into corruption became known – assumed particularly strong tones in Italy. This intersected with other sociopolitical, national and international issues pushing for change. Among these issues we can identify: the crisis of political representation and the rise of a new type of mass media representation; the crisis of some basics of the Constitutional Pact, such as the solidarity between rich and poor areas of the nation, expressed symbolically by the birth of the secessionist Northern League; the collapse of the international bipolar system in 1989 and the subsequent transformation of the PCI into the Democratic Party of the Left: the decline of the Fordist socio-industrial model and the rise of the post-Fordist model embodied by Fininvest, the television company belonging to Silvio Berlusconi. These were complex and diverse processes. They had for a long time probed the collective consciousness and unconscious and they warranted a thorough investigation into republican history, especially in the decade between 1968 and 1978, and how to resolve its political and institutional crises. This investigation never eventuated and the hasty version of the facts which was cobbled together in its place must bear some of the blame for the unfavourable outcome of the transition.

Earlier, I mentioned the dominant history's habitual tendency to diminish the complexities of real history according to the direction that a particular reading of the past intends to give to the present. A very good example of this is to be found in the way the mass media – both in print and on television – has conditioned the Italian transition. In fact, it has carried out a joint, three-way campaign, targeting the time span of the transition, the plurality of the subjects involved and the notion of politics at stake. Furthermore, by re-reading the past in such a manner, it has made a substantial contribution towards diminishing the scope of the subjectivity and meaning of politics, both now and in the future. This campaign established that everything began with *tangentopoli*. In this manner, it reduced the complexities of the ongoing investigation to a mere clash between 'the old' – in other words, the entire history of the First Republic – and 'the new' – a similarly poorly defined 'new beginning' that was supposed to offer a rebirth. It restricted its diagnosis solely to the institutional system, providing no insight into the social dynamics which went hand-in-hand with the political ones. It established that the cause of the political crisis was to be found in the lack of decision from an inept government, thereby encouraging an understanding of politics as merely an administrative tool of power. All the questions, subjects, opinions, excesses and perversities of politics that did not fit this concept were categorised as ungovernable 'disorder.' The *damnatio memoriae* of that 'dark decade' from 1968 onwards which, in Italy as in all western countries, questioned the traditional definition of politics was the result.

Conversely, since the early 1990s and right up to the present day, historical revisionists – both of the right and of the moderate left – have been boldly insisting on rewriting the history of the Republic's founding struggle. This struggle between fascism and anti-fascism has been turned into a story of 'national reconciliation' with the dual purpose of lifting the blame from Fascism and placing it on communism and of turning what was apparently a divisive and partisan national identity into a 'single' one that all 'Italians' can embrace.

Truth, however has won out in this revisionist attempt to alter the official account of Italian political history, by modifying the transition to suit its own ends. The 'new beginnings,' which many had hoped for, have undergone a substantial turnaround and have become a monolithic restoration. The question of legality did not prevent more than half of the Italian electorate from electing a prime minister who is the embodiment of illegality (but capable of presenting himself as *homo novus*, alternative leader-entrepreneur to the much-despised professional politicians). The desire for a more representative democracy had succumbed to the mirage of direct elections of the 'leaders' (from mayor to prime minister) and of the majority system which restricts rather than widens the democratic base. After the failed attempt at a 'reasonable' and bipartisan reform of the constitution, the constitutional crisis began to drift towards an accelerated 'de-constitutionalisation.'[16] In the meantime, skirting the truth and misconstruing the facts, the revisionists' narrative has had a profound effect on the nation's autobiography. 'The Italian people' felt that, for more than a decade, they had been made to look like a people who had lived under a corrupt regime for more than 40 years. Represented as having been held hostage to international bipolarism and especially to the Soviet Union, they felt themselves to be the victims of an ideological struggle which needed 'polishing up' into some new-found notion of 'patriotic unity,' possibly ratified by a military commitment. The funeral service for those Italian soldiers who died in Nassiriya last November was the defining moment of this project of sublimation of the ideological into the national identity.

However, like all the reinvented identities which crowd the world stage currently, this too was a cover-up for everything that the ascendant version of events was unable to explain. In actual fact, this version explains very little. It fails to explain how and why, in 30 years, Italy has gone from being the most advanced political laboratory concerning 'progressive democracy' to being the one most advanced showing the crisis of democracy. It also fails to explain something more insidious and ill-defined: that disillusioned and slightly melancholic attitude taken by those who, thirty years ago, had imagined another future for themselves and for Italy. In order to explain these and many other things, we must repudiate the notion which places the beginning of the transition in the early 1990s and in the political system. We must dispel the fable, very fashionable ten years ago, that the wish for change which occurred in the 1990s had its roots in our wish to free ourselves from the 1980s (the legacy that Berlusconi has inherited) and not, as has become clearer with the passing of time, from any wish to bury the 1970s. We must put back into the loop the personal and the political, our intimate selves and the public good, passions and reason, dreams and intentions. We must follow the course that may turn dreams into nightmares, we must judge both the terrorists who, by shooting at the state, dealt the dreamers a fatal blow, as well as the State which, by refusing to negotiate with the terrorists, dealt itself the fatal blow.

It should also be said that, having shattered our links with dreams, having attempted to deny politics its imaginative and symbolic dimension, as the party which arose from the ashes of the PCI has consistently done since 1989, we have allowed the likes of Berlusconi and his television companies unlimited access to the colonisation of the imaginary. By permitting a frenzied wish to control the dreamers to hold sway, by ignoring their pleas for liberty, we have only opened the doors to the liberal and liberty-destroying forces of the House of Freedom. The overturning of the 'Italian laboratory' cannot be explained by the short wave of a decade but must be traced back to the long-wave of a 30-year time span that began with a revolution in subjectivity which the left proved incapable of understanding and finished with the counter-revolution of a populist leader who measures everything against his own ego.

6. While I write these last pages, Silvio Berlusconi is appearing on television for the first time since he underwent plastic surgery of his face.[17] Looking at his pop image, a perfect example of a nation that has made a religion out of its 'look,' I am reminded of the face of Aldo Moro, both the real one and the one represented by Robert Herlitzka in Bellocchio's film, that tragic, lined mask and then his dead body, squeezed into the trunk of that red Renault in Via Caetani. And still I see the drawn faces, stiffened not by surgical lifts but by the sight of that dead body, doubled over, the petrified faces of Pietro Ingrao and Enrico Berlinguer and all the political leaders of the First Republic, captured at his funeral service and broadcast by a television which was still in black and white. Assembling those images at the conclusion of his film, Marco Bellocchio has succeeded in restoring to the people something which very few of us had dared to write in the 20 years since Moro's death: the 'First Republic' did not have to wait for *Tangentopoli* to crumble; it died that day in that church. It died together with the 'double body' of the king[18] which the terrorists had played with, by killing the secular body and putting the sacred one in the trunk like a useless suitcase: political authority began its demise in that trunk. The public, especially the young, came out moved and bewildered by that film. It is almost as if they had been confronted with something they knew nothing or very little about, like archaeology, and certainly not real Italian memories. According to the director, his intention in selecting Herlitzka for the role, was to emphasise the paternal figure of Moro – the very last father, I would say, of the First Republic. What has happened to all the fathers since then? And what has happened to patriarchy?

The fact that the breakdown in paternal authority was an important ingredient in the volatile mixture which characterised the Italian transition did not escape the notice of a few perspicacious observers in the early 1990s.[19] However, they failed to complete their analysis, thereby ignoring the role played by feminism, in changing that mixture. Italy in the 1990s requires this overlapping analysis, no less than Germany in the 1930s as viewed by Horkheimer and Virginia Woolf.[20] The crisis in Italian politics is indeed related to a much broader patriarchal crisis due to both the decline in masculine political authority and to the rise, in an unusual form, of a female political authority. This is the last piece that I want to add to the puzzle.

In 1994, the perspicacious observers whom I mentioned earlier, linked the breakdown of paternal authority to the deterioration of domestic politics, the disorientation of the managerial class and the Republican crisis – likened to a ship gone adrift, no longer able to refer to the founding fathers' compass. It was not a difficult conclusion, given the emergence of Berlusconi as a *homo novus* – more managerial and paternalistic that paternal – who managed to embody the shift to an Italy deprived of its lineage. However, Bellocchio's camera provides more information, not merely by identifying the death of Moro with the death of the Republic's last father but, in particular, because he points to the symbolic aspect of the father's death and links it to the symbolic procedure of a grieving process that was not elaborated. Italy has been fatherless since Moro's assassination, not because the fathers of the Republic have all died – a natural if painful occurrence in every generation and period – but because their deaths have not been worked through. Removed in death, their spirits still hang over the collective unconscious and nobody can take their place. The tragic death of Moro, assassinated by terrorists but left to be murdered – according to Bellocchio (and this is also my interpretation) – by the 'hard line'[21] adopted by the State, is subjected to this removal process in a distinctive manner. Beneath floods of words and conjecture regarding his abduction, the weakness of the political authority which the Red Brigades had exposed lies unmentioned, covered over by the hypocrisy of the state's 'firmness.' In other words, both at the time and in the intervening 25 years, no expression has been given to the crisis of political authority which Moro's abduction had so tragically revealed long before the farcical arrival on the scene of *tangentopoli,* the transition of the 1990s and Berlusconi. And Moro's murder is not the only example of that failure to grieve for the death of the father. Even the demise of the PCI, swamped by a flood of words which extolled what was to come and gave scant consideration to what was ending, was characterised by something similar in 1989. When the PCI changed its name and identity, its activists were prevented from ascertaining and evaluating the political and existential breakdown of a community and its symbolic order.

The failure to grieve for the death of father figures has continued, in some ways, to influence Italian political events. In my opinion, this is partly responsible not only for the wholesale confusion among the political classes but also for that particularly quarrelsome and fratricidal form that politics has assumed, not so much between the centre-right and centre-left alliances as deep within the centre-left coalition, heir to the political parties which founded the Republic, and within the main left-wing party, heir to the PCI. Almost as if, from a Freudian perspective, sons could not agree on a division of their father's estate because they had failed to grieve symbolically for his death. Almost as if that unsettled period of the Italian transition could only reinforce that old cliché of a people inclined to fraticide as Umberto Saba maintained in 1946.[22]

7. However, the scene is further complicated by an element which I have intentionally kept for last as I believe it to be the pivotal one. The *paternal* order of the First Republic was indeed a patriarchal one and the demise of paternal authority is interwoven, in Italian politics, with the end of patriarchy and with an extraordinary feminine and feminist growth. This fact profoundly alters the terms of the problem as we have studied them up until now and as they would have normally been studied. Even in the field of relations between the sexes, we come up against a mainstream narrative which is considerably misleading when compared with reality. It repeats the same old story: 1970s feminism was a great social revolution but it failed to make a breach in the world of politics which is still entirely a male bastion, impenetrable then and now to women, as is evidenced by the insignificant percentages of women in parliament and in top party or government jobs.[23] The story however has had its day: it believes that the effects of a feminist revolution on politics can be measured on that very same scale of power and that very same notion of politics that feminism has challenged so dramatically. This thesis needs to be overturned: Italian feminism has been and continues to be not only a social, but an intrinsically political movement. Not because it asserted women's right to enter politics, but because it demolished the traditional idea, scope and ways of politics. Moreover, its *criticism* of traditional politics cuts across the *crisis* of politics, thereby showing an alternative that did not mean adding women to an existing scenario but rather, creating a new scenario.

For obvious reasons, I will be unable to go into any detail regarding Italian feminism's deconstruction of the established concepts of contemporary politics: suffice to say that they have hurled the gendered subject composed of body and language, of reason and passion against the abstract notion of a rational and neutral individual on whom these concepts were based. This challenge has been carried through by protesting and rewriting, from here onwards and consequently, the notions of identity and difference, universality and equality, political rationality and intent, public and private, representation and state.[24] I would like to point out however that the progress made by Italian feminism on this front has taken place in the middle of a context – the 35 years from 1968 to the present day which we are examining through our three films – strongly marked by the crisis in modern politics. The ongoing struggle with this crisis has characterised the feminist course. The feminist movement was born from its very kernel, it reveals its deepest motives, interprets it and, I maintain, stamps it with its own shadow. I beg to differ from current views that either disregard the effect of the feminist revolution on Italian politics or point out the divergences between the outcomes of various events and feminist intentions. I am convinced that feminism has had a remarkable influence on the changes that have taken place in Italian society and politics even if – and this is the essence of the problem – its role has been often ignored or misconstrued. I am furthermore convinced that by following in these footsteps, changes in Italian society and politics will take a different direction, will reveal further contradictions and will take on a new transparency. We are speaking here about another, different account of the Italian transition which in part lends weight to the account of our three films and in part corrects it, makes it more complex and gives it a new position.

We are, in fact, particularly indebted to feminism for that redefinition of politics that all three films lay claim to just as it is also due to feminism, in large part, that there is a self-conscious narrative practice that claims its own intrinsic political character, and an intellectual practice that links thought to experience and the symbolic to the real.[25] This practice also creates a public space through a network of relationships (including the one between the author and his/her readers) which also does not depend on social hierarchy and traditional political mediation.[26] In all cases, it is not a matter of planting little flags as evidence of victory. Rather, we need to reformulate a correct lineage which has been corrected by the political crisis and by political criticism. We need to understand why it has been, and never could have been otherwise, a female-centred lineage, and draw the conclusions regarding the linked destinies of politics and the relations between the sexes.

The 'putting back into the loop' of the personal and the political, desires and intentions, the transformation of self and that of the world, of the unconscious with the rational as the three films reclaim, would have been impossible in the period around '68 (and would also have been an untellable tale today) if the subject of sexual difference had not erupted onto the public sphere. The collapse of the regime of dualities – between public and private, between ordered rationality and disordered irrationality – on which the long story of modern politics is founded, came about due to this eruption of women onto the public sphere. The fact that it happened to coincide with the period of '68 does not justify the current reading which interprets feminism as an 'offshoot' of '68, along the lines of the story of Eve being created from one of Adam's ribs. An accurate reconstruction of facts and documents reveals, more importantly, that the surge of feminism in Italy, as in the US, began before 1968. Furthermore, it is the very presence of the female subject and its criticism that goes to the very heart of the statute of modern politics that made the period of '68 so radical, and not vice versa. In fact, the groundswell of '68 returns ten years later and falls into those contradictions typical of male political history, primarily the use of violence. While the feminist groundswell has more distant origins – as manifested by its echoes in twentieth-century feminist (but also not feminist) thought in Virgina Woolf or Hannah Arendt – and it does not stop but rather grows stronger when, thanks to the 'big chill' of the 1980s, the mood of '68 is dampened and politics returns to the stifling confines of governability. Neither does it stop when the great crisis of the 1990s makes itself felt.

The point however is that the two paths are only seemingly parallel. In actual fact, since the 1970s, quite a strong thread links that swift narrowing of the traditional political horizon with the widening of the horizon of difference; the withdrawal of institutional politics into an all-male fratricidal enclave with the exponential growth of relations between women; the male regret for the lost paternal authority with the theoretical and practical female research on maternal authority.[27] That thread is the growth of female freedom which proceeds at the same pace as the decline of patriarchy and with the temporary subrogation of a fraternity that is both self-referencing and misogynist. It is, in fact, not only the death of the father that the generation of men who grew up within or alongside the movement of '68 is incapable of working through; it is also the public maternal authority and a sentiment of acknowledgement and reconciliation towards the tear inflicted by women on the rigid plot of politics.[28]

Not even our three films are capable of explaining and elaborating on this sentiment; even here, proving to be extremely indicative of a 'spirit of the times' which they help us to decipher. It is not an accident that the most complex characters, in all three films, are female; they drive the plot, they embody the stimulus for change and they liberate the ambivalence of the unconscious. But it is also no accident that this construction of the female characters stops short of the threshold of political acknowledgement. Again it is on the threshold which separates intimacy and History, passion and reason that the female, replete with her seductive powers and sway, is given her rightful place more so than in the sovereign place of a politics rewritten by intimacy and desire. Yet again, in Giordana's film which, unlike the others, has a chronological and pedagogical deliberateness, feminism – the single unnamed movement of those 20 years – is completely dismissed, while all the male filial gratitude is lavished on the mother, not as a measure of the world but as a guarantee for a return to the origins which she represents.

In this manner, the female political revolution is (not) enshrined in the Italian public memory; like a wellspring of change that has watered the earth and of which the earth bears an infinite number of traces, never returned in its entirety to its profile, often deforming or diminishing it or allowing it to evaporate. It is both a lot and a little, depending on how we women manage to make sense of this representation. But until the collective memory succeeds in drawing a more precised profile and in recognising its political expression, the narrative of the (un)making of the Italian identity will be full of defects, like a painting not shown in its best light.

Notes

1. Translated from the Italian by Denise Formica.

2. *La Meglio gioventù*, directed by Marco Tullio Giordana, screenplay by Sandro Petraglia and Stefano Rulli, with Luigi Lo Cascio, Adriana Asti, Sonia Bergamasco, Maya Sansa and Yasmine Trinca, produced by Raicinema. The film tells the story of two brothers, Nicola and Matteo Carati, who are linked by dreams, hopes, literature and friendships until they meet Giorgia, a young female inmate of a psychiatric institution. Now their interests are no longer similar: after a holiday in Sweden, Nicola becomes a psychiatrist and joins the protest movement while Matteo abandons his studies and joins the police force. Thus begin two life stories which are emblematic of two distinctive ways of living through the years that go from the Florence floods of 1967 to *tangentopoli*, through 1968, terrorism and the murder of Aldo Moro. Emblematically, every existential and political choice of the two main characters is marked by an encounter with a woman. The female figures in the film are ambivalent and affected by change to a greater degree than the male figures. The title of the film is taken from that of the poetry collection of the same name by Pierpaolo Pasolini from which the screenplay often draws inspiration.

3. In a well-known poem entitled *Il Pci ai giovani*, written the day after the confrontation between students and police in front of the Faculty of Architecture of Rome University in Valle Giulia in 1968, Pierpaolo Pasolini polemically declared that his sympathy lay with the policemen 'figli di poveri' (children of the poor) rather than with the students 'figli di papà' (children of the well-to-do).

4. Franco Basaglia is the psychiatrist to whom Italy is indebted for the abolition of mental institutions and Law 180 (1978) which revolutionised mental illness therapies. This law was one of the most important ones resulting from the cultural climate of 1968 and it is not a coincidence that, since 1980, it has been subjected to a series of drastic revisions.

5 See Note 7.

6. *The Dreamers*, directed by Bernardo Bertolucci, screenplay by Gilbert Adair, based on his novel *The Holy Innocents*, with Michael Pitt, Eva Green and Louis Garrel, produced by Jeremy Thomas. The film narrates the story of two Parisian twins, Théo and Isabel, and their American friend whom they meet through their shared passion for cinema in the days of the occupation of the *Cinematique di Parigi* marking the beginning of the '68 student protest in France. They then shut themselves in their parents' apartment where they normally lived and experimented living together and other forbidden things until a rock is hurled through the window, convincing them to join in the marches of the student protesters.

7. At the screening of his film at the Venice Film Festival in 2003, Bertolucci saluted his audience and critics with a clenched fist. In his introduction to *Sognando 'The Dreamers*,' a book of the film's images and screenplay edited by Fabian S.Gerard (Ubulibri), he states: "Natalia Aspesi asked me if that clenched fist was nostalgic. I said, yes. Perhaps nostalgia for an old provocation which I never acted upon. I sense a great deal of bewilderment around and I see sardonic sneers. What is happening? What is all this nonsense about the word 'nostalgia?' What is this chorus of historical-philosophical insults against the word 'Utopia?' Is it not a revisionist attempt to discredit the movement of '68 that had its very roots in Utopia?

8. *Buongiorno, notte* directed by Marco Bellocchio, screenplay based on *Il prigioniero*, Paola Tavella's book-length interview with Moro's warder, Maria Laura Braghetti, with Roberto Herlizka, Maya Sansa and Luigi Lo Cascio, produced by Marco Bellocchio and Sergio Pelone. The film narrates the abduction of the leader of the DC, Aldo Moro on 16 March 1978 and ends tragically with the prisoner's murder which is preceded by Chiara's dream in which he is liberated.

9. 'The Italian transition' is the name given in journalistic and political language to a process of political-institutional transformation which began in the early Nineties in Italy with the discovery of a system of bribes, known as *tangentopoli,* due to a series of investigations carried out by the Deputy Public Prosecutor in Milan, known as *mani pulite.* This brought about the collapse of the parties (especially the Christian Democrats and the Socialists) that had governed for the major part of the first 45 years of the Republic. However, as the rest of my argument will demonstrate, it is a conventional name for a process whose ends and scope are, in their own way, conventional and controversial. The use of the term First Republic is also conventional and controversial in the light of the political-institutional system that collapsed under *tangentopoli.* Strictly speaking, it is an unacceptable term insofar as the change of the political system did not lead either to a new Constitution or a Second Republic.

10. Olivia Guaraldo provides an exhaustive account of this debate in a critical review, *Politica e racconto.*

11. At the beginning of the 1990s, following a referendum and legislative reform, the Italian electoral system, previously one of proportional representation, became a system of majority representation. Consequently, a different association of the political forces which survived the upheaval of *tangentopoli* aligned into two opposite poles, one centre-right and the other centre-left.

12. In November 1989, the day after the fall of the Berlin Wall, Achille Occhetto, the then secretary of the PCI announced to the Bolognina branch in Bologna that it was necessary to change the PCI's name, character and political aims. The so-called 'svolta della Bolognina' began a transformation process which ended with the birth of the PDS (now DS) at the Rimini conference in February 1999.

13. See Posner 2001.

14. See Marazzi 1994.

15. On 3 February 2002, in Piazza Navona in Rome, at the end of a colourless demonstration by the leaders of the centre-left (who were pushed into opposition in June 2001, after five years in government, by Berlusconi's second victory and still shell-shocked by the electoral defeat), Nanni Moretti, much loved by left-wing audiences for his openly left-wing films (*Palombella rossa, Caro Diario, Aprile*) leapt onto the stage, took the microphone and uttered the still-famous phrase, "With these leaders we will never win." Immediately dismissed as the 'ravings of an artist,' Moretti's gesture forced the secretary of the DS, Piero Fassino to face the widespread disillusionment that Moretti represented. On 22 February, he organised a conference on the relations between the party and intellectuals. Subsequently, Nanni Moretti became one of the leaders of the so-called 'girotondi' (ring-a-ring-a-roses), a movement with the twin aims of defending lawfulness and the constitution from Berlusconi's attacks and of encouraging the centre-left to listen to ordinary people. Made up essentially of the so-called 'thinking middle class,' the movement's leaders, apart from Moretti, are all well-known personalities, the historian Paul Ginsborg, the town planner Francesco Pardi and the philosopher and director of the journal *Micromega,* Paolo Flores d'Arcais. We should underline the fact, however, that we owe the initial surge of the movement to their habit of playing 'girotondo' around the Law Courts and Rai and their recourse to email or their organisation of demonstrations. This was the work of a handful of women who, as soon as the media spotlight fell upon the movement, were relegated to the shadows. While I am writing this, in January 2004, negotiations are taking place between 'girotondo,' the core groups of the larger party caucuses and the acronyms that constitute the centre-left in the lists for the European elections to be held next June.

16. I cannot go into the political merit of these processes here. Refer to my 'Il ritorno della sovranità assoluta.'

17. On 24 January 2004, Forza Italia, the party founded by Silvio Berlusconi in 1994, celebrated its tenth anniversary with a well-organised television ceremony. For the occasion, after being out of circulation for more than a month, the Premier returned to the public arena exhibiting a new face, recently enhanced by plastic surgery.

18. The obvious reference is Kantorowitz's famous study *I due corpi del re.*

19. Scalfari and Eco, "È una destra senza legge."

20. See my 'Dai padri alle madri' in *Il futuro del Novecento.*

21. The 'hard line' of 'firmness' refers to the decision of the Italian state and notably of the Christian Democrats and the PCI not to negotiate with the Red Brigades about the liberation of Moro.

22. "Vi siete mai chiesti perché l'Italia non ha avuto, in tutta la sua storia – da Roma a oggi – una sola vera rivoluzione? La risposta – chiave che apre molte porte – è forse la storia d'Italia in poche righe. Gli italiani non sono parricidi: sono fratricidi. Romolo e Remo, Ferruccio e maramaldo, Mussolini e I socialisti, badaglio e Graziani. [...] gli italiani sono l'unico popolo (credo) che abbiano, alla base della loro storia (o della loro leggenda) un fratricidio. Ed è solo col patricidio (uccisione del vecchio) che si inizia una rivoluzione, [...] gli italiani voglioni darsi al padre, ed avere da lui, in cambio, il permesso di uccidere gli altri fratelli."

"Have you ever asked yourselves why Italy has not had, in its entire history – from Rome until now – a single real revolution? The response – a key that opens many doors – is perhaps the history of Italy in a few lines. Italians are not patricidal, they are fratricidal: Romulus and Remus, Ferruccio and Maramaldo, Mussolini and the socialists, Badoglio and Graziani [...] I believe that Italians are a people that have fratricide at the foundation of their history (or of their legends). And it is only with patricide (the murder of the old) that one commences a revolution. [...] Italians want to give themselves to the father and to have his permission to murder other brothers." (Saba, *Scorciatoie e raccontini*)

23. The percentage has never yet reached ten percent.

24. The bibliography on the subject is immense. Refer to my 'Il desiderio di politica'; 'L' eccedenza della libertà'; Boccia; and Diotima, *Oltre l'uguaglianza*.

25. See Diotima, *La sapienza di partire da sé*. See also Guaraldo, on the relation between an author and her public that is ignored by social hierarchies and traditional political mediations.

26. See Scarparo.

27. The category of 'maternal authority' is one of the most crucial and innovative ideas developed by Italian sexual difference feminist theory. It is not a question of equal and symmetrical authority although it is diverse and asymmetrical in terms of paternal authority. It refers to a symbolic order based on relations and trust rather than upon a hierarchy. Moreover, it serves to restore a public function to the mother beyond that of care that 'maternal' traditionally signifies. The mother, gives life and nourishment but also language to the world. See. Diotima, *Oltre l'uguaglianza. Le radici dell'autorità*.

28. See my 'L' eccedenza della libertà femminile.' See also "Nella piega del presente."

Contributors

Paola Bono teaches English theatre at the Università Roma Tre. Besides doing research in this field – with special attention to the Elizabethan period – she has also written about contemporary women writers with a comparative and interdisciplinary approach, as well as about the transformation of themes and stories through different cultures, media and historical periods. She is on the editorial board of the Italian feminist journal *DWFdonnawomanfemme*, and of *The European Journal of Women's Studies*, and is a member of the international Advisory Board of *Signs*. For more information see http://www.profonline.it/display.php?id_prof=9.

Suzanne Branciforte lives in Liguria and teaches at the University of Genoa. She is the author of *Parliamo italiano!* (1998, 2002), a multimedia program for learning Italian, and translator of Renata Viganò's collection of short stories, *Partisan Wedding* (1999). Her research and writing focuses on language, cultural identity and cultural mediation between Italy and the US. She has recently completed a memoir.

Mirna Cicioni has worked and studied in the United Kingdom and Australia, and is currently Senior Lecturer in Italian studies at Monash University. Her research publications and areas of interest include language and society in twentieth-century Italy, Italian feminism, and post-World War II Italian Jewish writers. She has written an introductory monograph on Primo Levi and is working on a study of autobiography and humour in the writings of Primo Levi, Natalia Ginzburg, Aldo Zargani and Clara Sereni.

Ida Dominijanni is a journalist and editor with the newspaper *Il manifesto*, and teaches political philosophy at the Università Roma Tre. She is also a member of the women's philosophical group Diotima at the University of Verona. She edited *Motivi della Libertà* (Franco Angeli, 2002), and she is the author of several essays on political theory and feminist theory, including "Nella piega del presente," in *Diotima, Approfittare dell'assenza* (Liguori 2002).

Paula Green is currently completing a doctoral thesis at the University of Auckland. She has had two volumes of poetry published by Auckland University Press, *Cookhouse* (1997) and *chrome* (2000), with a forthcoming volume, *Crosswind*, due in 2004. Her poetry and essays have appeared in journals in Australia, Canada, Great Britain, India, New Zealand and the USA.

Patrizia Guida, Professor of contemporary Italian literature at the University of Lecce, Italy, holds a Laurea in Lingue e Letterature Straniere from the University of Bari, and a PhD in Italian studies from the University of Lecce. She specialises in twentieth-century and contemporary Italian literature. In addition to numerous articles and reviews, her publications include *Invisibile Women Writers in Exile in the U.S.A.* (Peter Lang); *Letteratura femminile del Ventennio fascista* (Pensa Editore); *Oltre la linea gotica: Il Mondo di Bonsanti* (Pensa Editore); *Francesco Jovine. Scritti critici* (Milella). She is presently working on a book on the literature of Southern Italy after World War II.

Bernadette Luciano is head of the Italian Department and Coordinator of the Programme in European Studies at the University of Auckland, New Zealand. She has written numerous articles on Italian women writers, Italian film and dialect poetry. She is currently editing a book on New Zealand/European cultural studies.

Maria Cristina Mauceri is Cassamarca Lecturer in Italian studies at the University of Sydney. Before moving to Australia she lectured for a number of years in German Literature in Italy. In Australia she developed an interest in comparative literature as a way of bridging the gap between German and Italian literature. She has published on the history of literary themes, in particular on the double and youth. She is currently working on migrant writers in Italy and Italian writers living outside Italy. Her recent publications include an essay on "La straniera" by Younis Tawfik and an interview with Helga Schneider on Kuma (2003).

Maja Mikula is a lecturer in Italian studies at the Institute for International Studies, University of Technology, Sydney. Her research interests are in the areas of (trans)nationalism, gender and the new media. She has published a chapter on "Croatia's Independence and the Language Politics of the 1990s" in *Perspectives on Europe: Language Issues and Language Planning in Europe* (Melbourne: Language Australia Ltd, 2002). Recent articles include "Naked in the Gymnasium: Women as Agents of Social Change" (2004); "Gender and Videogames: The Political Valency of Lara Croft (2003); and "Virtual Landscapes of Memory" (2003).

Maria Pallotta-Chiarolli, PhD, is a Senior Lecturer in social diversity and health in the School of Health and Social Development at Deakin University, Melbourne, Australia. Maria teaches, writes and researches on cultural diversity, gender diversity and sexualities in education and health. She is also an external faculty member of Saybrook Graduate Research Centre, San Francisco. In 1999, Maria was honoured with the title of Lifelong Honorary Patron for PFLAG (Parents and Friends of Lesbians and Gays) Victoria, Australia. Her book *Tapestry* was short-listed for the NSW Premier's Award in the Ethnic Affairs Commission category and in the Children's Book Council Non-Fiction Award. *Boys' Stuff* was shortlisted for the Western Australian Premier's Award; won the Australian Book Design Award in the Educational Texts for Young People Category; and achieved a Highly Commended in the Australian Award for Excellence in Educational Publishing. It was also nominated for a Human Rights Award.

Dana Renga, an Assistant Professor of Italian at Colorado College, received her Ph.D. in Italian literature from the University of California at Los Angeles. Her fields of interest are nineteenth and twentieth-century Italian literature, cultural studies and Italian film with an emphasis on issues of historical and gender representation. She has published on Italo Calvino, Federico Fellini, Andrea Zanzotto, Guarino Guarini and Italian cinema under fascism. Her current research focuses on gender and cultural identity in Italian cinema.

Gabriella Romani teaches at Princeton. Her research focuses on nineteenth-century literature and culture, with particular attention to questions relating to gender representations and the formation of modern identities. She is coediting with Antonia Arslan an anthology in the English language of nineteenth-century short stories by Italian women writers and is working on a book on nineteenth-century women's epistolary narratives.

Susanna Scarparo is Cassamarca Lecturer in Italian studies at Monash University. She is the author of *Elusive Subjects: Biography as Gendered Metafiction* (Troubador, Forthcoming) and has written articles on women's life writing, historical fiction, Italian feminism and Italo-Australian studies.

Rita Wilson teaches in the School of Languages, Cultures and Linguistics, Monash University, and has published articles on avant-garde poetry, Italo Calvino and Antonio Tabucchi. She is the author of *Speculative Identities: Contemporary Italian Women's Narrative* (Northern Universities Press, 2000) and co-editor of *Spaces and Crossings. Essays on Literature and Culture from Africa and Beyond* (Peter Lang, 2001).

Works Cited

Aaron, Daniel. "The Hyphenate Writer and American Letters." *Rivista di Studi Anglo-Americani* 3.4-5 (1984/85): 11-28.

Aciman, Andrè. *Out of Egypt: A Memoir*. New York: Riverhead, 1994.

Adams, J.C., and P. Barile. *The Government of Republican Italy*. 3rd ed. Boston: Houghton Mifflin, 1972.

Agazzi, Elena, and Angelo Canavesi, eds. *Il segno dell'io. Romanzo e autobiografia nella tradizione moderna*. Udine: Campanotto, 1992.

Aleramo, Sibilla. *Andando e stando in gioie d'occasione e altre ancora*. Milan: Mondadori, 1954.

---. *Una donna*. Milan: Feltrinelli, 1980.

Alighieri, Dante. *Divine Comedy: Italian Text and Translation*. Trans. Charles Singleton. Princeton: Princeton UP, 1989.

Almansi, Guido. *Amica ironia*. Milan: Garzanti, 1984.

Altman, Janet Gurkin. *Epistolarity: Approaches to a Form*. Columbus: Ohio State UP, 1986.

Altork, Kate. "Walking the Fire Line: The Erotic Dimension of the Fieldwork Experience." *Taboo: Sex, Identity and Erotic Subjectivity in Anthropological Fieldwork*. Eds. D. Kulick and M. Willson. London: Routledge, 1995.

Anderson, Benedict. *Imagined Communities*. London: Verso, 1983.

Anzaldùa, Gloria. *Borderlands/La Frontera: The New Mestiza*. San Francisco: Spinsters/Aunt Lute, 1987.

Anzaldùa, Gloria, and Cherry Moraga, eds. *This Bridge Called My Back: Writings by Radical Women of Color*. Watertown, Mass.: Persephone Press, 1981.

Apter, Emily. "Comparative Exile. Competing Margins in the History of Comparative Literature." *Comparative Literature in the Age of Multiculturalism*. Ed. Charles Bernheimer. Baltimore: Johns Hopkins UP, 1995.

Armstrong, Nancy. *Desire and Domestic Fiction*. New York: Oxford UP, 1987.

Arru, Angelina, and Maria Teresa Chialant, eds. *Il racconto delle donne. Voci, autobiografie, figurazioni*. Naples: Liguori, 1990.

Aull, Katharina. *Verbunden und gebunden*. Frankfurt am Main: Peter Lang, 1993.

Baeri, Emma. *I lumi e il cerchio*. Rome: Editori Riuniti, 1992.

Baiardo, L. "Grazia Deledda. Amore e gloria." *Una donna un secolo*. Ed. S. Petrignani. Rome: Il Ventaglio, 1986.

Balducci, C. *A Self-made Woman: Biography of Nobel-Prize Winner Grazia Deledda*. Boston: Houghton Mifflin Co., 1975.

Banti, Alberto. *La nazione del Risorgimento*. Turin: Einaudi, 2000.

Banti, Anna. *Opinioni*. Milan: Il Saggiatore, 1961.

Bar-On, Dan. *Legacy of Silence: Encounters with Children of the Third Reich*. Cambridge, Mass.: Harvard UP, 1989.

Barthes, Roland. "Introduction to the Structural Analysis of Narratives." *Image-Music-Text*. London: Collins, 1977. 79-124.

Battistini, A. "L'autobiografia e il superego dei generi letterari." *Annali d'Italianistica* 4 (1986): 7-29.

Beaujour, Michel. *Poetics of the Literary Self-Portrai.* Trans. Yara Milos. New York: New York UP, 1991.

Beebee, Thomas. *Epistolary Fiction in Europe:1500-1850.* Cambridge: Cambridge UP, 1999.

Benjamin, Walter. "Theses on the Philosophy of History." Trans. Harry Zohn. *Illuminations.* New York: Schocken Books, 1969. 253-64.

Benstock, Shari, ed. *The Private Self: Theory And Practice Of Women's Autobiographical Writings.* London: Routledge, 1988.

Berger, Alan, and Naomi, Berger, eds. *Second Generation Voices. Reflections by Children of Holocaust Survivors and Perpetrators.* New York: Syracuse U P, 2001.

Bertolotti, Davide. *Epistolario ad uso della gioventù.* Milan, 1831.

Bianchetti, G. *Dello scrivere italiano.* Milan, 1844.

Bloom, Lynn Z. "Heritages: Dimensions of Mother-Daughter Relationships in Women's Autobiographies." *The Lost Tradition: Mothers and Daughters in Literature.* Eds. Cathy N. Davidson and E. M. Broner. New York: Frederik Ungar Publishing Co., 1980.

Boccia, Maria Luisa. *La differenza politica.* Milan: Il Saggiatore, 2002.

Boime, Albert. *The Art of Macchia and the Risorgimento.* Chicago: Chicago UP, 1993.

Bono, Paola. "La casa che non c'è. Topografia provvisoria del femminismo anglosassone." *Reti* 3 (1992): 3-8.

---, ed. *Questioni di teoria femminista.* Milano: La Tartaruga, 1993.

Bono, Paola, and Sandra Kemp, eds. *Italian Feminist Thought: A Reader.* Oxford: Basil Blackwell, 1991.

Booth, Wayne C. *A Rhetoric of Irony.* Chicago: U of Chicago P, 1974.

Boscagli, Maurizia. "Brushing Benjamin Against the Grain: Elsa Morante and the Jetztzeit of Marginal History." *Italian Women Writers from the Renaissance to the Present.* Ed. Maria Ornella Marotti. Pennsylvania: Pennsylvania State UP, 1996. 131-44.

Botteri, Inge. *Galateo e Galatei: La creanza e l'istituzione della società nella trattatistica italiana tra antico regime e stato liberale.* Rome: Bulzoni, 1999.

Bourque Johnson, Elizabeth. "Mothers at Work: Representations of Maternal Practice in Literature." *Mothers and Daughters: Connection, Empowerment & Transformation.* Eds. Andrea O'Reilly and Sharon Abbey. Lanham: Rowman & Littlefield Publishers, 2000. 21-35.

Braidotti, Rosi. *Nomadic Subjects: Embodiment and Sexual Difference in Contemporary Feminist Theory.* New York: Columbia UP, 1994.

Branciforte, Suzanne. "Politica radicale/pedagogia radicale: l'esperienza di un'italianista italo-americana." *Esilio, migrazione, e sogno americano.* Eds. Paolo A. Giordano and Anthony Julian Tamburri. Boca Raton: Bordighera Press, 2002. 60-73.

---. "Voyage to the Center of Mother Earth: On Italian American Identity." *America and the Mediterranean: Proceedings of the 16th Biennial International Conference of the AISNA (Associazione Italiana di Studi Nord-Americani).* Eds. Massimo Bacigalupo and Pierangelo Castagneto. Turin: Otto Editore, 2003.

Bregola, Davide. "Helena Janeczek: riuscire a trasmettere il gelo." *Da qui verso casa.* Rome: Edizioni Interculturali, 2002.

Brew, Angela. "Moving Beyond Paradigm Boundaries." *Writing Qualitative Research.* Ed. J. Higgs. Sydney: Centre for Professional Education Advancement, University of Sydney and Hampden Press, 1998.

Brewster, Anne. "Fictocriticism: Pedagogy and Practice." *Crossing Lines: Formations of Australian Culture.* Eds. P. Buttress, A. Nettelbeck and C. Guerin. Adelaide: Proceedings of the Association for the Study of Australian Literature Conference, 1995.

Briganti, P. "La cerchia infuocata. Per una tipologia dell'autobiografia letteraria italiana del Novecento." *Annali d'Italianistica* 4 (1986): 189-222.

Brodzsky, Bella. "Mothers, Displacement, and Language in the Autobiographies of Nathalie Sarraute and Christa Wolf." *Life/Lines. Theorizing Women's Autobiography.* Eds. Bella Brodzki and Celeste Schenck. Ithaca: Cornell UP, 1988.

Brodzsky, Bella, and Celeste Schenck, eds. *Life/Lines: Theorizing Women's Autobiography.* Ithaca: Cornell UP, 1988.

Bruck, Edith. *Chi ti ama di più.* Milan: Lerici, 1959.

Bruner, J. *La fabbrica delle storie. Diritto. Letteratura. Vita.* Bari: Laterza, 2002.

Bruss, Elizabeth W. *Autobiographical Acts: The Changing Situation Of A Literary Genre.* Baltimore: Johns Hopkins UP, 1976.

Bukiet, Melvin Jules, ed. *Nothing Makes You Free: Writings by Descendants of Jewish Holocaust Survivors.* New York: W.W. Norton, 2002.

Butler, Judith. "Imitation And Gender Insubordination." *Inside/Out: Lesbian Theories.* Ed. Diana Fuss. New York: Routledge, 1991.

Buttafuoco, Annarita. "Educazione e modelli di emancipazione nella stampa politica femminile del secondo Ottocento." *Cronache femminili.* Siena: Dipartimento di studi storico sociali e filosofici, 1988. 21-52.

Buttafuoco, Annarita, and Marina Zancan. *Svelamento.* Milan: Feltrinelli, 1988.

Cafagna, Josephine, et al. "Panel Discussion on Exploring Identity and Community through the Arts and Culture." *In Search of the Italian Australian into the New Millenium.* Eds. Piero Genovesi and Walter Musolino. Melbourne: Gro-Set Pty Ltd, 2000. 797-840.

Caizzi, Bruno. *Dalla Posta dei Re alla Posta di tutti: Territorio e comunicazioni in Italia dal XVI secolo all'Unità.* Milan: FrancoAngeli, 1993.

Cappiello, Rosa. *Oh Lucky Country.* Trans. G. Rando. Brisbane: U of Queensland P, 1984.

---. *Paese Fortunato.* Milan: Feltrinelli, 1981.

Capponi, Carla. *Con cuore di donna.* Milan: Il Saggiatore, 2000.

Cavarero, Adriana. "The Need for a Sexed Thought." Trans. Paola Bono and Sandra Kemp. *Italian Feminist Thought: A Reader.* 1986. Eds. Paola Bono and Sandra Kemp. Oxford: Basil Blackwell, 1991. 180-85.

---. *Nonostante Platone.* Rome: Riuniti, 1990.

---. *Tu che mi guardi, tu che mi racconti.* Milan: Feltrinelli, 1997.

Cecchi, E., ed. *Romanzi e novelle.* 4 vols. Milan: Mondadori, 1941.

Cherniavsky, Eva. *That Pale Mother Rising: Sentimental Discourses and the Imitation of Motherhood in 19th-century America.* Bloomington: Indiana UP, 1995.

Cicioni, Mirna, and Susan Walker. "Picking Up the Pieces: Clara Sereni's Recipes for Survival." *Novel Turns Towards 2000 - Critical Perspectives on Contemporary Narrative Writing from Western Europe.* Ed. John Gatt-Rutter. Melbourne: Voz Hispanica, 2000. 35-47.

Cigarini, Lia, and Luisa Muraro. "Politica e pratica politica." *Critica Marxista* 3 (1992). 13-17.

Cixous, Hélène. "The Laugh of the Medusa." Trans. Keith Cohen and Paula Cohen. Eds. Elaine Marks and Isabelle de Courtivron. Amherst: U of Massachusetts P, 1980.

---. "The Laugh of the Medusa." *Signs* 1 (1976): 875-99.

---. "Fiction and its Phantoms: A Reading of Freud's *Das Unheimliche* (The Uncanny)." *New Literary History.* 7:3 (1976): 525-48.

---. *Les rêveries de la femme sauvage, Scènes primitives.* Paris: Galilée, 2000.

---. *Osnabrück.* Paris: Des femmes, 1999.

Colombi, Marchesa. 1887. *Gente per bene.* Novara: Interlinea, 2000.

---. *Un Matrimonio in provincia.* Novara: Interlinea, 1999.

Cook, Elizabeth H. *Epistolary bodies.* Stanford, CA: Stanford UP, 1996.

Cope, Bill, and Mary Kalantzis. "Why Literacy Pedagogy Has to Change." *Education Australia* 30 (1995): 8-11.

Cotnoir, Louise. "Liminaire." *Tessera* 8 (1990).

Creed, Barbara. *The Monstrous-feminine: Film, Feminist and Psychoanalysis.* London: Routledge, 1993.

Daley, Mary. *Gyn/Ecology: The Metaethics of Radical Feminism.* Boston: Beacon Press, 1978.

D'Angeli, Concetta. "Il Paradiso nella Storia." *Studi Novecenteschi* 21. 47-48 (1994): 215-35.

Dappio, Carla. "I periodici femminili dell'800 in due biblioteche romane." *Memoria* 5 (1982): 118-21.

De Caldas Brito, Christiana. "Che cosa vuol dire essere uno scrittore migrante?" *Diaspore europee e lettere migranti.* Eds. Armando Gnisci and Nora Moll. Rome: Edizioni Interculturali, 2002.

De Clementi, Andreina. "Il racconto di sé tra rivelazione e dissimulazione." *Memoria* 33 (1991).

De Felice, Renzo. *Rosso e nero.* Milan: Baldini e Castoldi, 1995.

De Giovanni, Neria. *L'Ora di Lilith.* Rome: Ellemme, 1987.

---. *Carta di donna: Narratrici italiane del '900.* Turin: Società Editrice Internazionale, 1996.

De Lauretis, Teresa. *Alice Doesn't: Feminism, Semiotics, Cinema.* Bloomington, IN: Indiana U P, 1984.

---. "Eccentric Subjects: Feminist Theory and Historical Consciousness." *Feminist Studies* 16.1 (1990): 115-51.

---. "The Essence of the Triangle or, Taking the Risk of Essentialism Seriously: Feminist Theory in Italy, the U.S. and Britain." *Differences* 1.2 (1989): 3-38.

---. ed. *Feminist Studies: Critical Studies.* Bloomington, IN: Indiana UP, 1986.

---. *Sui generis: Scritti di teoria femminista.* Milan: Feltrinelli, 1996.

---. *Technologies of Gender: Essays in Theory, Film and Fiction.* Bloomington, IN: Indiana UP, 1987.

De Man, Paul. *The Rhetoric of Romanticism.* New York: Columbia UP, 1984.

De Michelis, E., ed. *Opere scelte.* Vol. 1. Milan: Modadori, 1964.

Deledda, Grazia. *Cosima.* 1936. Milan: Mondadori, 1975.

---. "Omaggio a G. Deledda." *Il Convegno* 7 (1959).

---. *Deledda: Lettere inedite (1891-1900)*. Milan: Fabbri, 1966.

Deleuze, Gilles, and Felix Guattari. *A Thousand Plateaus*. Trans. Brian Massumi. Minneapolis: U of Minnesota P, 1987.

Della Coletta, Cristina. *Plotting the Past: Metamorphoses of Historical Narrative in Modern Italian Fiction*. West Lafayette: Purdue UP, 1996.

Dell'Oso, Anna Maria. *Cats, Cradles and Chamomile Tea*. Hornsby: Random House Australia, 1989.

---. *Interview with Anna Maria Dell'Oso*. Dec. 1998 - Jan. 1999. Available: http://www. australiadonna.on.net/english/dellos.htm.

---. "The Sewing Machine." *Growing up Italian in Australia*. Ed. Barbara Walsh. Sydney: State Library of NSW Press, 1993. 43-63.

Dernedde, Renate. *Mutterschatten-Schattenmutter*. Frankfurt am Main: Peter Lang, 1994.

Derrida, Jacques. "The Ear of the Other. Otobiography, Transference, Translation." Ed. C.V. McDonald. New York: Schocken Books, 1985.

Dickie, John. "Imagined Italies." *Italian Cultural Studies: An Introduction*. Eds. David Forgacs and Robert Lumley. Oxford: Oxford UP, 1996. 19-33.

---. "The Notion of Italy." *The Cambridge Companion to Modern Italian Culture*. Eds. Zygmunt G. Baranski and Rebecca J. West. Cambridge: Cambridge UP, 2001. 17-33.

Dini, Francesca, ed. *I Macchiaioli*. Florence: Edizioni Polistampa, 2002.

Diotima. *La sapienza di partire da sé*. Naples: Liguori, 1996.

---. *Oltre l'uguaglianza. Le radici dell'autorità*. Naples: Liguori, 1995.

DiQuinzio, Patrice. *The Impossibility of Motherhood: Feminism, Individualism, and the Problem of Mothering*. London: Routledge, 1999.

Doglio, Maria Luisa. *Lettera e donna*. Rome: Bulzoni, 1993.

Dominijanni, Ida. "Dai padri alle madri." *Il futuro del Novecento*. Rome: manifestolibri, 2000.

---. "Il desiderio di politica." *La politica del desiderio*. Milan: Pratiche, 1995.

---. "Il ritorno della sovranità assoluta." *La forza e il diritto*. Ed. Alberto Burgio. Rome: Deriveapprodi, 2003.

---. "Language, Communication and Betrayal." *European Journal of Women's Studies* 1.1 (1992). 61-72.

---. "L' eccedenza della libertà femminile." *Motivi della libertà*. Ed. Ida Dominijanni. Milan: Franco angeli, 2001. 47-88.

---. "Nella piega del presente." *Approfittare dell'assenza*. Ed. Diotima. Naples: Liguori, 2002. 187-212.

---. "Politica del simbolico e mutamento." *IG Informazioni* 3 (1994). 131-58.

Durbè, Dario. "Painters of Italian life." *Macchiaioli*. Los Angeles: Frederick S. Wight Art Gallery, U of California P, 1986.

DWF, editorial board. *DWF: Genealogie del presente* 49 (2001).

---. "Biografie: effetti di ritorno." *DWF* 3 (1986): 5-6.

Eakin, P. *Fictions in Autobiography: Studies in the Art of Self-Invention*. Princeton: Princeton UP, 1985.

Eco, Umberto. *The Role of the Reader. Explorations in the Semiotics of Texts*. Bloomington: Indiana UP, 1979.

Ely, Margot, Margaret Anzul, Maryann Downing, and Ruth Vinz. *On Writing Qualitative Research: Living By Words*. London: Falmer Press, 1997.

Epstein, Helen. *Children of the Holocaust: Conversations with Sons and Daughters of Survivors*. New York: Penguin, 1979.

Evans, J. "A Short Paper About People, Power and Educational Reform. Authority and Representation in Ethnographic Research. Subjectivity, Ideology and Educational Reform: The Case of Physical Education." *Research in Physical Education and Sport*. Ed. A.C. Sparkes. London: Falmer Press, 1992.

Fanning, Ursula. "Mother in the Text, Mothering the Text: Francesca Santivale and Fabrizia Ramondino." *The Italianist* 14 (1994): 204-17.

Farinelli, Giuseppe, Ermanno Paccagnini, Giovanni Santambrogio, and Angela Ida Villa, eds. *Storia del giornalismo italiano*. Turin: Utet, 1997.

Featherstone, Mike. "Ed. Introduction." *Global Culture: Nationalism, Globalization and Modernity*. Thousand Oaks, CA: SAGE Publications, 1999. 1-14.

Fedele, Clemente. *La voce della posta: comunicazioni e società nell'Italia napoleonica*. Prato: Istituto di studi storici postali, 1996.

Ferreira, Maria Aline Seabra. "The Uncanny (M)other: Angela Carter's *The Passion of New Eve*." *Paradoxa*. 3. 3-4 (1997): 471-88.

Finocchi, Anna. *Lettrici: immagini della donna che legge nella pittura dell'Ottocento*. Nuoro: Ilisso, 1992.

Firenze, Centro Documentazione Donna di, ed. *Verso il luogo delle origini*. Milan: La Tartaruga, 1992.

Firestone, Shulamith. *The Dialectic of Sex: The Case for Feminist Revolution*. New York: Bantam Books, 1970.

Fitzgerald, Maureen H. "Ethnography." *Qualitative Research: Discourse on Methodologies*. Ed. J. Higgs. Sydney: Centre for Professional Education Advancement, University of Sydney and Hampden Press, 1997.

Fleishmann, A. *Figures of Autobiography*. Berkeley: U of California P, 1983.

Floris, A. *La prima Deledda*. Cagliari: Edizioni Castello, 1989.

Forster, E.M. *A Room with a View*. 1908. New York: Bantam Books, 1988.

Fortini, Laura. "I segni sul muro." *Ciao bella: Ventun percorsi dicritica letteraria femminile oggi*. Eds. Rosaria Guacci and Bruna Miorelli. Milan: Lupetti/Piero Manni Letteratura, 1996. 195-209.

Foucault, Michel. *The History of Sexuality: An Introduction*. Trans. Robert Hurley. Vol. I. New York: Vintage Books, 1978.

Franchini, Silvia. *Editori, lettrici e stampa di moda: giornali di moda e di famiglia a Milano dal "Corriere delle dame" agli editori dell'Italia unita*. Milan: FrancoAngeli, 2002.

Freire, Paolo. *Pedagogy of the Oppressed*. Harmondsworth: Penguin, 1972.

Freud, Sigmund. *The Interpretation of Dreams. The Standard Edition of the Complete Psychological Works of Sigmund Freud*. Trans. James Strachey. Vols. IV and V. London: The Hogarth Press, 1953-74.

---. "The Uncanny." *Standard Edition of the Complete Psychological Works*. Vol. 17 London: Hogarth Press, 1953-1974.

Fried, Robert C. *Planning the Eternal City: Roman Politics and Planning since World War II*. New Haven: Yale UP, 1973.

Friedman, Susan Sanford. "Women's Autobiographical Selves: Theory and Practice" *The Private Self: Theory and Practice of of Women's Autobiographical Writings*. Ed. Shari Benstock. London: Routledge, 1988. 34-62.

Friedan, Betty. *The Feminine Mystique*. New York: Norton, 1963.

Frye, N. *Anatomy of Criticism*. Princeton: Princeton UP, 1957.

Fuà Fusinato, Erminia. "Sulla educazione delle donne italiane." *Giornale delle donne* 23.8 (1876).

Gabelli, Aristide. "L'Italia e l'istruzione femminile." *Nuova Antologia* 15.9 (1870): 145-67.

Galli della Loggia, Ernesto. *La morte della patria*. Bari: Laterza, 1996.

---. *L'identità italiana*. Bologna: Il Mulino, 1998.

Gamba, B. *Lettere descrittive*. Marsilio: Venice, 1820.

Genette, G. *Figure III*. Turin: Einaudi, 1976.

Giacobbe Harder, M. *Grazia Deledda. Introduzione alla Sardegna*. Milan: Bompiani, 1974.

Giannatonio, Pompeo. "Matilde Serao tra giornalismo e letteratura." *Nuova Antologia* (1977): 150-58.

Gilbert, S. and S. Gubar,. *The Madwoman in the Attic: The Woman Writer and the Nineteenth-Century Literary Imagination*. New Haven: Yale UP, 1979.

Gilbert, Sandra M. "Mysteries of the Hyphen: Poetry, Pasta, and Identity Politics." *Beyond the Godfather: Italian American Writers on the Real Italian American Experience*. Eds. Kenneth Ciongoli and Jay Parini. Hanover: UP of New England, 1997.

Gilmore, Leigh. *Autobiographies. A Feminist Theory of Women's Self-Representation*. Ithaca: Cornell UP, 1994.

Gilroy, Amanda, and W. M. Verhoeven, eds. *Epistolary Histories: Letters, Fiction, Culture*. Charlottesville: UP of Virginia, 2000.

Ginzburg, Natalia. *Mai devi domandarmi*. Milan: Garzanti, 1970.

Giorgio, Adalgisa, ed. *Writing Mothers and Daughters, Renegotiating the Mother in Western European Narratives by Women*. New York: Berghahn, 2002.

---. "A Feminist Family Romance: Mother, Daughter and Female Genealogy in Fabrizia Ramondino's *Althénopis*." *The Italianist*. 11 (1991): 124-149.

Giunta, Edvige. *Writing with an Accent. Contemporary Italian American Women Authors*. New York: Palgrave, 2002.

Godard, Barbara. "Traduzione:soggetto/i in transito". *Questioni di teoria femminista*. Ed. Paola Bono. Milan: La Tartaruga, 1993.

Goldsmith, Elizabeth C. *Writing the Female Voice: Essays on Epistolary Writing*. Boston: Northeastern UP, 1989.

Golino, Enzo. "Cuor di mamma nazista." *L'Espresso* 5 April 2001: 135.

Goodfellow, Joy. "Constructing a Narrative." *Writing Qualitative Research*. Ed. J. Higgs. Sydney: Centre for Professional Education Advancement, University of Sydney and Hampden Press, 1998.

Gordon, Mary. "The Parable of the Cave or: In Praise of Watercolors." *The Woman Writer on her Work*. Ed. Janet Sternburg. New York: Norton, 1980.

Gozzi, G. *Segretario moderno o ammaestramento ed esempi per ogni sorta di lettere tratte dai più illustri scrittori*. Padova, 1820.

Green, Paula. *chrome*. Auckland: U of Auckland P, 2000.

Guaraldo, Olivia. *Politica e racconto*. Rome: Meltemi, 2003.

Guglielminetti, M. "Per un'antologia degli autobiografi del Settecento." *Annali d'italianistica* 4 (1986): 140-51.

Gunew, Sneja. "Denaturalizing Cultural Nationalisms: Multicultural Readings of 'Australia.'" *Nation and Narration*. Ed. H.K. Bhabha. London: Routledge, 1990.

---. *Framing Marginality: Multicultural Literary Studies*. Melbourne: Melbourne UP, 1994.

Habermas, Jürgen. *The Structural Transformation of the Public Sphere*. Cambridge, MA: MIT Press, 1988.

Hall, Stuart. "Encoding/Decoding." *Media Texts: Authors and Readers*. 1980. Eds. David Graddol and Oliver Boyd-Barrett. Clevedon: The Open University, 1994. 200-11.

Hall, Stuart, David Held, and Tony McGrew, eds. *Modernity and Its Futures*. Cambridge: Cambridge UP, 1992.

Hart, F. "Notes for an Anatomy of Modern Autobiography." *New Literary History* 1 (1970): 485-511.

Heilbrun, Carolyn G. *Writing a Woman's Life*. W.W. Norton: New York, 1988.

Hirsch, Marianne. "Novel of Formation as Genre: Between Great Expectations and Lost Illusions." *Genre* 3 (1979): 293-311.

---. "Maternity and Rememory: Toni Morrison's *Beloved*." *Representations of Motherhood*. Eds. Donna Basin, Margaret Honey, and Meryle Mahrer Kaplan. New Haven: Yale UP 1994. 92-110.

---. *The Mother/Daughter Plot, Narrative, Psychoanalysis, Feminism*. Bloomington: Indiana UP, 1989.

Holub, Renate. "Between the United States and Italy: Critical Reflections on Diotima's Feminist/Feminine Ethics." *Feminine Feminists: Cultural Practices in Italy*. Ed. Giovanna Miceli Jeffries. Minneapolis: U of Minnesota P, 1994. 233-60.

---. "For the Record: The Non-Language of Italian Feminist Philosophy." *Romance Language Annual* 1 (1990): 133-40.

---. "The Politics of Diotima." *Diffferentia* 5 (1991): 161-71.

Hooks, Bell. *Feminist Theory: From Margins to Center*. Boston: South End Press, 1984.

---. *Outlaw Culture: Resisting Representations*. New York: Routledge, 1994.

Hooton, Joy. "Autobiography and Gender." *Writing Lives: Feminist Biography & Autobiography*. Ed. Susan Magarey. Adelaide: Australian Feminist Studies, 1992. 25-40.

Horne, Donald. *The Lucky Country: Australia in the Sixties*. Harmondsworth: Penguin, 1966.

Hull, Gloria T., Patricia Bell Scott, and Barbara Smith, eds. *All the Women Are White, All the Blacks Are Men, But Some of Us Are Brave*. Old Westbury, N.Y.: The Feminist Press, 1982.

Hutcheon, Linda. *Irony's Edge. The Theory and Politics of Irony*. London: Routledge, 1994.

Irigaray, Luce. *Ce sexe qui n'en est pas un*. Paris: Minuit, 1977.

---. *Le corps à corps avec la mère*. Ottawa: Les editions de la pleine lune, 1981.

---. *This Sex Which is Not One*. 1977. Ithaca: Cornell UP, 1985.

Iser, Wolfgang. *The Act of Reading. A Theory of Aesthetic Response*. Baltimore: Johns Hopkins UP, 1978.

Lite, Shere. "I Hope I'm Not Like My Mother." *Motherhood: A Feminist Perspective*. Eds. Jane Price Knowles and Ellen Cole. New York: The Haworth Press, 1990. 13-30.

Janeczek, Helena. *Cibo*. Milan: Mondadori, 2002.

---. *Lezioni di tenebra*. Milan: Mondadori, 1997.

--- with M. C. Mauceri. "Unpublished Interview." 9 January 2003.

Jauss, Robert Hans. "Identity of the Poetic Text in the Changing Horizon of Understanding." *Reception Study: From Literary Theory to Cultural Studies*. Eds. James L. Machor and Philip Goldstein. New York: Routledge, 2001. 7-28.

Jay, Paul. *Being in the Text: Self-Representation from Wordsworth to Roland Barthes*. Ithaca, NY: Cornell UP, 1984.

Jelinek, E., ed. *Women's Autobiography: Essays in Criticism*. Bloomington, IN: Indiana UP, 1980.

Kantorowitz, E. *I due corpi del re*. Turin: Einaudi, 1989.

Kaplan, Caren. *Questions of Travel: Postmodern Discourses of Displacement*. Durham: Duke UP, 1996.

---. "Resisting Autobiography: Out-Law Genres and Transnational Feminist Subjects." *Women, Autobiography, Theory: A Reader*. Eds. Sidonie Smith and Julia Watson. Madison: U of Wisconsin P, 1998. 208-21.

Kemp, Sandra and Paola Bono, ed. *The Lonely Mirror: Italian Perspectives on Feminist Theory*. London and New York: Routledge, 1993.

King, Noel, Toby Miller, and Stephen Muecke. "Off the Planet: On Fictocriticism". Unpublished Paper courtesy of Stephen Muecke, University of Technology, 1994.

Klein, Melanie. *Love, Guilt and Reparation and other Works, 1921-1945*. New York: Doubleday, 1997.

Kolsky, Stephen. "Clara Sereni's *Casalinghitudine*: The Politics of Writing. Structure and Intertextuality." *Italian Quarterly* 133-134 (1997): 47-58.

Kristeva, Julia. "Women's Time." *Feminisms: An Anthology of Literary Theory and Criticism*. New Brunswick: Rutgers UP, 1997. 860-79.

Kroha, Lucienne. *The Woman Writer in Late-Nineteenth-Century Italy*. New York: The Edwin Mellen Press, 1992.

Lacan, Jacques. "The Mirror Stage as Formative Function of the I." Trans. Alan Sheridan. *Écrits*. New York: W.W. Norton & Co., 1977. 1-7.

Lagorio, Gina. *Inventario*. Milan: Rizzoli, 1997.

---. *Penelope senza tela argomenti e testi*. Ed. F. Mollia. Ravenna: Longo, 1984.

Lanaro, Silvio. *Nazione e lavoro. Saggio sulla cultura borghese in Italia 1870-1925*. Venice: Marsilio Editori, 1979.

Lang, Candace. *Irony/Humour: Critical Paradigms*. Baltimore: Johns Hopkins UP, 1988.

Lanser, Susan Sniader. *Fictions of Authority: Women Writers and Narrative Voice*. Ithaca: Cornell UP, 1992.

Lazzaro-Weis, Carol. *From Margins to Mainstream: Feminism and Fictional Modes in Italian Women's Writing 1968-1990*. Philadelphia: U of Pennsylvania P, 1993.

Lejeune, Philippe. *Le pacte autobiographique*. Paris: Seuil, 1975.

Libreria delle donne di Milano. *Non credere di avere dei diritti*. Turin: Rosenberg e Sellier, 1987.

---. *Sexual Difference: A Theory of Socio-Symbolic Practice*. 1987. Trans. Teresa De Lauretis and Patrizia Cicogna. Bloomington: Indiana UP, 1991.

---. "Un filo di felicità." *Sottosopra* (1986).

Lincoln, Yvonna S. "I and Thou: Method, Voice, and Roles in Research with the Silenced." *Naming Silenced Lives: Personal Narratives and Processes of Educational Change*. Eds. D. McLaughlin and W.G.Tierney. New York: Routledge, 1993.

Lionnet, Francoise. *Autobiographical Voices: Race, Gender, Self-Portraiture*. Ithaca: Cornell UP, 1989.

Livi, Grazia. *Le lettere del mio nome*. Milan: La Tartaruga, 1992.

Lombardi, O. *Invito alla lettura di Grazia Deledda*. Milan: Ist. Propaganda libraria, 1986.

Lorde, Audre. *Sister Outsider: Essays and Speeches*. Trumansburg, N.Y.: The Crossing Press, 1984.

---. *Zami: A New Spelling of My Name*. Trumansburg, N.Y.: The Crossing Press, 1983.

Lugones, Maria. "Purity, Impurity, and Separation." *Signs* 19.2 (1994): 458-79.

Madrignani, Carlo. *Alle origini del romanzo in Italia: Il "celebre Abate Chiari"*. Naples: Liguori, 2000.

Maggi, Stefano. *Le ferrovie*. Bologna: Il Mulino, 2003.

Majorana, Quirino. "Cenni storici sul graduale sviluppo degli impianti in Italia." *Cinquant'anni di storia italiana*. Milan: Ulrico Hoepli Editore della Real Casa e della R. Accademia dei Lincei, 1911.

Manin, Giuseppina. "Travolti da un insolito destino Giannini e Melato fanno il bis." *Corriere della Sera* 11 July 2003: 24.

Mantegazza, Paolo. *Fisiologia della donna*. Milan: Treves, 1883.

Manzini, Gianna. *Album di ritratti*. Milan: Mondadori, 1964.

---. *Ritratti e pretesti*. Milan: Il Saggiatore, 1960.

Marazzi, Christian. *Il posto dei calzini: La svolta linguistica nell'economia e i suoi effetti nella politica*. Bellinzona: Casagrande, 1994.

Marotti, Maria Ornella. "Filial Discourses: Feminism and Femininity in Italian Women's Autobiography." *Feminine Feminists: Cultural Practices in Italy*. Ed. Giovanna Miceli Jeffries. Minneapolis: U of Minnesota P, 1994. 65-85.

Martindale, Kathleen. "L'in-discreto soggetto lesbica si rifiuta di negoziare". *Questioni di teoria femminista*. Ed. Paola Bono. Milan: La Tartaruga, 1993.

Martino, Wayne, and Maria Pallotta-Chiarolli. *Boys' Stuff: Boys Talking About What Matters*. Sydney: Allen & Unwin, 2001.

---. *So What's A Boy? Issues of Masculinity in Schooling*. Maidenhead: Open University Press, 2003.

Masi, Paola. "Autoscatti: lettura della figurazione di sé nel femminismo." *DWF*. Spring 1 (1986): 11-21.

Mattesini, Luana. "Scrivere di sé: una rassegna critica sull'autobiografia femminile." *DWF* 2-3 (1993): 18-19.

Mauceri, M. Cristina. *Helga Schneider: la scrittura come testimonianza*. 6 April 2003. Available: http://www.disp.let.uniroma1.it/kuma/SEZIONI/POETICA/mauceripoeticakuma6.htm

Mehlman, James. *A Structural Study of Autobiography*. Ithaca: Cornell UP, 1974.

Melillo, Enrico. *La Posta nei Secoli*. Naples: Liguori, 1895.

Menozzi, Giuliana. "Food and Subjectivity in Clara Sereni's *Casalinghitudine*." *Italica* 71.2 (1994): 217-27.

Mestica, Giovanni. *Istituzioni di letteratura*. Florence: G. Barbera Editore, 1882.

Miccinesi, M. *Deledda*. Florence: Il Castoro, 1975.

Miceli Jeffries, Giovanna. "Unsigned History: Silent, Micro-'Technologies of Gender' in the Narratives of the Quotidian." *Gendering Italian Fiction. Feminist Revisions of Italian History*. Eds. Maria Ornella Marotti and Gabriella Brooke. London: Associated University Presses, 1999. 71-84.

Miller, Nancy. "Teaching Autobiography." *Women, Autobiography, Theory: A Reader*. Eds. Sidonie Smith and Julia Watson. Madison: The U of Wisconsin P, 1998. 461-70.

Miller, Nancy K. "Decades." *Feminist Theory: An International Debate*. Eds. Gayle Greene and Coppelia Kahn. London: Routledge, 1991.

---. *Getting Personal. Feminist Occasions and Other Autobiographical Acts*. New York and London: Routledge, 1991.

---. "Representing Others: Gender and Subjects of Autobiography." *Differences* 6.1 (1994): 1-27.

Minh-ha, Trinh T. "Other Than Myself/my Other Self." *Travellers' Tales: Narrative of Home and Displacement*. Eds. George Robertson et al. London: Routledge, 1994. 9-26.

---. *Woman, Native, Other: Writing Postcoloniality and Feminism*. Bloomington: Indiana UP, 1989.

---. *When The Moon Waxes Red*. New York: Routledge, 1991.

Misch, G. *Geschichte der Autobiographie*. Frankfurt: G. Schulte-Bulmke, 1955.

Mizzau, Marina. *Eco e Narciso: Parole e silenzi nel conflitto uomo-donna*. 1979. Turin: Bollati Boringhieri, 1988.

---. "La qualità dell'ironia." *Semiotica: Storia Teoria Interpretazione. Saggi intorno a Umberto Eco*. Eds. Giovanni Manetti, Patrizia Magli and Patrizia Violi. Milan: Bompiani, 1992. 187-200.

---. *L'ironia. La contraddizione consentita*. Milan: Feltrinelli, 1984.

Moi, Toril. *Sexual/Textual Politics: Feminist Literary Theory*. 1985. London: Routledge, 1990.

Molina, Maria Luisa "Papusa. Fragmentations: Meditations on Separatism." *Signs* 19.2 (1994): 449-57.

Mondello, Elisabetta. *La nuova italiana: La donna nella stampa e nella cultura del Ventennio*. Rome: Editori Riuniti, 1987.

Montanari, Giuseppe Ignazio. *L'arte di scriver lettere dedotta dall'analisi de' classici*. Naples, 1845.

Moraga, Cherrie. *Loving in the War Years*. Boston: South End Press, 1983.

---. *Loving in the War Years: Lo que nunca paso por sus labios*. Boston: South End Press, 1984.

Morante, Elsa. *History: A Novel*. 1974. Trans. William Weaver. South Royalton: Steerforth Italia, 2000.

---. *La storia: romanzo*. Turin: Einaudi, 1974.

---. *Il mondo salvato dai ragazzini*. Turin: Einaudi, 1968.

Moretti, F. *Il romanzo di formazione*. Turin: Einaudi, 1986.

Morgan, Janice. "Subject to Subject: Voice to Voice: Twentieth-Century Autobiographical Fiction by Women Writers." *Gender & Genre in Literature: Redefining Autobiography in Twentieth-

Century Women's Fiction. Eds. Janice Morgan and Colette T. Hall. New York: Garland, 1991. 3-19.

Mottier, Véronique. "Narratives of National Identity: Sexuality, Race, and the Swiss 'Dream of Order.'" *ECPR Joint Sessions*. Mannheim, 1999.

Muraro, Luisa. *L'ordine simbolico della madre*. Milan: La Tartaruga, 1992.

---. "The Narrow Door." *Gendered Contexts: New Perspectives in Italian Cultural Studies*. Eds. Julia. L. Hairston and Laura Benedetti, and Silvia M. Ross. New York: Peter Lang, 1996. 7-17.

Neera. *Profili, impressioni e Ricordi*. Milan: Cogliati, 1919.

Nelson, K., ed. *Narratives from the Crib*. Cambridge, MA: Harvard UP, 1989.

Nestle, Joan. *A Restricted Country*. Ithaca, N.Y.: Firebrand, 1987.

Olney, J. *Metaphors of Self: The Meaning of Autobiography*. Princeton: Princeton UP, 1972.

---., ed. *Autobiography: Essays Theoretical and Critical*. Princeton: Princeton UP, 1980.

Palazzolo, Maria Iolanda. "Le donne e la lettura." *Dimensione e problemi della ricerca storica* 2 (1991): 87-96.

Pallotta-Chiarolli, Maria. *Girls' Talk: Young Women Speak Their Hearts and Minds*. Lane Cove, Syndey: Finch Publishing, 1998.

---. *Someone You Know: A Friend's Farewell*. 1991. Adelaide: Wakefield Press, 2002.

---. *Tapestry: Interweaving Lives*. Sydney: Random House, 1999.

Parati, Graziella. *Public History, Private Stories: Italian Women's Autobiography*. Minneapolis: U of Minnesota P, 1996.

Pascal, Roy. *Design and Truth in Autobiography*. Cambridge, Mass.: Harvard UP, 1960.

Passatempo: letture per il Gentil sesso. Vol. I. Torino: Tipografia G. Candeletti Successore Cassone, 1869-1872.

Passerini, Luisa. *Autoritratto di gruppo*. Florence: Giunti, 1988.

---. *Storia di donne e femministe*. Turin: Rosenberg & Sellier, 1991.

Patterson, O. "The Nature, Causes, and Implications of Ethnic Identification." *Minorities: Community and Identity*. Ed. C. Fried. Berlin: Springer-Verlag, 1983.

Personal Narratives Group. *Interpreting Women's Lives: Feminist Theory*. Bloomington: Indiana UP, 1989.

Perugi, Giampaolo. *Educazione e politica in Italia 1860-1900*. Turin: Loescher Editore, 1978.

Petrignani, Sandra. *Le signore della scrittura*. Milan: La Tartaruga, 1984.

Petronio, G. "Grazia Deledda." *Letteratura italiana. I contemporanei*. Vol. 1. Milan: Marzorati, 1963. 137-58.

Picci, Giuseppe. *Guida alla studio delle Belle Lettere e al comporre con un manuale dello stile epistolare*. Milan: Eredi di Ernesto Oliva Editore, 1883.

Pickering-Iazzi, Robin. "Images of Motherhood in Aleramo, Morante, Maraini and Fallaci." *Annali d'italianistica* 7 (1989): 329-34.

---. "The Politics of Gender and Genre in Italian Women's Autobiography of the Interwar Years." *Italica* 71 (1994): 176-97.

Pike, B. "Time in Autobiography." *Comparative Literature* 28 (1976).

Pilling, John. *Autobiography and Imagination: Studies in Self-Scrutiny*. London: Routledge & Kegan Paul, 1981.

Piromalli, A. *Grazia Deledda*. Florence: La Nuova Italia, 1968.

Pizzorusso, A. *Ai margini dell'autobiografia*. Bologna: Il Mulino, 1986.

Portelli, Alessandro. *L'ordine è già stato eseguito: Roma, le Fosse Ardeatine, la memoria*. Rome: Donzelli, 1999.

Porter, Roger. "Autobiography, Exile, Home: The Egyptian Memoirs of Gini Alhadeff, Andrè Aciman, and Edward Said." *Biography* 24.1 (2001): 302-13.

Posner, Richard A. *Public Intellectuals: A Study of Decline*. Cambridge: Harvard UP, 2001.

Prima Relazione sul Servizio Postale in Italia, Anno 1863. Turin: Tipografia Fodratti, 1864.

Properzi Nelsen, Elisabetta. "Clara Sereni and Contemporary Italian-Jewish Literature." *The Most Ancient of Minorities - The Jews of Italy*. Ed. Stanislao G. Pugliese. Westport: Greenwood Press, 2002. 157-67.

Ramondino, Fabrizia. *Althénopis*. 1981. Turin: Einaudi, 1995.

---. *Althénopis*. Trans. Michael Sullivan. Manchester: Carcanet, 1988.

---. "In *Althénopis* ci sono tutte le mie esperienze." *Lettere/2*. July (1991): 1-6.

Re, Lucia. "Passion and Sexual Difference: The Risorgimento and the Gendering of Writing in Nineteenth-Century Italian Culture." *Making and Remaking Italy: The Cultivation of National Identity around the Risorgimento*. Eds. Albert Russell Ascoli and Krystyna von Hennerberg. Oxford: Berg, 2001.

---. "Utopian Longing and the Constraints of Racial and Sexual Difference in Elsa Morante's *La Storia*." *Italica* 70.3 (1993): 361-75.

Rich, Adrienne. *Of Woman Born. Motherhood as Experience and Institution*. New York: W.W. Norton, 1976.

Robb, Simon. "Academic Divination is Not a Mysticism: Fictocriticism, Pedagogy and Hypertext." *Crossing Lines: Formations of Australian Culture*. Eds. P. Buttress, A. Nettelbeck and C. Guerin. Adelaide: Proceedings of the Association for the Study of Australian Literature Conference, 1995.

Romano, Lalla. *Un sogno del nord. Tutte le opere*. Vol. 2. Milan: Mondadori, 1992.

---. *Una giovinezza inventata*. Turin: Einaudi, 1995.

Rorty, Richard. *Contingency, Irony and Solidarity*. Cambridge: Cambridge UP, 1989.

Rosselli, Carlo. *Socialismo liberale*. Turin: Einaudi, 1979.

Ruddick, Sara. "Thinking Mothers/Conceiving Birth." *Representations of Motherhood*. Eds. Donna Basin, Margaret Honey, and Meryle Mahrer Kaplan. New Haven: Yale UP 1994. 29-45.

Rusconi, Gian Enrico. *Patria e Repubblica*. Bologna: Il Mulino, 1997.

---. *Resistenza e Postfascismo*. Bologna: Il Mulino, 1995.

---. *Se cessiamo di essere una nazione: tra etnodemocrazie regionali e cittadinanza europea*. Bologna: Il Mulino, 1993.

---. "Will Italy Remain a Nation?" *Italy*. Ed. Mark Donovan. Vol. 1. Aldershot: Ashgate, 1999. 309-21.

Rusconi, Marisa. "Nuovi percorsi tra esperienza e scrittura." *Ciao bella: Ventun percorsi di critica letteraria femminile oggi*. Eds. Rosaria Guacci and Bruna Miorelli. Milan: Lupetti/Piero Manni Letteratura, 1996. 155-72.

Saba, Umberto. *Scorciatoie e raccontini*. 1946. Milan: Mondadori, 1963.

Said, Edward. "The Mind of Winter: Reflections on Life in Exile." *Harper's Magazine* September 1984: 49-55.

---. *Out of Place: A Memoir.* London: Granta, 1999.

---. *Reflections on Exile and Other Essays.* Cambridge: Harvard UP, 2000.

Sapegno, N. *Pagine di storia letteraria.* Palermo: Manfredi, 1960.

---, ed. *Romanzi e novelle.* Milan: Mondadori, 1971.

Sarup, Madan. "Home and Identity." *Travellers' Tales: Narrative of Home and Displacement.* Eds. George Robertson et al. London: Routledge, 1994. 93-104.

Saunders, Nona. "Tapestry I and II." *Miscegenation Blues: Voices of Mixed Race Women.* Ed. C. Camper. Toronto: SisterVision, 1994.

Saywell, Shelley. *Women in War.* Harmondsworth: Penguin, 1986.

Scalfari, Eugenio, and Umberto Eco. "È una destra senza legge." *Repubblica* 21 (1994).

Scano, A., ed. *Versi e prose giovanili.* 1938. Milan: Treves, 1972.

Scappaticci, Tommaso. *Introduzione a Serao.* Rome-Bari: Editori Laterza, 1995.

Scarparo, Susanna. "Feminist Intellectuals as Public Figures in Contemporary Italy." *Australian Feminist Studies* 19.44 (2004): 201-12.

Schneider, Helga. *Il piccolo Adolfo non aveva le ciglia.* Milan: Rizzoli, 1998.

---. *Il rogo di Berlino.* Milan: Adelphi, 1995.

---. *La bambola decapitata.* Bologna: Perndragon, 1993.

---. *Lasciami andare, madre.* Milan: Adelphi, 2001.

---. *Porta di Brandeburgo. Storie berlinesi 1945-1947.* Milan: Rizzoli, 1997.

---. *Stelle di cannella.* Milan: Salani, 2002.

Sereni, Clara. *Casalinghitudine.* Turin: Einaudi, 1987.

---. *Da un grigio all'altro.* Rome: Di Renzo, 1998.

---. *Eppure.* Milan: Feltrinelli, 1995.

---. *Il gioco dei Regni.* Florence: Giunti, 1993.

---. *Manicomio primavera.* Florence: Giunti, 1989.

---. *Passami il sale.* Milan: Rizzoli, 2002.

---. "Primavera anche all'inferno." Interview with Bia Sarasini. *Noi Donne* (May 1989): 76-78.

---. *Taccuino di un'ultimista.* Milan: Feltrinelli, 1998.

Seyhan, Azade. *Writing Outside the Nation.* Princeton: Princeton UP, 2001.

Shemek, Deanna. "Prisoners of Passion: Women and Desire in Matilde Serao's *Romanzi d'Amore.*" *Italiana* (1986): 243-54.

Shumaker, Wayne. *English Autobiography: Its Emergence, Materials, and Forms.* Berkeley: U of California P, 1954.

Simon, Catherine. *Helga Schneider, fille de SS.* 15 March 2002. Available: http://www.fsa.ulaval. ca/personnel/vernag/EH/F/ethique/lectures/Helga_Schneider_fille_de_SS.htm.

Sinopoli, Franca. "Diaspora e migrazione intraeuropee in Luigi Meneghello, Carmine Abate, Jarmila Ockayova." *Diaspore europee e lettere migranti.* Eds. Armando Gnisci and Nora Moll. Rome: Edizioni interculturali, 2002.

---. "Poetiche della migrazione nella letteratura italiana contemporanea: il discorso autobiografico." *Studi (e testi) italiani. Semestrale del Dipartimento di Italianistica e Spettacolo dell'Università di Roma 'La Sapienza'* 7: 189-206.

Skrbis, Zlatko. "A Neglected Issue: Ethnic Group or Ethnic Community?" *Progress Went West.* Eds. H. Smith, L. Gardiner, and J. Wooding. University of Western Sydney, Nepean: Papers from the Third Annual Postgraduate Work in Progress Conference, 1994.

Slaughter, Jane. *Women and the Italian Resistance 1943-1945.* Denver: Arden Press, 1997.

Smith, Barbara, ed. *Home Girls: A Black Feminist Anthology.* New York: Kitchen Table, Women of Color Press, 1983.

Smith, Sidonie. *A Poetics of Women's Autobiography: Marginality and the Fictions of Self-Representation.* Bloomington, IN: Indiana UP, 1987.

---. *Subjectivity, Identity, and the Body. Women's Autobiographical Practices in the Twentieth Century.* Bloomington, IN: Indiana UP, 1993.

Smith, Sidonie and Julia Watson, eds. *De/Colonizing the Subject: The Politics of Gender in Women's Autobiography.* Minneapolis, MN: U of Minnesota P, 1992.

---. *Reading Autobiography. A Guide for Interpreting Life Narratives.* Minneapolis: The U of Minnesota P, 2001.

Smith, Sidonie. *A Poetics of Women's Autobiography: Marginality and the Fictions of Self-Representation.* Bloomington, IN: Indiana UP, 1987.

---. *Subjectivity, Identity, and the Body. Women's Autobiographical Practices in the Twentieth Century.* Bloomington, IN: Indiana UP, 1993.

Somers, Margaret. "The Narrative Constitution of Identity: A Relational and Network Approach." *Theory and Society* 23 (1994): 605-49.

Spacks Patricia. "Selves in Hiding." *Women's Autobiography: Essays in Criticism.* Ed. E. Jelinek. Bloomington: Indiana UP, 1980.

---. *Imagining a Self: Autobiography and Novel in Eighteenth-Century England.* Cambridge, Mass.: Harvard UP, 1976.

Spengemann, William C. *The Forms of Autobiography: Episodes in the History of a Literary Genre.* New Haven: Yale UP, 1980.

Spivak, Gayatri. *In Other Worlds: Essays in Cultural Politics.* New York: Methuen, 1987.

---. *Woman, Native, Other. Writing Postcoloniality and Feminism.* Bloomington: Indiana UP, 1989.

---. *The Post-Colonial Critic.* New York: Routledge, 1990.

Springer, Elisa. *Il silenzio dei vivi.* Venice: Marsilio, 1997.

Stanton, Domna C., ed. *The Female Autograph: Theory and Practice of Autobiography from the Tenth to the Twentieth Century.* Chicago: U of Chicago P, 1987.

Starobinski, J. "The Style of Autobiography." *Autobiography: Essays Theoretical and Critical.* Ed. J. Olney. Princeton: Princeton UP, 1980. 73-83.

Steedman, Carolyn. *Landscape for a Good Woman.* New Brunswick: Rutgers UP, 1987.

Stowers, Cath. "Journeying Back to Mother: Pilgrimages of Maternal Redemption in the Fiction of Michèle Roberts." *Mothers and Daughters: Connection, Empowerment & Transformation.* Eds. Andrea O'Reilly and Sharon Abbey. Lanham: Rowman & Littlefield Publishers, 2000. 61-74.

Swindells, Julia. "Liberating the Subject? Autobiography and 'Women's History': A Reading of the Diaries of Hannah Cullwick." Personal Narratives Group.

Taylor, Charles. *Sources of the Self.* Cambridge, MA: Harvard UP, 1989.

Thompkins, Jane P., ed. *Reader-Response Criticism: From Formalism to Post-Structuralism.* Baltimore: Johns Hopkins UP, 1980.

Todorov, Tzvetan. *The Poetics of Prose.* Ithaca: Cornell UP, 1977.

Tortorelli, Gianfranco. "I Libri più letti dal popolo italiano: un'inchiesta del 1906." *Studi di storia dell'editoria.* Bologna: Il Mulino, 1989.

Traniello, Francesco. "Sulla definizione della Resistenza come 'Secondo Risorgimento.'" *Le idee costituzionali della Resistenza.* Eds. S. Guerrieri and G. Monina C. Franceschini. Rome: Presidenza del Consiglio dei Ministri, 1996. 17-25.

Travella, Paola. *Il prigioniero.* Milan: Mondadori, 1978.

Undicesima Relazione sul Servizio Postale in Italia:1873. Rome: Tipografia Eredi Botta, 1875.

Vasta, Ellie. "Multiculturalism and Ethnic Identity: The Relationship Between Racism and Resistance." *Australian and New Zealand Journal of Sociology* 29.2 (1993): 209-25.

Vattimo, Gianni, and P. A. Rovatti, ed. *Il pensiero debole.* Milan: Feltrinelli, 1983.

Veneziani, Marcello. "The 'Case of Italy' on the Eve of European Integration." *The International Spectator* 33.1: 15-23.

Viroli, Maurizio. *For Love of Country: An Essay on Patriotism and Nationalism.* Oxford: Clarendon Press, 1995.

Wajnryb, Ruth. *The Silence. How Tragedy Shapes Talk.* Crows Nest, NSW: Allen and Unwin, 2001.

Ward Jouve, Nicole. *White Woman Speaks with Forked Tongue: Criticism as Autobiography.* New York: Routledge, 1991.

Wood, Sharon. "Clytemnestra or Electra: Renegotiating Motherhood." *Italian Women's Writing: 1860–1994.* London: Athlone Press, 1995. 232- 97.

Woolf, Virginia. *A Room of One's Own.* 1929. London: Grafton Books, 1977.

Yuval-Davis, Nira. "Women, Ethnicity and Empowerment." *Feminism and Psychology* 4.1 (1994): 179-97.

Zaccaria, Paola. *Mappe senza frontiere. Cartografie letterarie dal Modernismo al Transnazionalismo.* Bari: Palomar, 1999.

Zambon, Patrizia. *Le donne a scuola: l'educazione femminile nell'Italia dell'Ottocento.* Mostra documentaria e iconografica, Florence: Tipografia "Il Sedicesimo", 1987.

---. *Letteratura e stampa nel secondo Ottocento.* Alessandria: Edizioni dell'Orso, 1993.

Zancan, Marina. *Il doppio itinerario della scrittura. La donna nella tradizione letteraria italiana.* Turin: Einaudi, 1998.

---. "La donna." *Letteratura italiana.* Ed. Alberto Asor Rosa. Vol. V: Le questioni. Turin: Einaudi, 1986. 765-827.

---. *Le scrittrici e i loro testi.* 1996. Ed. Maria Ida Gaeta. Available: http://rmcisadu.let.uniroma1.it/crilet/mostra900/zancan.htm. July 15 2002.

Zarri, Gabriella, ed. *Per lettera.* Rome: Viella, 1999.